WILLIAM
AND
MARY

ALSO BY JOHN VAN DER KISTE

Published by Sutton unless stated otherwise

Frederick III, German Emperor 1888 (1981)

Queen Victoria's Family: a select bibliography (Clover, 1982)

Dearest Affie: Alfred, Duke of Edinburgh, Queen Victoria's second son, 1844–1900 [with Bee Jordaan] (1984, n.e. 1995)

Queen Victoria's Children (1986; large print ISIS, 1987)

Windsor and Habsburg: the British and Austrian reigning houses 1848–1922 (1987)

Edward VII's Children (1989)

Princess Victoria Melita, Grand Duchess Cyril of Russia, 1876–1936 (1991)

George V's Children (1991)

George III's Children (1992)

Crowns in a Changing World: the British and European monarchies 1901–36 (1993)

Kings of the Hellenes: The Greek Kings 1863–1974 (1994)

Childhood at Court 1819–1914 (1995)

Northern Crowns: The Kings of modern Scandinavia (1996)

King George II and Queen Caroline (1997)

The Romanovs 1818–1959: Alexander II of Russia and his family (1998)

Kaiser Wilhelm II: Germany's last Emperor (1999)

The Georgian Princesses (2000)

Gilbert & Sullivan's Christmas (2000)

Dearest Vicky, Darling Fritz: Queen Victoria's eldest daughter and the German Emperor (2001)

Royal Visits in Devon and Cornwall (Halsgrove, 2002)

Once a Grand Duchess: Xenia, sister of Nicholas II [with Coryne Hall] (2002)

WILLIAM AND MARY

JOHN VAN DER KISTE

SUTTON PUBLISHING

First published in the United Kingdom in 2003 by
Sutton Publishing Limited · Phoenix Mill
Thrupp · Stroud · Gloucestershire · GL5 2BU

British Library Cataloguing in Publication Data
A catalogue record for this book is available from the British
Library.

ISBN 0-7509-3048-9

Typeset in 11/14.5pt Sabon.
Typesetting and origination by
Sutton Publishing Limited.
Printed and bound in England by
J.H. Haynes & Co. Ltd, Sparkford.

Contents

List of Plates

Preface

In 1677 Lady Mary (by which title she was then known), niece of King Charles II and second in line to the English throne, wept bitterly when told she was going to marry her cousin Prince William of Orange. Their wedding in a private ceremony at St James's Palace, on William's twenty-seventh birthday, represented a symbolic union of the English and Dutch in providing resistance to French ambitions and the designs of King Louis XIV. The proceedings were remembered partly for the tearful face of the bride and her unsmiling husband, and partly for the jovial banter of King Charles. As he gave his niece away he urged the officiating Archbishop not to lose any time, lest the heir's heavily pregnant wife should 'disappoint' the marriage by presenting the kingdom with a son; and when the groom turned solemnly to his bride, presenting her with a handful of coins and the assurance that all his worldly goods he thus endowed her, the King told her to pocket them at once 'for it was all clear gain'.

Despite these inauspicious beginnings, the marriage became a successful partnership in personal and dynastic terms. Though Mary was unable to have children, they soon came to love and respect each other deeply. She was second in line of succession to the throne, and as matters stood he would be only her consort. Yet through her selflessness and also the demands of state, some eleven years later they became the only joint sovereigns ever to occupy the English throne.

Their place in the succession was, however, far from straight-forward. Charles II had no legitimate children. Mary's father, Charles's only surviving brother James, Duke of York, was already showing signs of the obstinacy and drive towards Catholicism that threatened to make his position as heir untenable. If he and his second wife Princess Mary Beatrice were to have a son, Mary would forfeit her position in the line of succession and in due course would probably be displaced by a Catholic dynasty descended from her half-brother. This was a situation which her husband was anxious to avoid, not merely for reasons of avarice or personal ambition but in order to check the pre-eminence of France throughout Europe.

As had been already suspected by a few far-sighted individuals, once he became king James rapidly alienated what support he had ever had, and the birth of his son James, Prince of Wales – generally believed to be a 'warming-pan baby', smuggled in as a substitute for an infant who was born dead or died prematurely, or possibly even as the result of a sham pregnancy – cost him his crown. William was invited to come to England in order to help restore the country's basic freedoms, and the circumstances in which he and Mary, still the true heir to the throne, became joint sovereigns were and remain unparalleled in English history.

In this biography I have endeavoured to present them as personalities caught up in a remarkable chain of events. This is the story of two very different characters, an outwardly cold, taciturn man and his affectionate, warm-hearted cousin, who married for reasons of state, whose lives – as so often in royal circles – became circumscribed by duty and ceremonial, and who left their home in Holland with some reluctance. Yet they reigned over a short period of significant change, and in the process left the standing of the British monarchy in 1702 in a far better position than it had been in 1688.

Throughout the seventeenth century England used the Julian calendar, which was ten days behind that of Europe, where the calendar reforms introduced by Pope Gregory XIII were observed. This discrepancy increased to eleven days in 1700. In accordance with common practice, I have dated events in England according to the Old Style and those on the continent according to the New Style, with both separated by an oblique stroke in cases where confusion might otherwise result.

Contemporary letters are quoted in the text with their original spelling.

Acknowledgements

My thanks for help, support and advice in various ways throughout the writing of this book are due to my friends, Kim-Elisabeth Geldard; Coryne Hall; Karen Roth; Shirley Stapley; Sue Woolmans; Phil Lindsey-Clark; to the staff of the Kensington and Chelsea Borough Libraries; and to my editors at Sutton, Jaqueline Mitchell and Alison Miles. As ever, my particular thanks and gratitude go to my mother Kate Van der Kiste, for her tireless assistance, encouragement, and her painstaking reading of the final draft manuscript.

ONE

'Piccinion'

On 31 October 1650 William II, Prince of Orange, returned from a hunting expedition to his home at Binnenhof Palace, The Hague. He was unwell, but as his wife Mary was expecting their first child in a few days he did not wish to alarm her. Next day he was worse, and that evening his doctors confirmed that he had smallpox. Panic-stricken, she wanted to go to his side immediately, but her attendants told her that she must not jeopardize the life of her unborn infant, and she had to be held back by force. Within a week William, only twenty-four, was dead. His grief-stricken young widow was inconsolable, and the household feared she might follow him to the grave. In her short life she had already lost a husband and a father, for it was less than two years since the latter, King Charles I of England, had been executed.

Her apartments were hung with black, even the bed in which she was to bear her child and the waiting cradle. The confinement was expected at the end of the month, but the shock of her husband's death caused her to go into labour early. On the evening of 14 November, her nineteenth birthday, a young prince was born. A nurse present at the birth claimed afterwards that, during the first moments of the baby's life, a draught blew out the candles in the bedchamber, and she saw three circles of light shining round his head. Far beyond the palace walls, the bells of The Hague were rung. Even in the Dutch Republic, it was customary to celebrate such a royal birth as if a future king had been born.

In the seventeenth century the Princes of Orange traditionally held the greatest offices in the Dutch Republic which, after an eighty-year struggle, had won its independence from Spain, then the most powerful nation in Europe, to become a leading maritime and trading nation. The Republic was a federation of seven of the seventeen provinces of the Low Countries under Habsburg rule, the remaining ten still being under Spanish government. Each province had its own law, customs and representative assembly, and sent a delegation to the States-General of the United Provinces.

The Princes of Orange were the Republic's richest citizens, owning large estates in the Netherlands and Germany. As sovereign princes in their own right, they took their title from the small principality of Orange on the Rhône. Their outlook was more cosmopolitan than that of most Dutchmen, and French was usually spoken at their court. Though exercising semi-royal power, these princes did not hold the title of king. The offices of Stadholder and Captain General were not strictly hereditary, but had always been conferred on the head of the house of Orange. In the seventeenth century some suspected that the Princes of Orange planned to proclaim themselves kings. When Frederick Henry married his son William Henry to Mary Stuart in 1641, he hoped that her father would in due course help him to establish an Orange monarchy. Such plans had been thwarted by his father-in-law's troubles, culminating in the English civil war, his execution and the declaration of a commonwealth in Britain.

The offices of Stadholder and Captain General lapsed with William II's death. While most Dutchmen expected his infant son to succeed to them in due course, many regents felt that the two offices, civil and military, conferred too much power and should not be granted to one man. The establishment of a centralized monarchy could jeopardize municipal rights and the traditional liberty and tolerance of Dutch society. Pensionary Johan de Witt, the leading figure in the States of Holland, saw himself as the defender of Dutch liberty and institutions against the aspirations of the house of Orange. Within the next few years the struggles of William and his supporters, who controlled several of the smaller provinces, to secure his elevation to these offices would figure prominently in Dutch politics throughout the early years of his life, and would have a formative influence on his character and political outlook.

* * *

By the time the baby prince was three days old, the household were anxious about the young mother who lay distraught and weeping, and about her puny child who seemed to grow weaker by the day. The first nurse chosen for him had been unsuitable, and another foster mother was found. He rallied slowly, but still seemed so delicate that few expected him to survive infancy.

On 21 January 1651 he was christened at the Grote Kerk, The Hague. Mary wanted to call him Charles, after her father and brother, but at the insistence of her mother-in-law Amalia von Solms-Braunfels, he was given the traditional Orange names of William Henry. Denied the right to choose his names, she refused to attend the ceremony. It was an unhappy occasion, for many of the congregation had been waiting for hours in the snowy streets of the city to see their new prince. The presence of a large crowd which grew restive during the long service in the freezing building unnerved the choir, who sang out of tune, and the noise forced the preacher to abandon his sermon.

Since her arrival in the Dutch Republic as a homesick young bride of twelve, Mary Stuart had neither liked the people of her husband's country, nor regarded it as home. The Dutch found her haughty and arrogant, sensing that she thought herself too good for them. Widowed at nineteen, she felt herself surrounded by enemies, and made no effort to conceal her devotion to England and her favourite brother Charles, an exiled sovereign-in-waiting. As a Stuart she saw it as her duty to help restore him to his rightful position as King of England, and then to persuade him to use his power to have William raised to a suitable position. She regularly lent Charles and James money she could ill afford. When the English Parliament sent their youngest brother Henry, Duke of Gloucester, to Holland, observers thought she treated him with affection in marked contrast to the scant attention she paid her only child.

The closest of her husband's relatives was her mother-in-law, the Dowager Princess Amalia von Solms-Braunfels, widow of Prince Frederick Henry of Orange. She tried to obtain custody of her grandson, partly as a family duty towards the state, and partly as she sensed her daughter-in-law had little maternal love for the boy.

3

The anti-Orangists, led by Johan de Witt, considered him as a Child of the State, and maintained he should be brought up as a Calvinist and a servant of the Republic. The tendencies of the Netherlands were republican, and William's close Stuart connection counted against him. But as a race the Dutch were fiercely loyal to the house of Orange, and feeling in his favour was so strong that he was nearly named Captain General of Holland at the age of three. A year later Oliver Cromwell, Lord Protector of England, signed a treaty with the States that neither William nor his descendants should ever be appointed to the chief command of their armies or fleets.

Nicknamed 'Piccinion' by his mother,[1] William was a weak, undersized child. The Nassaus were a sickly family with a high incidence of fever, tubercular trouble and a generally short life expectancy, and he grew into a pale, thin boy with asthma, a dry cough and a visibly humped back. As an adult he always had to wear a cuirass, a device incorporating a breastplate and backplate fastened together, to help him hold himself up straight on horseback. All his life he had a poor appetite, and would eat little when tired or ill, thus depleting his reserves of strength still further. His tutors had to sit with him at mealtimes to make sure he ate properly, which he did with reluctance. As an adult, of course, there would be no compulsion to follow this necessary but tiresome rule. He went early to bed, a routine to which he would always adhere. His tutors taught him never to trust doctors, which was probably as well in view of the barbaric remedies they normally prescribed. The amount of exercise he took was strictly controlled, as his guardians thought him too weak to be taxed as strongly as other children of his age. He was introduced to tennis and fencing a little later than usual, and perhaps because of this he never really enjoyed them. The only sport he really liked was hunting, which took him out into the open air, gave him relief from his asthma and also brought him a degree of privacy which other sports did not. A natural tendency towards outward coldness, a taciturn demeanour and his firm self-control were reinforced by his lonely, self-contained childhood.

William's first years were overshadowed by ill-health and by disputes among the older generation who seemed to regard him almost as a trophy. His mother distrusted and feared her mother-in-law and the machinations of the Dutch government, which saw him as the chief hostage in their efforts to establish their constitution on a firmer footing. To them he was the representative of a great leader of the previous century, William the Silent, and he personified their hopes for the future. His mother secured the appointment of an Englishwoman, Lady Stanhope, as the governess of his first household. Despite Mary's protests, when William was six Pastor Trigland began to instruct him in the Reformed faith, and thus laid the basis of William's committed Calvinism.

Around 1656 there were rumours that the Princess of Orange was considering taking a second husband. Her mother Queen Henrietta Maria hoped she might arrange a match for her with the young King Louis XIV, now aged eighteen. Mary was accordingly invited to Paris and, while nothing came of any plans to make her Queen of France by marriage, she showed no inclination to return to Holland before necessary. Eventually she left France after receiving a message that William was seriously ill, but on reaching Bruges she learned that he only had measles and was making a good recovery, so she dallied there for several weeks. There are conflicting accounts of how much or how little she cared for him. Some say that by now she had more or less given up the struggle for control of him, preferring to spend much of her time abroad, and that by the time he reached his ninth year and was enrolled as a student at Leyden University she did not object, as they were already estranged and on formal terms. Others maintain that despite her haughty attitude and quick temper, she was devoted to him and ever keen to do what she could in helping to reclaim ancestral dignities on his behalf.

At the age of eight he formed a lifelong friendship with his cousin Princess Elisabeth Charlotte, or 'Liselotte', one year his junior, the niece of Sophie, Duchess of Brunswick and later Electress of Hanover. They both came on a long visit to Binnenhof, and one day at a reception Liselotte became separated from her aunt. Seeing a lady who looked as if she was suffering from a severe cold, she asked William the identity of the woman with 'the fiery nose'. That, he told her solemnly, was his mother. She looked at him apologetically and he burst into giggles at this childish *faux pas*. For the rest of her stay they were almost inseparable playmates, and the older generation whispered among themselves that William might have found his future wife.

In November 1659 William was provided with his own establishment at Leiden, in the building which had been the convent of St Barbara. He was looked after by a household including three governors (of whom one, William Frederick of Nassau-Zuylenstein, was a natural son of William's grandfather Prince William Henry), two young pages, a chamberlain, a physician, two gentlemen-in-waiting and a domestic staff of eleven. Constantine Huygens, a former secretary to his father and grandfather, was appointed his domestic governor, his duties including ensuring that the practical affairs of the household were run with order and efficiency, and that his young charge behaved with the utmost decorum. There was to be no blasphemy, unseemly behaviour or unpleasant conversation; gluttony and drunkenness, it was inculcated in him, were inappropriate to persons of honour. He was to study his Bible regularly, attend church twice on Sundays and answer questions afterwards in front of the servants. As well as English, which he learned from his mother, he spoke French, Dutch, German, Latin and Spanish.

His daily routine was drawn up in some detail. He was to rise between 7 and 8 a.m., and after saying his prayers had a light breakfast. Morning prayers were followed by study for the rest of the morning, divided into short periods for different subjects, including history, mathematics, geography, religious knowledge, philosophy, French, English and Latin. Next came dancing lessons, designed to produce a good carriage and grace of movement, particularly important for a boy who suffered from a hunched back. At dinner Huygens had to ensure that conversation was kept polite and seemly, and directed towards interesting themes. Part of the afternoon was to be spent in walking, riding or driving, followed by another hour or two of study before supper. This was followed by more recreation, perhaps billiards or a similar game, then evening prayers with the household, private devotions and bed between

9 and 10 p.m. Every day he read the Bible, and was required to learn a psalm by heart.

* * *

Meanwhile in England the death of Cromwell in September 1658 had given the Stuarts cause for hope. Some twenty months later Charles, who had been *de jure* king and tacitly acknowledged as such by his supporters since his father's execution, was recalled from exile to his kingdom. Before he set sail the States-General invited him to Holland, and for a few days the family were partly reunited at The Hague, surrounded by Dutch well-wishers and jubilant English exiles, many of whom would also cross the Channel in due course. At nine William was too young to participate in all the ceremonies, but he was brought from his establishment at Leiden to join in this display of family unity. On the day of his uncle's state entry into The Hague, amid a fanfare of bells and cannon, he, his mother and uncles James, Duke of York, and Henry, Duke of Gloucester, were among those in the crowded coach, as he perched on James's knee. That evening a great dinner was held at the Mauritshuis, cannon were fired after every toast, and the festivities and gifts to the new king and his family cost over two million guilders. On 23 May William was part of the company on the shore at Scheveningen and Charles embraced him tenderly before setting sail for England.

Now there was a possibility that, in addition to holding high office in Holland, William might also succeed to the English throne. Mary decided the time had come to introduce him to the people, and several cities invited them as honoured guests. Amsterdam went *en fête* with arches of laurels and streets hung with flags and tapestries, and they entered the city in a kind of royal progress, to the pealing of bells and the sound of trumpets. Triumphal cars paraded tableaux from Stuart and Nassau history. One showed William as a hero, represented by a figure attended by Hope and Religion, and surrounded by a group of children who offered him symbols of the arts and sciences, while winged figures of the Liberal

Arts hovered over them. In front of him an orange tree, bearing a single fruit, shaded an altar from which a phoenix arose from the ashes. Another was less well-judged, showing as it did a realistic representation of the execution of King Charles I. When Mary saw the poised axe, she was so shocked she almost fainted.

William's few months at Leiden had made him more assured and better mannered, and he took part in the proceedings with a sense of diplomacy and grace which would have done credit to a boy considerably older than nine. On the next day of the visit he made a sightseeing tour of the city on horseback, and then went to see the magnificent yacht which the States-General had prepared as a present for his uncle. On the Sunday William and his mother attended divine service in the Nieuwe Kerk, and the following morning after more festivities they returned to The Hague. There they were welcomed back with due ceremony and enthusiasm, and with what was probably for William the highlight of their tour. As their coach drove up to the Binnenhof, a troop of small boys with wooden swords at their sides and plumes of orange paper in their hats stood to attention, while their leader stepped forward, saluted and greeted William as their general. He accepted this honour with all due gravity, then turned to his mother and asked, 'Could they all be invited in?' When given permission, the group of eager small boys swarmed into the palace where they were given drinks and fruit. As they left again in orderly fashion, all smiling, William stood at the door and handed each a gingerbread cake.[2]

After this short tour William returned to Leiden to study. In September he came back to The Hague to spend a few days with his mother before she left to visit her brother in England. Ever since leaving from Dover in the spring of 1642, a homesick girl of ten, Mary had longed to return to the country of her birth. Now her prayers for her brother's restoration had been answered, and she meant to go back to England for a while to share in this family triumph. She had made careful provision for William's well-being in her absence, asking the States to appoint commissioners to supervise his education, in consultation with his guardians, as well as taking care of 'the being who is dearest to us in the world'.[3] To his great-aunt Elizabeth, the 'Winter Queen of Bohemia', she commended him anxiously. On 29 September mother and son said farewell. Barely had she stepped on board the yacht when she was told that Henry, Duke of Gloucester, had been taken ill and succumbed to smallpox several days earlier. Overwhelmed with misery at the parting from her son and the loss of a brother, she withdrew to her cabin and spoke very little during the voyage.

Grief turned to anger soon after her arrival in England when she learnt that James, now heir to their eldest brother's throne, had secretly married one of her former maids of honour, Anne Hyde (*see* p. 30). Already feeling unwell after a dense fog in London that autumn, so unlike the clear air of Holland, she had second thoughts about a plan she had formulated for making her headquarters in England. Their mother Henrietta Maria had also been angered by James's marriage, and was about to arrive in England either to try to prove the marriage was invalid, or to have it declared thus. She would wait for her mother, Mary insisted, and then she would return to Holland. Mother and daughter fulminated against the union, but in vain. Yet an even greater calamity was to come, when Mary fell ill of the dreaded contagion, took to her bed at Whitehall and died on 24 December 1660. She left a letter to the States-General, begging them to take care of 'the being who is dearest to us in the world'.[4]

Elizabeth broke the news to the orphan of ten, and for several days he was bitterly upset. Among those who tried to comfort him was his French tutor, a close personal friend of Mary. Through his tears, the boy looked at him and said, 'I'm sorry for you too. My mother was a good friend to you, and I'm too young to do very much.'[5]

Mary had hoped William might become the ward of his uncle Charles. Had he been taken over to England and brought up in the nursery that was soon to be filled with the generally short-lived children of James, Duke of York, his life would have taken a very different course, but it was now inevitable that he would stay in Holland as the jealously guarded treasure of his father's people.

Early in 1661 he fell seriously ill. A combination of asthma, violent headaches and recurrent fainting fits confined him to bed for some time; at one stage the doctors feared for his life, and a rumour even went out that he had died. There were fears that he would grow up severely deformed, and for a while he had to wear a supporting harness in order to try to prevent deformity. Perhaps the experience of grief, brooding on his loss without playmates of his own age, and surrounded only by members of the elder generation clad in deepest black like the drapes in his rooms, had left its mark on the sensitive young child. Whether it left him with a lifelong disposition to melancholy, or strengthened him and placed an old head on young shoulders is open to question.

By April he was convalescent, and his grandmother decided to take him with her to stay with their Brandenburg relations at Cleves. It was the first time he had been out of Holland, and after such a bleak winter he must have benefited from a change. The Elector, Frederick William, and Electress Louise both treated him with a kindness he would never forget. For six weeks he was to enjoy being part of a normal family unit, somewhat spoiled, allowed to do nothing but play games with his young cousins, and spending much of his time outdoors. He was introduced to the delights of riding, and went hunting for the first time. The Elector found him a remarkable child, and detected an understanding beyond his years. Elizabeth, Queen of Bohemia, called him 'a verie extraordinarie child and verie good natured'.[6] His health improved at once; the Elector's physicians reported that there was no longer any serious risk of deformity, and gave him a less restricting corselet to wear.

On his way back to Leiden from the holiday which he was reluctant to leave, he spent four days at Utrecht as guest of the provincial States. There was a full programme of official functions, including a parade of the militia, a concert in the Dom Kerk, a long civic banquet and services in the cathedral. After this break, it was back to the routine of studying at Leiden. That winter he was unwell again, but his condition was apparently not life-threatening and the physicians were not alarmed. His grandmother thought he might be outgrowing his strength, so he was brought back to The Hague in June 1662 to live at the palace again. His frail physique did not prevent him from revelling in sports and outdoor activities. He took great pride in his hounds, horses and a flight of falcons, a gift from

10

King Frederik III of Denmark, while he also learnt fencing and tennis and in winter enjoyed skating on the lake.

At the age of thirteen he developed a passion for art, especially books on the cities and wonders of Italy. Jan Mytens, one of the main painters at court, was appointed his agent, and helped him to buy pictures, especially portraits, and golden Chinese caskets. His modest allowance of 200 guilders a month (raised to 400 in 1666 and 600 two years later) was insufficient for a patron of Old Masters. Soon he was in debt and Amalia wrote to Mytens, ordering him to make no more purchases for His Highness without her prior approval. As he was expected to live within his means, personal extravagance was discouraged in dress as well as in collecting art, and on his grandmother's orders his dress allowance was restricted to 3,500 guilders a year. Though he enjoyed acquiring paintings, he was bored by having to sit still for long periods for his own portrait to be painted, however, with so many relatives requesting them, it was a duty he could not shirk.

Naturally shy and self-effacing, he was taught to be polite and affable to others. In adult life he was phlegmatic and rarely lost his temper in public, though he was not above kicking his servants when in a bad mood. As befitted a man born to be a soldier and ruler, he was given practical instruction in military theory, and was taught to appreciate the greatness and glory of the house of Orange. It was impressed on him that he must put duty before pleasure, and this gave him a strong feeling of his family's rank and glory and of the rights and obligations that these entailed. Literature and the arts were not considered essential, but in later years he was always interested in fine painting, landscape gardening and architecture. With his connoisseur's eye for detail, he learnt how to distinguish original paintings and marbles from copies.

By the age of nineteen he was precociously mature and self-possessed. Naturally intelligent, he was a sound judge of character, knew how to hide his feelings and tended to be taciturn while those around him talked freely. Unfailingly calm and polite, he applied himself unstintingly to hard work and business, and above all to managing his interests with skill.

As a young adult he had his own small court. His household kept early hours, with the daily provision of food, fuel and light being comfortable but not lavish. Each day throughout the winter months he was allowed two white wax candles and a night-light in his bedroom, with a turf fire lit morning and evening. By 1665 his personal suite numbered thirty-three, excluding kitchen staff, cleaners and outdoor servants. They met twice daily for common prayer, and ate together in the dining room. There were three tables, with William, Zuylenstein, Bornius and the chief household officers, plus maybe a few distinguished guests at dinner, at the first or high table; the pages, their governor and gentlemen-in-waiting at the second; and lackeys, supervised by the porter, at the third. The high table had a few extra amenities, such as a wider choice of beverages – Rhenish, claret and French wine (the others just had French wine and beer) – and white rolls instead of ordinary bread, but otherwise the same fare was served to all. Breakfast was between 6 and 7 a.m. in summer, an hour later in winter. The first course at dinner consisted of four dishes of *potages*, including soups, stews and entrées, the second a similar provision of roasts and green vegetables, with dessert consisting of four courses of fruit – fresh, cooked or candied. Supper, on simpler lines, was a family meal without any visitors present.

By now William had outgrown much of the ill-health which had dogged his earlier years. Apart from a chronic cough at times and bouts of asthma, as a young man he was comparatively fit and well. Descriptions of a hunchbacked dwarf, handed down to posterity, seem to be an exaggeration. Though it was ironic that he should eventually marry a woman 4 inches taller than him, as an adult he stood 5ft 6½in, 1½ inches taller than his contemporary King Louis XIV and 6½ inches taller than the diminutive King Charles I.

* * *

Now that his mother was dead and his uncle restored to the British throne, Prince William of Orange was a more important figure in the Republic. England was Holland's greatest commercial rival in

Europe, and the regents suspected that William might take after his father and seek English support in trying to declare himself king. Charles II was amenable, perhaps even anxious, to support any move for William's elevation to the Stadholderate, but not without ulterior motive. The advantages of having a tame sovereign prince ruling a leading rival European power were self-evident.

Ironically, Holland and England would soon find themselves embroiled in conflict. At the behest of his Parliament, eager to check Dutch shipping and trading leadership, a reluctant King Charles declared war on Holland in March 1665. A minor campaign on land, in which Charles's ally, the Prince-Bishop of Cologne, invaded the eastern provinces, was mirrored in a desultory conflict at sea. There was an indecisive battle in June 1666, and a Dutch attack the next year in which seventeen ships sailed up the Medway, raided Sheerness, hoisted the flag of the United Provinces over the naval dockyards and captured a British flagship as a show of strength. In July an inconclusive peace treaty was signed at Breda, merely confirming the ownership of one or two colonial possessions which had long been taken for granted. The man who was Prince William's uncle and might regard himself as his guardian had technically been his enemy, though more in theory than in practice.

It made no difference to William's upbringing. By the age of fourteen he was taking a greater part in general society life, attending evening parties at various great houses in Holland, carefully supervised gatherings where there would be cards, conversation, music and dancing until about 8 p.m. He was regarded as almost adult, and during the new year festivities of 1666 gave his first independent dinner party, attended by about fifty guests. All the older generation spoke well of him, and some distant relatives were beginning to see him as an eligible bridegroom for their marriageable younger princesses. Duchess Sophie of Brunswick had not forgotten the friendly childish encounter between him and Liselotte, and made tentative enquiries. However, William's political prospects still seemed modest, and Sophie's husband Duke Ernest did not pursue the scheme.

Another distant kinswoman, Emilia, Princess of Tarentum, visited The Hague in the spring of 1666, accompanied by her daughter Charlotte, who was much the same age as William. The girl was wearing a *barette*, a head-dress, and in a teasing mood one day William tried to snatch it off. Too quick for him, Charlotte ducked and ran away and he chased after her to try to catch it. Both ran around the room, giggling helplessly, until Emilia winked at her daughter – who promptly feigned breathlessness and let him catch her. Maybe Emilia had hoped that this might be a step towards the boy becoming her son-in-law, but it never was.

In March 1666 Johan de Witt approached the Princess Dowager with new proposals for her grandson's future. With the war going badly for the Dutch, at a time of impending national crisis it was important to have a figure of importance, and there were growing demands for the raising of the Prince's status. Zeeland, the most Orangist of the provinces, introduced a proposal in the States-General for giving him a seat in the Council of State, and it was suggested that one of the French marshals, preferably Turenne, should command the land forces, with William given a subordinate command under him. Though he had only reached the tender age of fifteen, such a proposal was natural for the standards of the day, especially as the Prince had a reputation for intelligence and thinking for himself, and would probably make a worthy military officer. It was not to be.

Nevertheless Amalia, the Princess Dowager, saw these proposals as a way to advance her grandson's dignity. She had always wanted to break his connection with Zuylenstein and here was her chance, especially as she believed she was acting for William's good. The States had acknowledged that he was a figure of national concern, and they were keen to bring him into public life; and whatever he might ultimately achieve, it would be necessary for him 'to live in good intelligence with the States'. In April new commissioners were appointed to supervise his education. His household was restructured, with Zuylenstein, Chapuzeau, Trigland and several Dutch and English attendants being dismissed. Bornius was appointed to a post in the Prince's treasury while the new governor, who replaced Zuylenstein, was Jan van Gent.

Distraught at being deprived of his friends and confidants, William appealed to his grandmother, but in vain. The intelligent, tactful Zuylenstein had become more like an elder brother than a tutor, making him aware of his heritage and potentialities and of the fact that Huygens was trying to recover for him the ancient principality of Orange, then an isolated Protestant stronghold, from the French monarchy. Johan de Witt resented these demonstrations of royalist feeling, and countered them by establishing the Prince under his own eye at The Hague. William was so upset at losing Zuylenstein that he went in tears to beg the French ambassador to plead for his reinstatement, but in vain. William concealed his grief and temper under an austere reserve and dignity; it was useless to protest, and it would not do to harm his prospects or the well-being of his friends by antagonizing those who held power over him. Witt himself took on the job as William's tutor and saw him regularly. While gaining further experience of hiding his feelings and accepting the new regime with good grace, William also absorbed some of Witt's learning and patriotism.

While his education continued apace, he took part in various entertainments and ceremonial functions. He was present at reviews of the fleet, military parades and regimental march-pasts. On his birthdays and other occasions of family celebration or mourning, such as births and deaths of close relations, he received the appropriate courtesies from official deputations. In January 1667 he was confirmed in the Groote Kerk, and to mark the occasion he presented a silver chalice to the chapel of a local almshouse and a stained-glass window to the church at Oudshoorn. Later that year he laid the foundation stone of a new village church at Terheyde, where he was presented with a silver trowel and a silver-mounted mallet.

In these years, as the older generation tussled for supremacy, William received Witt's visits and absorbed his teachings with a respect and courtesy that would have deceived most experienced statesmen. Meanwhile, the older man met his pupil's carefully planned manoeuvres for his restoration as head of the Republic with an arbitrary exercise of power that would have discouraged a less assertive individual. Even so, William silently resented all efforts to control him, and at length turned the tables. A few years previously the Provincial States of Zeeland had acknowledged him as Premier Noble of the Province, a dignity held by his predecessors. Now that he had reached his majority the Zeelanders asked him to come and take his seat in the Assembly. In September 1668, while Gent (with whom his relations had become increasingly strained) was on leave of absence, William left The Hague, apparently for Breda on a short hunting expedition, taking only a small amount of baggage and a few attendants. Everything had been carefully planned, and on 17 September he made a triumphal entry into Middelburg, Zeeland, escorted in an ornate coach drawn by six horses. Local militia lined the route, and the people roared their welcome. That night he was lodged in the medieval abbey buildings, but the crowds kept up their cheering and singing for several hours, while the city's great bell rang continuously above them. Next morning he took the oath as Premier Noble, and thanked the Diet of the States of Zeeland in a short speech. After several days of official functions (again, all carefully and secretly planned beforehand) at Zeeland and Breda, he returned to The Hague on 9 October. His old friend and tutor Huygens, who had helped to organize these events and welcomed him in the reception at Middelburg, wrote to the Princess Dowager telling her of his joy at the success of the venture.

The Loevesteiners were furious at having been bested, especially as they were powerless to do anything about it, and complained that he had been received not as Premier Noble or Governor, but as a king. Through gritted teeth, the States politely congratulated him on his elevation. He returned quietly to his studies, and his coming of age in November was marked modestly by a small concert given by the trained bands outside his palace, a small dinner party and callers coming to present their good wishes. More substantial was a gift of fine English hounds sent by King Charles.

Coming of age made no immediate difference to William's public position, and he was still nominally the ward of the States. His weekly sessions with Witt continued for a while, though the older man realized that his charge had a mind of his own and also enjoyed considerable public support. The increasingly powerless and ineffectual Gent retained his title and salary for another eighteen months or so, but fortunately for William they rarely saw each other except at meals. Thanks to his relatives, he was gradually assuming his responsibilities as sovereign ruler of Orange, as well as taking over management of his household and private estates.

* * *

Meanwhile beyond the borders of Holland rival European powers continued to pose a threat. In 1667 Louis XIV had attacked the Spanish Netherlands, with the immediate aim of extending France's frontiers and with long-term hopes of seizing some if not all of the Spanish empire. The sickly King Carlos II was childless, and Louis's wife was one of the major claimants to his throne. Suspecting that Carlos would soon die, Louis took advantage of the complex and varied laws of inheritance of the provinces of the Spanish Netherlands by seizing various territories in his wife's name. This made his frontier more feasible and put him in a better position to seize and hold the remaining provinces when Carlos died. On this occasion Louis's aggression was held in check by the formation of the Triple Alliance of England, the Dutch and Sweden, but Louis soon persuaded Charles II of the advantages of a joint war against the Dutch. Under the secret Treaty of Dover of 1670, both kings agreed to attack and partition the Republic. Charles hoped to take as much as possible of the Dutch trade and colonial possessions and to avenge what he regarded as his defeat, or rather lack of victory, in the war of 1665–7, while Louis's motives were more complex. The Dutch had shown in 1668 that they, not the Spanish, were the main obstacle to a French conquest of the Spanish Netherlands, and Louis intended to punish this upstart Calvinist Republic for having opposed him. In addition France wanted to seize and reopen the great port of Antwerp which, he hoped, would lead to the eclipse of both Amsterdam and London as commercial centres.

Charles planned to use William and his supporters to harass the States party, which he regarded as their common enemy. Like his late sister Mary, he looked upon William as an Englishman and a Stuart,

17

and expected him to follow English policy. Expressing an interest in William's elevation, he invited him to England. William had his own motives for visiting the country, as he wanted his uncle to repay the money he had borrowed from the coffers of the house of Orange, as well as the rest of his late mother's dowry, much of which had been promised but not yet paid. In addition, he hoped to enlist Charles's help in his struggle with Witt.

The idea of William's trip to England was met with dismay by most of those in Holland. Relatives reminded him of the deaths of his mother, of Elizabeth, Queen of Bohemia, and more recently of his aunt Henrietta of Orleans, who had all died within a few months of visiting England. Others viewed with suspicion any closer contact between the houses of England, believing that if he went he would surely never come back. The Duchess of York, they said, would arrange for one of her agents to poison him, as he might displace her daughters in the succession.

Refusing to be dissuaded, William continued with preparations for what was to be his first sea voyage. After a rough crossing he arrived at Margate on 6 November 1670, accompanied by Zuylenstein, Huygens, his lifelong friend Bentinck, Overkirke and a large suite. They stayed for four months, during which time he was royally feasted by the City of London and received honorary degrees from the universities of Oxford and Cambridge. Part of his mother's dowry was obtained from the treasury, and William was also given vague promises and assurances of loyalty and friendship. At first Charles received him emotionally, embracing him repeatedly with tears in his eyes. After a few days his mood changed, and he declared to William that the Protestant interest in Europe was no more than a factious body. He wished that his nephew would take pains to look at things himself, 'and not be led by your Dutch blockheads'.[7] William was perturbed, but out of respect to family loyalty held his tongue.

There is no evidence that any meeting took place between him and his eight-year-old cousin Mary, then still in the schoolroom, at this stage. Yet some at court were already beginning to suggest that a marriage of state between them would be prudent when she was old enough, and at the same time William was formally acknowledged as successor to the throne after the Duke of York and his children, given precedence over all of them apart from the duke. He was guest of honour at a reception held by the University of Oxford, which he attended wearing a red academic gown, and at which he was made a Doctor of Civil Laws. He accepted these honours politely but unresponsively, refused to commit himself over his marriage and found it difficult to conceal his contempt for the glib chatter and squalid splendour of his uncle's court.

Some admired his serious, upright demeanour, while others found him gloomy and priggish. Sir William Temple, the ambassador, had nothing but praise for him, finding him:

> in earnest a most extreme hopeful Prince, and to speak more plainly, something much better than I expected, and a young man of more parts than ordinary, and of the better sort; that is, not lying in that kind of wit which is neither of use to one's self nor to any body else, but in good plain sense, with show of application if he had business that deserved it, and that with extreme good agreeable humour and dispositions; and thus far of his way without any vice.[8]

He was bored by the horse-racing at Newmarket and by his uncles' endless eating and drinking. King Charles found him reserved, plainly dressed and rather more 'Dutch' than he had expected.

Efforts were made to break down his self-possession. At a supper party given by the Duke of Buckingham, the King and his rakes persuaded William to have one glass of wine too many. Normally sober, the Prince of Orange soon became more belligerently merry than the rest of them. To their amazement he broke the windows of the Queen's maids of honour's rooms, 'and had got into some of their apartments had they not been timely rescued'.[9] As they were responsible for the ignominious spectacle, his hosts took it in their stride. But William had a hangover for several days, and only a pick-me-up of eggs beaten in milk and chocolate, supplied on the orders of a thoughtful King Charles, an expert in such cures, hastened his recovery. He never forgot this embarrassing initiation into the world

19

of English debauchery – indeed, he probably never forgave Charles and his courtiers for it – and the incident only increased his scorn for the dissolute English court.

By early 1672, as King Louis XIV's military preparations became apparent, events within the Dutch Republic moved towards crisis. The Orangists and their popular supporters, encouraged by English agents, urged that William should be made Captain General so that he could use his influence with Charles to keep England apart from France. Though widely shared, this view took no account of the fickle Charles's intentions. Witt and the States party resisted William's elevation, first as they feared that William was ambitious for royal power, and secondly as they believed him to be the pawn of his uncle. There was in fact little substance behind these fears; William himself was unaware of the extent of Charles's commitment to France, and hoped he could prevail upon his uncle to help him secure the support he believed was his by right. His desire for power increased as the French menace grew, as he felt he needed power to defend his country, a task he believed the States party was either unable or unwilling to do, and he was ready to take risks in order to secure it.

In January 1672 he wrote to King Charles, suggesting that there would never be a better chance for him to obtain from the States whatever he required in the way of support. Should His Majesty be prepared to let him know what he wanted, he [William] was confident that, as long as such aspirations were not directly hostile to the foundations of the Dutch Republic, he would be able to obtain them for him in spite of any hostile designs by Witt and his cabal, who would thereby be worsted while he and his more trustworthy friends took the lead. He ended by assuring the King that, as long as he had any authority in the state, he would be utterly devoted to His Majesty's interests, as far as his honour and the faith which he owed to his country would allow him. His offer of submission was qualified with an insistence that the foundations of the Republic should be preserved. Though these assurances were not within his power to give, the letter remained secret. It was quite likely that William was treading a fine line by calling Charles's bluff, staking his safety on the probability that the latter would not be able to deliver.

Meanwhile deadlock between Holland and the other six provinces on the question of William's elevation paralysed the Republic's preparations for war. While the navy, mostly provided by Holland, was in good shape and helped to save the Republic, the army was in a bad state. William was at last made Captain General for one year, but after hearing that the mighty French army was making preparations as well, he was unsure of his chances.

Late in April 1672 Louis began his campaign, which soon became less of a war and more of a stately progress, as one garrison after another surrendered without fighting. In May Witt ordered the dykes to be cut, in order to create a last line of defence for the province of Holland. In June William's little army, now numbering only nine thousand, withdrew behind this 'waterline', which was still far from complete, and there seemed little hope of holding it as the French overran the province of Utrecht. If Louis had attacked the waterline at once he would probably have broken through, but he had wasted time overpowering the garrisons in his way, and he probably believed he had already done enough. He did not want to annex the Republic, only to inflict such a heavy defeat on the Dutch that they would no longer be able to hinder French military or commercial expansion. Convinced that the Dutch would have to accept whatever terms he imposed, he pushed his demands higher and higher. By the time the Dutch rejected them and broke off negotiations on 27 June, the waterline had grown stronger and William's numerically inferior army had grown in size and determination.

Holland was now in a better condition to resist the French, but its internal situation was alarming. With each humiliation, the people's anger grew and they sought scapegoats among the regents, although Orangists in the army had often showed themselves the most cowardly and defeatist. English and Orangist propaganda insisted that the kindly Charles II had made war only because the selfish regents of Holland had stubbornly refused to give William his rightful offices. The States party, it was alleged, would sooner sell the Republic to the French than accept the ambitious but deserving Prince William as Stadholder. Many believed that once he was elevated to the position, England would join with the Dutch against

France. The States of Holland bowed to the pressure; on 24 June William was confirmed as Stadholder and the States-General made him Captain General for life. His powers were mainly advisory rather than sovereign, however, and he would still meet with obstruction and opposition.

To defeat the French, William believed that he needed more effective and unhindered power, and that it was vital for him to break the opposition of the States party. To this end he pursued two distinct policies. First, he continued to try to do a deal with Charles II to take England out of the war and strengthen his position in the Republic. Secondly, he showed himself ready to exploit, even encourage, popular violence against his political opponents. His negotiations with Charles came to nothing, as although the King was ready to help him secure sovereignty over the United Provinces, his price in the form of large territorial and commercial concessions was too high. William was reported to have said that he preferred the title of Stadholder which the States had given him, and that he believed himself under an obligation not to place his interest before his obligations.

As events in the Republic turned more and more in his favour, he realized that he did not need his uncle's help. William's reaction to the upsurge of popular violence was mixed. Like most of the rioters, he had no time for democracy and he had no wish to encourage disorder. But the riots had already assisted his elevation and they were directed against his political enemies. The temptation to exploit the disturbances further was great and William yielded to it, doing little to stop the violence or the clamour for the punishment of Witt. He pointedly refused to declare that Witt was innocent of the crimes with which Orangist pamphlets charged him. Witt resigned his post as Grand Pensionary of Holland and was replaced by William's supporter Gaspar Fagel. In August 1672 a letter from Charles II to William was published, blaming the States party for the war and alleging that Charles's sole aim in making war had been to secure William's just rights. William did not directly order the letter's publication, but he had sent it to Fagel to use as he thought fit, and Fagel had had it read in the States-General and the States of

Holland. As one contemporary remarked, those who ordered its publication must have had some intention of bringing the men at the helm into disrepute and abandoning them to mob rule.

Witt's brother Cornelis was already in prison at The Hague on a trumped-up charge of treason. On 10 August Johan de Witt was lured to the prison by a forged letter which purported to come from his brother. Both were trapped inside and the crowds in the streets nearby broke down the doors, dragged the brothers outside, murdered them and savagely mutilated their bodies. The lynching had clearly been carefully organized. Leading Orangists like Zuylenstein were present, and the local clergy welcomed God's vengeance on these two sinners. William himself had neither directly authorized nor openly approved of the murders, but he had not discouraged the popular movement and had given it some implicit encouragement. The publication of Charles's letter was seen as especially provocative. He did nothing to punish those responsible for the outrage, telling a deputy of the States of Holland that he could not proceed as the crime had been committed by some of the leading citizens, and in due course he even appointed some of the ringleaders to government posts.

The Witts' murder led directly to the removal of the last barriers to William's seizure of effective power. A week later the States of Holland authorized him to change as many of the members of the town councils as he thought fit. They were encouraged to do so by Fagel's threat that it was better to forgo a mere formality than to allow the commonalty to impose order. Less than a third of the regents of Holland were dismissed, to be replaced by men of similar social standing. All William's opponents were removed or silenced, and in many towns the independence and civic spirit of the regents were permanently damaged. His rise to power was now complete. He held the offices of his ancestors, which were made hereditary in 1674, and he had for a time reduced the likelihood of opposition to his direction of war and diplomacy. In 1672 he began to take the offensive against France, and by the end of the following year most of the French troops had left Dutch soil. William had deservedly won for himself the title of Redeemer of the Fatherland.

From then to his dying day thirty years later, his main concern was the containment of France. His primary interests, war and diplomacy, were the main responsibilities of any seventeenth-century prince of senior rank. There was often, however, a difference between the patriotism and integrity of the motives behind his foreign policy and the sometimes unscrupulous methods which he used against opponents at home. He was always passionately convinced of his own right to rule, of the purity of his intentions and of his own rightness, convictions that had their roots partly in his personality and religious faith and partly in his upbringing. They made him intolerant of the opinions of others if those opinions led them to obstruct what he saw as his European mission. Always a statesman rather than a politician, he had little respect for politicians with their wheeling and dealing, their selfish ambitions and their obsession with local and sectional interests, and treated them with the contempt and lack of scruple which he thought they deserved.

With these authoritarian tendencies, in an ideal world he probably saw himself as an absolute monarch. However, in order to have the free hand abroad he required, William was ready to compromise at home, both in Holland and in England. In domestic affairs he was prepared to delegate responsibility, to work within the existing system and to use to the full the powers that he possessed, officially or unofficially.

Now Stadholder of most of the Provinces and Captain General of the Republic's armies by popular acclaim, William stood alone. It was up to him to save his country from the enemy, as his great-grandfather had done a century earlier. This was the start of his lifelong struggle against the might of French imperialism, just as the first William had struggled all his life against the might of Spanish imperialism; like him, by sheer stubborn refusal to admit defeat and often very little else, he managed to hold disaster at bay. Contrary to expectations William clung with grim loyalty to his 'Dutch blockheads', prepared if necessary to die on the last dyke in their defence, and defiantly rejected his designated role of puppet prince dependent on French and English patronage.

England's part in the wars had consisted of little more than two unsuccessful naval excursions, and by 1674 the strength of anti-French, anti-Catholic feeling in Parliament had forced King Charles to sue for a separate peace. The war went on without him but it was clear that, even with Spain and the Habsburgs as allies, the United Provinces would never be mighty enough to force a decision on the battlefield. Soon they too would have to accept a negotiated peace, and though William had learned not to trust his uncle he hoped that a solution to his problems might be found across the North Sea. His English friends were keeping him informed and, despite Temple's assurances, he knew that Charles's pro-French policy was very unpopular in the country. Parliament was spoiling for a war with France, while angry suspicions about the King's religious sympathies were exacerbated by the refusal of his Catholic brother and heir James, Duke of York, to attend Anglican services.

* * *

William's political apprenticeship was more or less complete by 1672, and now it was time for him to acquire some experience of a soldier's life. He enjoyed being on military campaigns, and those around him saw he became 'all fire', hardly recognizing in him the reserved young man he was at court. His education had already included a basic course of military theory, underlined by the lesson that he should always remember his responsibilities to family and country. A strong religious faith gave him physical courage. In battle he led by example, always wearing the conspicuous star of the Order of the Garter, and ignoring the pleas of others to be a little more cautious. Sometimes he was slightly wounded, but it seemed he led a charmed life, especially at Saint Denis when only the sharp shooting of his cousin Overkirke saved his life.

As a general he was less gifted, less cautious than some of his contemporaries who appreciated the virtues of manoeuvring with care and skill, never giving battle until sure of victory. He never fully mastered the finer details of siege warfare, relying instead on repeated and often costly assaults, tending to give battle too readily, often under unfavourable conditions which meant fighting and losing several small, unnecessary contests. Though this was partly a consequence of his impatient temperament, he also had disadvantages which Louis XIV's marshals did not. In 1672 the Dutch army was riddled with cowardice, indiscipline and incompetence, leading to sustained efforts by William and his lieutenant and mentor, Count George von Waldeck, to mould the men into a superior fighting force. Secondly, William was generally on the battlefield as leader of a coalition, and it was no easy task coordinating the various multinational armies. Thirdly, while Louis had a well-organized defence system and cooperative treasury, William depended on the States-General for money and men, and could not afford to spend the campaigning season on inconclusive manoeuvres; he had to fight, and if possible win, in order to maintain Dutch support for the war. Considering that his armies were smaller and of poorer quality than those of the French, he did well to achieve any success at all. He might be a hero and a saviour to his countrymen and allies, but he was still often forced to seek the help of Charles II, and this most equivocal supporter offered him help at the price of becoming a puppet king under the jurisdiction of an Anglo-French tyranny.

At one stage William sought to undermine his intractable uncle by supporting the opposition within England to the court and to the alliance with France. The war, the alliance, the Declaration of Indulgence of 1672 which extended toleration to all religious dissenters, including Catholics, the Duke of York's conversion to Catholicism and the quartering of troops near London had all created anxiety in England, making it easy for Dutch agents and propaganda to suggest they were part of a great plot to impose 'Popery and arbitrary government' in England and to exterminate Protestantism in Europe. Most seventeenth-century Englishmen looked askance at Catholicism and absolutism, and Charles's new ally, Louis XIV, personified both.

In February 1674, when Charles made peace with the Dutch, William was certainly behind some of the Dutch propaganda and political agitation; while he disapproved on principle of fomenting opposition to lawful authority, he was often driven by expediency to act contrary to his principles. But he kept his connections with the English opposition secret, in order to avoid compromising himself in the eyes of his uncles. Meanwhile in Europe he managed to secure the neutrality of Louis's other allies to build up a coalition against France, its chief members being the Dutch and the two Habsburg rulers, King Carlos of Spain and Leopold, the Holy Roman Emperor. Neither was a particularly useful ally, as the King was too weak to defend the Spanish Netherlands without considerable outside help, and the powerful Leopold was more interested in the well-being of Germany, his main concern being to check French aggression in the Rhineland, in which he was largely successful. The imperial generals were reluctant to risk heavy casualties in the Netherlands.

With the formation of an anti-French coalition, the pattern of the war changed. William's aim was now not to defend the Republic itself but rather to limit French gains in the Spanish Netherlands. Louis abandoned his hopes of crushing the Dutch and concentrated on rationalizing his northern frontier. When the war became a heavy burden on the French economy, with high taxes and bad harvests provoking unrest, an anxious Louis put forward several peace proposals to the Dutch. William hoped to make Louis relinquish all his conquests made since 1659, but this was over-optimistic, and the French King's army continued to capture more towns. William faced problems at home, with the war placing a strain on the Dutch Republic's economy and disrupting the trade on which the Dutch depended, while England was profiting from her neutrality. Once all danger to the Republic's territory had been removed, the war seemed expensive and unnecessary.

In March 1675 William was taken ill with fever, and within a day or two the illness was diagnosed as smallpox. As his father had died of the same disease at twenty-four, his supporters held their breath lest history should repeat itself. The Stadholder had no heir, and with no prince to survive him there would be no focus of loyalty or hope for the future. William was already respected as a courageous and astute leader, and any internal collapse within the Dutch

Republic would have a grave effect on European politics. King
Charles II and King Louis XIV both expressed their concern, and
asked to be kept informed of his progress.

Fortunately he was a sensible patient. In his darkened room he
refused to see any unnecessary visitors. The select circle of four
friends on whom he relied to nurse him, and his doctors, were the
only ones admitted, for fear of spreading the contagion unnecessarily. There was a tradition that if a healthy person shared the
bed of a smallpox patient, it would lessen the force of the attack. As
his most devoted friend, Bentinck was said to have slept in the bed,
and risked his life by contracting the disease just as William was
beginning to recover. Fortunately, by the end of April both had
almost completely recovered.

William was impatient to resume his normal routine. 'What
distressed me most during my illness was having to spend three
weeks without doing anything whatever,' he wrote to Count
Waldeck. 'You can imagine how much was neglected during that
time – but it was the will of heaven and one must be patient.'[10]

On his recovery he returned to the field, but the French remained
victorious. After wresting several fortresses from the French armies,
William felt he could consider the general peace urged on him by
Charles, who wanted to mediate between him and Louis XIV, while
secretly allying himself with Louis against William. Yet in the
absence of a consensus between the belligerent nations, and
William's reluctance to abandon his allies, the conflict continued.
Throughout Europe, Louis XIV's position seemed unassailable.

Doubts in Holland about the wisdom of William's foreign policy
were linked with anxiety about his ambitions at home, and fears
that he wanted to proclaim himself king. In 1675 he had been
offered the title of Duke of Gelderland, which would have given him
sovereign power in that province, but he reluctantly rejected the
offer when Holland and Zeeland made their opposition clear.
Opposition to his foreign policy and domestic ambitions was led by
Holland and above all by Amsterdam. The regents there had played
along with him in 1672–3; as his popularity waned with heavy
taxation and the interruption of trade, they insisted on peace. His

pursuance of the war depended on making the Dutch believe that victory was possible by bringing more forces to the allied side. As matters stood, the odds were against him; he was now twenty-five, the time had come to think seriously about marriage, and a dynastic alliance with England had to be considered.

Charles had no desire to put his 'strict friendship' with France at risk, at least while there was still any financial gain to be had. Nevertheless, encouraged by Temple and Lord Treasurer Danby, he could see advantages in an understanding with his nephew. There would be no better way to soothe general Protestant disquiet than by a marriage between his niece Mary and such an illustrious Protestant champion as the Prince of Orange. Moreover, if he could be persuaded to agree to a sensible understanding with France, then perhaps everyone would be satisfied.

TWO

'Mary Clorin'

Mary Stuart was born on 30 April 1662, the second child and first daughter of the Duke and Duchess of York. Her parents' marriage had not taken place in the happiest of circumstances. In 1652 Anne, eldest surviving child of the royalist exile Sir Edward Hyde, had been attached to the court of The Hague, becoming maid of honour to the widowed Princess Mary of Orange. Clever, lively and popular, she might have stayed with her mistress longer had it not been for the restoration of the monarchy in England. She and her father returned to their homeland, where Sir Edward was appointed Chancellor by King Charles II.

Soon after this, Sir Edward learnt that Anne was with child by the King's brother and heir James, Duke of York, who had confessed to 'a great affection for her'. Enraged, he declared that he would rather his daughter was the duke's whore than his wife, that he would turn her out of his house and never set eyes on her again, and that he hoped the King would send her to the Tower. His enemies lost no time in putting it about that his daughter was a loose woman and it was said that York, having been trapped, intended to repudiate her. Others said the King was forcing his younger brother into a hasty marriage, and that the Queen Mother was coming from France to prevent such an undignified alliance. Mary of Orange was angry at the idea that her former maid of honour would take precedence over her whenever she visited the court in England. Then it was revealed that a marriage had apparently already taken place at Breda, on 24 November 1659, in the presence of witnesses. Under English law the child would be James's legitimate heir, but even so Sir Edward insisted that another marriage must take place on British soil, to dispel any doubts that his daughter was the heir's wife and not his

30

mistress. James and Anne went through a second ceremony on 5 September 1660, and six weeks later their son was born. Named Charles and given the title Duke of Cambridge, he was always sickly and died at the age of seven months.

The birth of a daughter was a disappointment as they had dearly wanted a second son and, according to the diarist Samuel Pepys, nobody was pleased. Mary was not considered politically important. While King Charles II and his consort Queen Catherine were still childless, it was expected that she would soon provide him with children. Mary would also surely have a brother or two who would precede her in the line of succession; or alternatively, another revolution might send the Stuart dynasty into exile a second time.

Aged twenty-eight when his eldest daughter was born, James was an efficient and brave Lord High Admiral. Unlike King Charles, who was always affability itself, even flippant, ready to put people at ease with a diplomatic, sometimes teasing phrase, James was over-earnest and humourless, taking his religion seriously with a sense of purpose which became more devout if not bigoted in later life. Yet like his elder brother he never denied himself the pleasures of the flesh, and in addition to the twenty children (including stillbirths) born of both his marriages, he fathered at least seven children by two of his mistresses.[1]

Six more children were born to the Duke and Duchess of York, all puny infants of whom only Anne, born on 6 February 1665, survived infancy. Neither daughter was ever robust. In particular they suffered from 'sore eyes', though Mary was apparently less afflicted, and throughout her life had a passion for reading. Anne developed a squint, and though she may have been less naturally bookish than her sister, from childhood her poor eyesight was always a convenient excuse for rarely picking up a book, though she was always a devoted letter-writer. Their ill-health, and that of their siblings, has sometimes been laid at the door of their promiscuous father. Assertions that he suffered from venereal disease are probably scurrilous gossip, and the children's problems were more likely inherited from their mother, who developed breast cancer while they were still small. On the other hand, one recent biographer has suggested that Mary, being a daughter 'and therefore undervalued', enjoyed better health than her siblings as she escaped the attention of well-meaning doctors during childhood.[2] She took after her father in complexion, with heavy curls and dark eyes.

They were brought up mainly at St James's and the Duke of York doted on his eldest daughter. He enjoyed playing with her and showing her off to courtiers at St James's and Whitehall. The duchess seems to have shown her children less affection. Preoccupied with one pregnancy after another, humiliated by an unfaithful husband who plainly regarded her as little more than a brood mare, and often unwell, she found solace in fashionable dresses and overeating. When she had what was apparently no more than a mild flirtation with the good-looking Henry Sidney, her husband's Groom of the Bedchamber and her own Master of the Horse, the duke took gross exception. Husband and wife quarrelled, but it brought James to his senses for a while, and afterwards he played the part of a faithful husband – until the next mistress came along.

Though it was customary for most aristocratic children to be kept apart from their parents at meals, Mary and Anne dined regularly with their parents. The duchess spoilt Anne endlessly with titbits at table until she took after the duchess in becoming extremely fat, a problem, like myopia and gout, which plagued her to the grave.

By the time Mary was aged nine, her mother had lost what beauty she had ever possessed. Corpulent and disease-ridden, she knew that she was not long for this world. On 30 March 1671 she and her husband dined heartily with friends in Piccadilly, and on their return to St James's she collapsed in agony and was put to bed, where she died a few hours later. She was buried in the Chapel of Henry VII, at Westminster Abbey, but neither her husband nor their four remaining children attended or were represented at the ceremony.

Within a few months the two younger infants, Edgar and Katherine, also died. Mary had never been close to her mother and, having lost so many siblings, death in the family had become a sadly commonplace experience. She was growing up a pretty child with large brown eyes, dark auburn curls and a delicate complexion, the more lively minded and engaging of the girls. Maybe Anne, now aged six, felt at a disadvantage in having a quick-witted elder sister with whom to compete, and did not have the strength of spirit to try. Yet she had always seemed quiet and dull to those around her, and she never changed.

Both were declared Children of the State, and their education became the responsibility of the King and his advisers. He guaranteed that they would be brought up as members of the Church of England, and thus promised the House of Commons that the Protestant succession would be assured. They were moved to an establishment created for them at Richmond, a Thames-side palace built by King Henry VII, in the charge of Cavalier veteran Colonel Edward Villiers and his wife Lady Frances, who had been governess to the York children since 1661. Here they were away from the court and from their father's contagious Popery. Although James often saw the girls, he was wise enough not to make any serious efforts to foist his religion on to them for the moment. The only tension arose when Charles appointed as Mary's spiritual mentor the theologian Henry Compton, Bishop of London, an outspoken anti-papist. His first task was to persuade James to allow him to prepare Mary for confirmation; he succeeded, but only at the cost of creating a certain amount of bad feeling on both sides.

The Villiers daughters were brought up with the princesses, and between them formed the nucleus of a select royal school, where they were all taught to speak and read French, and had drawing, music and dancing lessons. There was also time for games of cards, walks and gossip. They were given a thorough grounding in the teachings of the Church of England, strict religious observance was enforced and the importance of saying prayers regularly was impressed on them. The conscientious Mary showed considerable aptitude in each subject, while Anne was lazy and difficult to interest in anything.

Intelligent, sensitive and emotional, beyond her books and lessons Mary had little to occupy her mind apart from the world of court gossip. Deprived of male company and friendship, a bored, lonely adolescent with a lively imagination, she needed someone to look up to and identified herself with the lovesick heroines she met in her reading; she became unnaturally fond of a girl nine years her elder, Frances Apsley, elder daughter of Sir Allen and Lady Apsley. Sir Allen had fought against the Dutch under the Duke of York in 1665, and was now Treasurer of the Household to Charles II and Receiver-General to the duke. The Princess's affectionate soul sought comfort and release in long passionate letters to the older girl. There was no question of formality, or emphasis on difference of rank between any of the girls. Mary and Anne, whose favourite reading was poetic drama, assumed for themselves and their confidantes names from plays. Mary named herself Mary Clorin or Clorine, after the eponymous character in John Fletcher's play *Faithful Shepherdess*, while Frances was Aurelia, after a flirtatious character in John Dryden's comedy, *An Evening's Love*.

Without other friends or playmates Mary became totally absorbed in this fourteen-year correspondence, a fantasy world inspired by plays she saw and novels she read. Her first surviving letter to Frances Apsley begins 'dear husband' and ends 'your loving wife'. She strove 'to tel my dearest dear husband how much I love her wold be but to make you weiree of it for al the paper books and parchments in the world wo'd not hold half the love I have for you'.[3] All these letters were badly written, poorly spelt, oddly punctuated and effusively sentimental; in another she described herself as 'your humbel servant to kiss the ground where you go to be your dog in a string your fish in a net your bird in a cage your humbel trout'.[4] They were phrased with such passion that later generations were tempted to suspect a lesbian relationship, but this theory is not worth taking seriously. It is hard to read anything more than a schoolgirl crush and a highly imaginative turn of phrase in these colourfully expressed but innocent outpourings of a warm and loving adolescent, merely seeking an outlet for her emotions within an all-female environment. The girls were, however, well aware that if their letters were to be seen by curious adult eyes, there might be trouble. No footman was trusted with them, and they were usually delivered and collected by Mr Gibsone the drawing master. Yet after a while Frances became embarrassed by the younger girl's effusive turn of phrase, and the correspondence shocked her father when he was alerted to it.

The only male character to feature in these letters was her cousin James, Duke of Monmouth, the illegitimate son of King Charles II. He was fourteen years older than Mary, and her interest may have been partly hero-worship for a man who played a prominent role in military campaigns abroad, partly natural affection for a close male relative and partly fascination with his tangled extra-marital liaisons. Like his father, he never understood the meaning of the word fidelity. Though married to the heiress Lady Anna Scott of Buccleuch, he was also involved with a mistress, Eleanor Needham, a friend of Mary and Frances, who was found to be carrying his child and had left court, saying that 'nobody should ever hear of her more'. Nevertheless, their affair resulted in several more children.

A year after his wife's death the Duke of York was engaged as Admiral of the Fleet in a short war with the Dutch, one of the few episodes of his long life in which he really distinguished himself. In peacetime he lived at Richmond or St James's Palace, where he often had his daughters to stay with him. He leaned increasingly towards the Catholic church but, as a result of the passing of the Test Act in the spring of 1673, by which only practising Anglicans could hold any civil or military office under the crown, he was forced to relinquish all his commands. Increasingly unpopular, he was now known as 'Squire James' by the people of London. Despite a procession of mistresses he intended to marry again, and his eye fell on one Lady Bellasyse, a widow of seventeen, who was at least Protestant, but singularly plain and with no royal blood. The King refused to countenance such a marriage, telling him indignantly that he had 'played the fool once, it is not to be borne, and at such an age!'[5]

James sent emissaries to inspect various eligible princesses abroad, and received good reports of Mary Beatrice d'Este of Modena's disposition and appearance. At fifteen she was attractive but pious, with strong family ties to the Pope. Born and raised in Italy, she had never heard of England until she became engaged to be married to the heir, and she had begged to be left to become a nun in the Carmelite convent where she had been educated.

A proxy marriage took place between the Princess and the Earl of Peterborough. She wept throughout the ceremony, begged not to be parted from her mother and developed a nervous fever that delayed her crossing the Channel. On arrival at Dover she was met by a husband whom she detested on sight; he was more than twice her age, tended to stammer when nervous and, as contemporaries unanimously agreed, had a rather cruel expression about the mouth. His child bride could therefore be excused for initially bursting into tears whenever she looked at him. Nevertheless they were married at Dover on 21 November 1673. On the night of her arrival in England a party marched through the streets with an effigy of the Pope which was then burnt on a bonfire in protest. The Commons objected to the match, but by the time they had placed their petition for a Protestant alliance before the King, James was already the husband of Mary Beatrice.

Mary and Anne liked their young stepmother, scarcely more than a child herself. When the duke told his daughters that he had provided them with a playfellow, he was quite right. Overwhelmed by the sophistication of this somewhat decadent court, Mary Beatrice was far more at ease with these two girls who seemed like younger sisters. Once she had got over her homesickness they found her likeable and high-spirited, happy to join in with their games of blind-man's-buff and cards, even on Sundays, despite the disapproval of their chaplain, Dr Lake. They were glad that she did not seem nearly so serious about her religion as their father, and that she was open-minded enough not to try to persuade them to join the Catholic church. Her friendship brought a change for the better into their young lives. However, remarriage to a young and pretty princess did nothing to cure the duke of his womanizing ways. Like a good wife she soon came to be fond of her husband, and it grieved her that he should seek comfort and pleasures in the arms of other women such as Arabella Churchill.

In the autumn of 1674, King Charles decided to commission a masque, to be acted at Whitehall, in which his nieces would be the main performers. John Crowne, a protégé of the Duke of Rochester and a playwright who was understandably modest about his unexceptional writing talents, was ordered to pen a suitable dramatic vehicle for the Duke of York's daughters. Taking his theme from Ovid's *Metamorphoses*, he chose to write a masque titled *Calisto, or The Chaste Nymph*, with Mary in the title role and Anne as her friend Nyphe. Everyone praised Mary's performance, not least Crowne himself, who said that she 'spoke to the eyes and souls of all who saw her'.[6] It would have been remarkable if he had said anything else.

The duke did not neglect his duties as a husband. In January 1675, fourteen months after their wedding, Mary Beatrice gave birth to a first child, named Catherine Laura. At her parents' behest she was christened in the Catholic faith, and a disapproving King Charles immediately arranged an Anglican christening for his little niece, at which twelve-year-old Mary was proud to be one of her stepsister's godmothers. Mary and Anne remained Mary Beatrice's closest friends at court, and were a great comfort when the baby princess died in October after a fit of convulsions.

* * *

In April 1677 Mary was fifteen: her sheltered years were coming to an end and her future had to be considered. It was clear that King Charles II's consort, Queen Catherine, would never bear a child, and after four years of marriage the second Duchess of York had had two miscarriages and two daughters, one of whom had died in infancy and the other, Isabella, was a sickly child unlikely to survive long.* Moreover the duke's open conversion to Roman Catholicism had already begun to raise doubts about his succession to the throne, and that of his family after him. The marriage of his elder daughter was therefore a matter of no little dynastic concern. Her cousin William was regarded by King Charles and his ministers as a likely candidate for her hand, and it was considered a matter of major importance that he should be in no doubt about her doctrinal allegiance.

---

*   She died in March 1681, aged four.

From William's own point of view, marriage to Mary would have slender advantages. She was next in line to the British throne after her father, and he would be unlikely to offer much of a dowry, though the thrifty William hardly needed money. Marriage to another Mary Stuart would probably be unpopular in Holland, where his mother was remembered with little affection. William himself shared his mother's contempt for the low birth of Mary's mother, who had, after all, been one of her servants; he suspected that the mother's lowly status might prejudice her daughter's claim to the throne. Added to this was a belief that the Duke of York was diseased, perhaps venereally, and incapable of begetting a child who would live to maturity. Advisers in Holland suggested that he would do better to consider either a Danish princess or perhaps the widowed Queen of Poland.

In spite of these discouraging omens, William would surely improve his chance of succeeding to his uncle Charles's throne if he did marry Mary, but it was still remote – and unlikely for a good many years. The only immediate benefit he could hope for was the hypothetical one that the marriage would give him enough extra influence with Charles to enable him to bring England in to the alliance against France. Although this policy had the support of some of Charles's ministers, notably the Earl of Danby, Lord High Treasurer, it was to prove a failure.

In April 1676 William invited Sir William Temple, English Ambassador to The Hague and one of the few Englishmen he liked and trusted, to Honselaarsdijk Palace to discuss the possibility of such a marriage. Temple was favourably impressed by William; he respected the Prince's common sense and ready application to business so lacking in his uncle King Charles II, and was delighted that the Prince was considering an English marriage, which would be entirely in his interest and would bring him nearer the crown. He knew it would be unwise to try to rush matters. In considering his prospects, William said he was often pressed by friends to think of marrying, that many persons had proposed to him and he was considering marrying an English rather than a German or a French princess.

When Temple expressed approval, William requested reassurance on two points, and asked that he should give it 'not as an ambassador, but as a friend or at least an indifferent person'. Some of his friends, or those who pretended to be his friends, were very much against any thought of his marrying in England, telling him that 'he would by it lose all the esteem and interest he had there, and be believed to run wholly into the dispositions and designs of the Court, which were generally thought to run so different from those of the nation, especially upon the point of religion'.[7] They had made him fear that it was only a matter of time before there was another anti-monarchical revolution, as likely as not on the grounds of religious differences. It would be as well for his reputation if he avoided becoming too closely identified with the crypto-Catholic court of England. Moreover, he wanted to know something more about 'the persons and disposition of the young lady'. While he appreciated that it was not for princes to pay too much attention to personal details, he himself considered it important.

Temple replied that he was delighted by the Prince's decision. Politically, he foresaw no disadvantages, as the King and his nephew would benefit from a closer relationship. William would be one degree nearer the crown, which, despite the issue of religion, stood on much firmer foundations in England than before. William was less interested in the English crown than in gaining extra influence with Charles and thus enlisting the support of the English army and navy in the alliance against France. As for the character of Princess Mary herself, Temple had no personal knowledge, but his wife and sister both thought well of her, were friends of her governess and could vouch for the fact that considerable trouble had been taken over her upbringing. As far as he knew, the girl was modest, pious and healthy. William needed no further encouragement, and promptly wrote to the King and the Duke of York for permission to visit England, while asking Temple to instruct his wife and sister to confirm their opinion of the Princess through Lady Frances Villiers. He then agreed to put the matter on one side, and left for the summer campaign.

On his return in January 1677 terms of peace between the Republic, her allies and France were again discussed with Temple. As the French conditions were impossible, Temple again suggested that the Republic should consider making a separate peace and deserting Austria and Spain, but William would not hear of it and Temple told his master that the Prince would not be separated from his allies. Charles had no desire to put his 'strict friendship' with France at risk, at least while there was still any financial gain to be had. He put forward a proposal suggested by Louis, of splitting the combination formed against France. William listened to the terms, then said dismissively that dinner was ready and they would talk of it when they had dined. He would rather die than accept such terms, and he recognized the hand of the French ambassador behind them. A few hours later he told Temple, with a touch of cold irony, that his dinner had been spoiled. He had not expected such a return for his overtures, and had been insulted by the written offer of the Anglo-French terms coming from the hand of the English Secretary of State, Arlington, whom he detested, and who had written to him as if he were a child.

A month later William announced that a peaceful solution was not yet possible and he would continue with the war rather than break his contract with Austria and Spain. He pursued his campaign against the French, with varying success, until July, when he was able to come home from the front for a short time. Persuaded by Temple and Danby, King Charles could see the advantages of an understanding with his nephew. There would be no more certain way to soothe general Protestant disquiet than by a marriage between his niece and such an illustrious Protestant champion as the Prince of Orange. It would also help reinforce William's attachment to the Stuart family interest away from the opposition party, now growing dangerously in self-confidence and organization. Added to that, maybe the Prince could be parted from his European allies and persuaded to agree to a sensible accommodation with France.

The King now offered terms that had not been dictated by Louis, and William agreed to come to England to discuss them. In October 1677 he arrived at Harwich and travelled to Newmarket, joining his uncles who had gone there for the autumn race meeting. Charles had been hoping to use his niece as a prize to be withheld until he had won his own terms from his nephew regarding peace, but soon realized that the young man was not to be deflected from his purpose.

With his hooked nose, fragile physique and asthmatic cough, William was hardly an ideal bridegroom for a sentimental, fifteen-year-old girl. A professional soldier and a 'plain man', as he regarded himself, William had neither the desire nor the facility for anything but formal politeness or a direct interchange of plans and ideas. It never occurred to him to enlarge on the interests, such as architecture, gardening and interior decoration that, along with his hunting, were his sole relaxation. On this occasion the Prince's reserve was more than usually impenetrable, and he was much criticized by the English statesmen. As self-possessed as ever, he was at the same time in too much of a hurry and too preoccupied with the burden of a nation at war to attempt any effort at the interchange of hyperbolic compliments that decorated conversational openings at the court of Whitehall. He despised the display, sycophancy and wild behaviour that took the place of sociability among his uncle's courtiers. But he could at least offer the peace that Charles desired to arrange and the means to enforce his own requirements. He also had a supporter whose integrity and acuteness were equalled by his own.

One man, arguably the most important male character in William's life, was present at all these discussions. Willem Bentinck, who had come to England shortly before, had already been his master's closest friend and confidant for some ten years. The most intelligent and capable of William's immediate circle, he had gained the highest place in his master's affections; though neither handsome, fascinating nor accomplished, he was extremely shrewd and more adept than William at flattering those with whom they did business, and at making himself at home with the gossip which was so essential to a man of society in the European courts of the seventeenth century.

William was twelve years older than Mary, almost a generation apart, and had been schooled in a tough environment, born to shoulder responsibility almost as soon as he came of age, while she had had a highly emotional, enclosed development in the nursery, the schoolroom and the presence-chamber. Temple thought that William seemed 'like a hasty lover'[8] at Newmarket coming to claim his bride. Though he might have begrudged his absence from the autumn campaign on mainland Europe, he was still determined not to make the separate peace Charles still secretly hoped for, and he wanted to meet the Princess before discussing terms. Temple was his unequivocal English ally, and among his other potential supporters the astute Danby, not only Lord Treasurer but also the most powerful minister in the Council, would prove to be the most dependable. Danby wanted to turn the course of European politics by abandoning the Anglo-French alliance and joining with the States-General in their conflict against Louis XIV, seeing it as the only way to achieve England's independence and his own ambitions. He had tried to free Charles from financial dependence on Louis for some time, and a marriage between William and Mary would be a step towards putting the scheme into practice. Moreover, he was relieved that the King seemed to approve of the Anglo-Dutch alliance.

William had to reckon with the Duke of York, who now saw any chance of a Catholic marriage for Mary slipping away. Although he had sent William an affectionate letter of greeting when his visit was first proposed, he told Danby that he knew what was going on and was sure that the marriage plans would fall through, as the King had promised he would not consent to any marriage for Mary without his full consent. When Danby reported this to the King, he replied that he had indeed given his brother such a promise, but that 'he must consent'. While James opposed the Dutch marriage, he had no allies except for M. Barillon, the French Ambassador. His sense of loyalty and duty to king and country prevailed, and permission was extracted from him by Charles for Mary's hand, and he reluctantly told Barillon that they must accept the inevitable. Unaware how far matters had gone, the ambassador urged the duke to stand his ground. James half-heartedly suggested that Charles should be approached and appealed to by his mistress the Duchess of

Portsmouth, who for the past seven years had been Louis's unofficial representative. Barillon was given a private audience, but before he could even begin to discuss the matter the King explained that this marriage would quell any suspicions held by his subjects that the alliance he had with France had no other foundation than a change of religion. It was the Duke of York's conduct that had given rise to suspicion.

William also had to take into account the presence of the maverick Duke of Monmouth, who had to be considered as a possible if unlikely claimant to the English throne. Charles was now allowing Monmouth and his supporters to believe that he might one day acknowledge him as his legitimate heir, though his official declarations categorically denied any such thing. In fact, the King was using his son as a sop to Protestant feeling and a weapon against Louis and James, when the demands of the one and the suggestions of the other became inconvenient. Monmouth believed, perhaps correctly, that his mother, Lucy Walter, had been privately married to the King during exile. Though he had led the victorious Franco-British forces against William at the siege of Maastricht, he was now ready to join him in a war against Louis XIV. There was never any major difference of opinion between William and Monmouth, who admired and respected each other's abilities, even though William might consider the older man's ambitions and judgement to be at fault.

William arrived at Newmarket to find Arlington, Danby and Temple waiting to escort him to the presence-chamber. King Charles and the Duke of York received their nephew cordially, and a few days passed with the usual amusements and hospitality. Charles made several efforts to draw William into conversation, but was disappointed to find him so evasive. Afterwards he asked Temple to find out what the problem was, and learned that the Prince of Orange had no intention of discussing anything, either about the marriage or about European affairs, until he had met Princess Mary. Now more amused than disturbed, and evidently impressed with the young man's determination, the King yielded good-humouredly, instructing the court to leave Newmarket and return to London.

At this stage William was at last formally introduced to his cousin Mary. It appears that he was not yet spoken of to her as a prospective suitor, though she must have been intelligent enough to realize that plans were being made. She received him with a becoming lack of self-consciousness. Maybe she was disappointed by her first sight of William, a good 4 inches shorter than herself and eleven years older, a thin, unremarkable man with a hunched back, a pockmarked face still bearing the telltale signs of smallpox, melancholy dark eyes and a long nose. He was almost comically unfashionable in appearance, wearing his own thick dark brown hair in preference to a wig. Beside the dashing, good-looking Duke of Monmouth, the only other male cousin whom she yet knew, he must have cut a very nondescript figure. His public manner was stiff and reserved and he was not given to making extravagant speeches, or indulging in displays of gallantry which Mary's favourite reading of romantic plays and novels had led her to expect in a suitor. Yet his manners were courteous, he flattered her with intelligent conversation and treated her as an adult instead of the young girl barely out of the schoolroom which she still was. Over the next few days they were present together at several functions. It was evident to all that she had made a great impression on him. At fifteen she was attractive, tall, slender and graceful, rather diffident but with charming manners and an appealing air of gentleness – everything a young bachelor could wish for.

King Charles was pleased but not surprised. On the other hand the Duke of York had secretly hoped it might come to nothing, but as a model subject of his brother and sovereign he knew he had to accept the inevitable. While his consent was necessary to grant the hand of his daughter in marriage, this was a formality he could not reasonably refuse. For an unpleasant moment Charles feared that his brother's obstinacy might put paid to the scheme altogether. He said as much to Danby, who persuaded the King that it would be in the duke's best interests, and added that there was great enthusiasm for the marriage throughout the nation, particularly as another Protestant alliance would be an additional bulwark against Catholic France. In a mood of gloom Charles said his brother would probably never consent to it, to which Danby answered that he, the King, would have to overrule him and command it. This stiffening of Charles's resolve worked, and when the Duke of York complained to him about the arbitrary manner in which he was being treated, he found no sympathy.

Even so, the King and his heir still had the national interest at heart, and James wholeheartedly supported his brother's wish to discuss the terms of peace before the marriage contract. William was caught between conflicting loyalties, as the argument continued for nearly a week, while Temple and Danby steeled themselves for the – admittedly remote – possibility of a breaking-off of all negotiations. Nobody was more anxious for the marriage than Charles, who continued to play an unwilling and half-hearted part in peace talks, mainly for the benefit of the suspicious French Ambassador. Emphasizing the conflicting loyalties between which he was torn, James sent desperate messages to King Louis, and again the question of a separate peace was raised. William said he realized that he and his allies would get hard terms, and he had no intention of selling his honour for a wife.

Charles still wanted to settle the outstanding political issues before giving his consent to the marriage, and now that William was evidently taken with Mary he felt his case had been strengthened. While he was eager to give his assent to such a match, the issue of peace with France had to be settled before any betrothal could be announced. William was obdurate; he would get married first and then discuss an end to hostilities. While under no illusions that he and his allies would not get the easiest of terms from the French, he would not give anybody the satisfaction of saying behind his back that he had sold his honour simply for a marriage alliance.

For several days neither side would give way, and on the evening of 19 October William received Temple in his lodgings at Whitehall, telling him morosely that he greatly regretted ever having come to England. Unless the King gave up his plan of discussing peace before the marriage, he himself would return to Holland in two days' time. First, the King must choose what their future personal relationship was to be. Were they to be the greatest friends – or sworn enemies?

Knowing that William had several influential contacts among the opposition, Temple went to see the King next day, repeating William's ultimatum. A breach between uncle and nephew, he emphasized, would be disastrous for all concerned; he resisted the temptation to add that it might suit the Duke of York but nobody else.

It was probably just as the King expected, and he conceded with apparent, probably feigned, spontaneity. He felt it would be prudent to convey the impression that he was giving in against his will. With the good-tempered resignation of a man who knows when he is beaten, he said he never yet was deceived in judging a man's honesty, 'and if I am not deceived in the Prince's face, he is the honestest man in the world, and I will trust him, and he shall have his wife, and you shall go immediately and tell my brother so, and that it is a thing I am resolved on'.[9] The Duke of York, he said, would do as he was told and he did, albeit reluctantly; prepared for bad news, James expressed surprise and then remarked philosophically that as a loyal member of the royal house he had no choice but to accept the King's authority.

When Temple went to tell William the news, the young man refused to believe a word of it at first. Once persuaded that it was not yet another trap set by his uncle, he embraced Temple and said that he had 'made him a very happy man, and very unexpectedly'.[10] While the negotiators were congratulating one another the Duke of York, having dined at Whitehall, went to St James's to see his daughter who, as legend would have it, wept all afternoon and throughout the following day. Marrying a man whom she had only met a few days before, and leaving home and friends to live in a foreign country, was a shock. However, the settlement of affairs can hardly have been unexpected. She had always known that any marriage arranged for her would be an affair of state, and she must also have been aware that the Prince of Orange was the most likely candidate for her hand.

That he possessed many fine qualities was not in question, but courage, integrity and steadfastness of purpose may not necessarily have been the sort of qualities likely to appeal to an immature, over-emotional girl of fifteen. In any case, throughout her childhood she had been used to hearing everyone and everything from Holland being ridiculed at court, especially by the pro-French party, and she was aware that her father resented any kind of Dutch connection. The Duke of York wanted a Catholic son-in-law for his favourite daughter, did not like William and cared for his Calvinism even less. He had doubtless done his best to paint a thoroughly negative picture of her future in a joyless Dutch desert inhabited by ill-bred, boorish republicans, for he and Charles had sometimes received less than hospitable treatment from the States during their years of exile. Yet nobody shared her distress; on the contrary, news of her engagement was well received.

Then James sent for Lady Frances, telling her that the King thought fit to bestow his daughter upon the Prince of Orange, and that she must now prepare the Princess for instant departure into Holland. There would be a fortnight in which she needed to help choose her trousseau, as well as the inevitable programme of entertainments and rejoicings in which she was expected to take part. The most picturesque of these was on 29 October when the city entertained the royal family to a vast banquet at the Guildhall.

The wedding was arranged to take place on 4 November, William's twenty-seventh birthday, at 9 p.m. He insisted on rejecting an elaborate ceremony performed in the midst of a large crowd in a warm building, on the grounds that it would have probably precipitated a severe fit of coughing. Instead it was a small, private and sombre affair, held in Mary's bedchamber at St James's Palace with only their closest relatives present, the Bishop of London, Henry Compton, officiating, and Bentinck as best man. The misery of the bride, the cold correctness of the bridegroom, the grim resignation of the Duke of York and the tears of the duchess, who dreaded parting from her favourite stepdaughter and was heavily pregnant with her fourth child, were portents of gloom long remembered by Dr Lake. The bride's sister Anne, who had worked up a little-sister resentment against the man who had come to steal her beloved only sister away from her, and Lady Frances Villiers were unable to attend as they were sickening for smallpox. Only the King was his usual cheerful if tactless self, trying to enliven proceedings with characteristic pleasantries. On giving away his niece he advised Dr Compton to make haste, lest the Duchess of York should bring them a boy and so 'disappoint' the marriage. When William turned to Mary and put down some coins with the solemn words 'all my worldly goods I thee endow', the King told her to pick them up and put them in her pocket, 'for it was all clear gain'.[11]

When the service was over and the bride and bridegroom had received the congratulations of their relatives, the court and all the foreign ambassadors, cakes and hot possets were handed round. Then Mary, who had withdrawn to another room to be undressed by Queen Catherine, the Duchess of York and the Duchess of Monmouth, was put to bed beside her husband. Charles himself drew the curtains round the bed, saying 'Now nephew, to your work! Hey! St George for England!'[12] They had to be up early next morning, to receive the Mayor and Aldermen of London who came to bring their best wishes in person. William then presented jewels worth £40,000, the groom's traditional present to the bride. It was late as their arrival from Holland had been delayed. The finest, and the one she would always treasure most, was a small ruby and diamond ring.

As the ministers had known all along, the marriage was popular in England; it seemed to show that the nation was escaping at last from her subordination to France, and it was a cause for rejoicing that 'the Eldest Daughter of the Crown should sleep in Protestant Arms'.[13] By this time the bells of St James's and of every church from Chelsea to the Tower of London were pealing out and fresh bonfires were being prepared. The jubilation throughout the capital was in sharp contrast to the gloom of the newly-weds. William had not secured the alliance against France that he wanted, and he feared that his marriage might not have given him the extra influence with his uncle which he had expected.

Though the States-General had given their consent to the marriage, they were just as unenthusiastic. The small dowry was just enough to pay for the jewels William had given Mary as a wedding present. On 7 November the Duchess of York gave birth to a son, much to the delight of her husband who felt that they had wrong-footed everyone else. The Pope sent his congratulations to the couple, and in France the birth was seen as a good omen for the prospects of a Catholic succession. Mary was not in the least disappointed at being ousted in the succession, unlike her husband. Already irritated by the King's refusal to grant him a dukedom, William was even more put out when asked to stand as godfather (as was the King himself) to the child, though he knew he could hardly refuse. The child was christened the next day by Dr Crewe, Bishop of Durham. He was named Charles and given the title Duke of Cambridge.

At first the baby thrived, but within five weeks he was dead. While convalescing from smallpox, Anne had visited her stepmother in the lying-in chamber. Bending over the cradle, she had given her baby brother a kiss, and thus unwittingly passed on the contagion to him. Mary's governess, Frances Villiers, also fell ill and William, still in his apartments at Whitehall, recalling his brush with the disease two years earlier, ordered his wife to leave the infected surroundings of St James's. Defiantly she retorted that her first duty was to nurse her sister. Husband and wife quarrelled, and when her chaplain, Edward Lake, went to say goodbye to her, he found her in tears, 'not only for her sister's illness, but also for some discontent occasioned by the Prince's urging her to remove her lodgings to Whitehall'.[14] William managed to prevent Dr Lake from going to one and then the other of the sisters to read prayers; it was decided that the chaplain should remain in attendance on Mary for two more days.

William found the superficial atmosphere and general claustrophobia of Charles's court increasingly irritating. Moreover, matters in Holland called for his attention; he was impatient to go home, and redoubled his efforts to get his wife away from the country he detested and the relatives he despised. Even so, his marriage appeared to have made one change for the better with his in-laws, with the Duke of York now appearing more sympathetic and ready to listen to him than the King. On 15 November a ball was held to celebrate Queen Catherine's birthday. Mary was dressed in all her new jewellery, and she and William danced together. But it was noted that he did not seem to have much to say to her throughout the evening, and barely gave her a second glance. Worst of all, it emerged that he had not even been to visit her the previous day. Bored beyond endurance with England and preoccupied with getting away, he took little notice of her until after the party was over, when he ordered her to get ready for their departure at once.

All the family came to take their leave of her with some emotion. As luck would have it, a fierce gale was blowing and they had to wait in town for another four days. William grew increasingly sullen and impatient, and everyone noticed that he seemed to be taking no notice of his Princess, or making any effort to go and see her at St James's. On one of her last evenings in England Mary had a last short and sad meeting with Frances Apsley, but she was tired and overwrought, and Frances had to leave in a hurry as her father was ill. Mary wrote miserably, 'I hope you will keep your word with me and not forget your pore Clorine that loves you better then can be exprest.'[15]

The wind changed favourably on 19 November. A tearful Mary begged the Duchess of Monmouth to look after her little sister, still recovering from smallpox and unable to join the party who had come to see her off, and said her last goodbyes to Queen Catherine and to the Duchess of York. The Queen tried to comfort her by remarking that when she had first arrived in the country to be married, she had not even seen her future husband. 'But, madam,' replied Mary, 'you came into England; but I am going out of England.'[16]

King Charles and the Duke of York accompanied the Prince and Princess of Orange down river in the royal barge to Erith, where they had a farewell dinner together. The young couple then went on board the yacht *Mary* and did not disembark until within sight of Gravesend. William urged the captain to make haste, but the weather was deteriorating rapidly. The captain refused to cross the North Sea in such conditions and he landed the Prince and Princess at Sheerness, where they were offered hospitality by the governor. Impatient to return to Holland to help prepare his military budget and other business, and unable to face another round of emotional farewells, William refused to return to London, so they waited at Canterbury until the weather improved. On Sunday morning he and Mary attended divine service at Canterbury Cathedral. He had made no allowances for any further travelling expenses in England after his departure from London, and as he had to provide accommodation for the suite for several days his money was running low. The Mayor of Canterbury respectfully declined to lend them funds and Dr Tillotson, Dean of the Cathedral, came to their rescue. Homesick and desperately missing her family, Mary spent much of the time in her room. Still worried by Anne's illness, she was even more distressed to learn that her governess Lady Frances Villiers, whom she had intended to take to Holland as part of the English household of forty persons as stipulated in her marriage contract, had died.

At last, on the morning of 28 November, they set sail from Margate. Husband and wife travelled in separate ships, Mary in the *Katherine*, William in the *Mary*. The sea was still very rough, and by the time the convoy came within sight of the Dutch coast twenty-four stormy hours later, everyone on board was soaked and prostrate with seasickness or exhaustion or both. Ice floes in the River Maas prevented them from landing at Rotterdam and they had to go ashore at the small fishing village of Terheyde, where William carried his exhausted bride across the beach. This first view of Holland, with fierce waves crashing on a deserted beach in midwinter, was hardly an inviting one. Only a few cold and wet villagers had come to welcome the bedraggled company, who had to walk several miles over frostbound, rutted lanes. Coaches were hurriedly summoned to collect them. At last they reached the gates at the end of a long drive which took them to the palace at Honselaardijk, where the household had been alerted to their impending arrival and were ready to greet them with blazing fires, lighted candles and dinner.

THREE

Prince and Princess of Orange

On 14 December 1677 the Prince and Princess of Orange made their state entry into The Hague. Church bells were ringing and guns were firing as they drove in a golden coach, drawn by six piebald horses, along streets decorated with garlands and triumphal arches and lined with cheering crowds. A guard of honour was provided by young girls dressed in white strewing sweet herbs along their path. They were greeted at the gates by twelve companies of burghers, then they crossed over the bridge into the city decorated with garlands, and passed under an arch adorned with foliage and representations of their coats of arms above two clasped hands. In the evening they stood together at a window in the Binnenhof to watch a spectacular firework display, and next day the States-General laid on a formal reception for them. With her youthful charm and manners, Mary made a very good impression, and the general verdict was that she was a great improvement on the last Mary Stuart, Princess of Orange.

After two days of official engagements they resumed their interrupted honeymoon at Honselaardijk, which was to be their principal residence. William's Dutch entourage had been surprised by the unhygienic conditions they found in England, and everything was much cleaner in Holland. When dining with a friend one evening, Sir William Temple thought nothing of spitting on the floor, and was startled to see a servant in the room immediately wipe it up with a clean cloth. He was even more taken aback when his friend warned him that, had his wife been present, she would probably have asked him to leave the house at once for fouling her floor. Sir William and Lady Temple were among William's closest friends, and he used to dine with them once or twice a week.

Early in January Mary undertook her first ceremonial duty on her own, receiving the ladies of The Hague in audience. For her it was a timely introduction to the snobbery prevalent in Dutch public life. In order to pander to their petty-minded whims, William had agreed with the noblemen that the Princess should only kiss married women if they were of noble birth, and spinsters if they were related to William and his family. When some of the ladies realized they would not be greeted with the royal kiss, they complained to their husbands. William was told that their wives were entitled to a kiss by virtue of their husband's office, which surely gave them the necessary rank. Refusing to be dictated to, he insisted that the office did not ennoble the holder, and that his wife had behaved correctly. Nevertheless, there were mutterings that this latest English Princess to marry into the Orange family might be just as haughty as her late unlamented mother-in-law.

For a few weeks husband and wife were alone at last in their home, and had a chance to get to know one another properly. At twenty-seven, William was already mature, seasoned by experience, an old head on fairly young shoulders. Yet with a young, comparatively childlike wife, at last there was some feminine company in his life to help make good the vacuum. He had had no sisters, and had hardly known his mother or his grandmother. It was no wonder that the apparently grim, unbending and reserved man that Mary had met in England became more good-humoured and affectionate in his home environment. At ease in the surroundings where he had grown up, away from what he regarded as the lax, tiresome court of St James's, he was immediately transformed. Mary now realized that her cousin and husband was not the ogre she had feared and dreaded.

It did not take her long to appreciate the fundamental cultural differences between the easy-going English and the comparatively grave Dutch. Now it was clear why William had cut such a puritanical figure at the court of St James's. The English loved to dress up and dazzle one another with their fashionable finery, while the thrifty, down-to-earth Dutch wore sober colours which hardly changed from one year to the next, preferring to spend their money on houses and furnishings instead. Thanks to his grandmother's prudent financial sense, William was comfortably off, though his mother had spent much of what she possessed in supporting her eldest brothers during their years of exile. By nature he preferred the simple life to one of ostentation, and his preoccupation with the political and military affairs of Holland left him with little time or energy for the hated business of lavish entertaining.

During his adult bachelor years he had spent much of his time in the company of other men, dining with officers of The Hague garrison or foreign diplomats. Apart from Bentinck (who later married Anne Villiers, one of Mary's ladies), his closest friends included Overkirke and Odijk, sons of Heer van Beverweerd, the illegitimate son of William's great-uncle Prince Maurice, and their distant kinsman by marriage, the Earl of Ossory. Unlike his uncles in England, he loathed the formality and conviviality of court life, much preferring male company and the camaraderie of camp and hunting field. Mary was a poor horsewoman, and never enjoyed riding. Shy by nature, he preferred the company of men whom he knew well to that of women. As his name was not to be linked with that of another woman, apart from his wife, for several years, it was easy for his enemies to suggest that he was homosexual, a slander which some did not hesitate to stoop to in his later years.

Married life did not mean the total abandonment of his bachelor routines. He continued to hold what might have been regarded as business luncheons with these friends, advisers and ministers. Mary accepted without demur his midday meals which she was not invited to attend, ostensibly on the grounds that it would not have been right for her to sit down and eat with her social inferiors. It was probably more true to say that a woman's presence would have restricted the frequently bawdy male conversation. William spent much of the afternoon engaged in military or government business, while Mary was 'at home' to people who came to play cards or perhaps dance. After they had gone, husband and wife would have supper together. As William had been preoccupied with state affairs most of the day, Mary was tactful enough to avoid serious topics, entertaining him instead with lighthearted gossip and trivia. Realizing that serious business took up so much of his time with others, she knew that he was glad to put it all behind him when he was at home. Their marriage had hardly been a love match, but if the testimony of most contemporaries is to be believed, they had evidently fallen in love with each other not long after their wedding. Moreover, in the early weeks of 1678 Mary realized that she was expecting a child.

William was careful to keep some other news from her until the last possible moment. For there was no avoiding the consequences of the war which still continued far beyond the castle walls of Honselaardijk. He was aware that the French were once more on the move in Flanders; the towns of Ghent and Bruges soon fell to them and in March 1678 he left hurriedly for the front after an emotional goodbye. Mary's uncle Laurence Hyde had just arrived at The Hague, and thought that William left in the best of spirits, as if he could not wait to get away from his wife.

For the first time since her marriage, Mary had time to write a long letter home to Frances Apsley. The old Mary Clorin had changed from a tearful rebellious bride into a young woman very much in love with her husband. Once she had thought that leaving her own country, friends and relatives was the worst thing that could happen to her, but now instead she had the loneliness of seeing him go to war. The reality of life as the wife of a military commander who had responsibilities to country and army – the prolonged absences and the uncertainty of knowing whether he was safe or not – hit her hard. 'What can be more cruell in the world than parting with what on loves and nott ondly comon parting but parting so as may be never to meet again to be perpetually in fear . . . for god knows when I may see him or whethere he is not now at this instant in a batell.'[1]

The days until they were able to meet again, when she was allowed to join him in Antwerp for two weeks at the end of March, seemed like a lifetime. They had another reunion at Breda for a short period early in April, 'for that is so neer the Army he can live in the town and go to it at any time at a quarter of an hour warning when I am there if I dont ritt dont wonder for may be I shant have time or twenty things may happen'.[2] The long coach journey to

Breda proved unexpectedly rough. A combination of several days' discomfort and not resting enough on her arrival was probably responsible for a miscarriage, and she was seriously ill for several weeks afterwards. It was a grave disappointment to husband and wife, and she received an anxious letter from the Duke of York, begging her to take greater care of herself.

In the middle of May William came back from the battlefront to be present at a series of vital debates in the Assembly of the States-General of Holland, which often went on late into the evening. All the time he was expecting to be summoned back to the army, as French troops were preparing for a new onslaught. Yet the odds were against the Dutch, and early in June they sought a truce. Though dissatisfied by the terms of the Franco-Dutch peace treaty, leaving France in possession of the Franche Comte and several key towns in the Spanish Netherlands, he was overruled. But Mary was glad to have him safely at home again. For much of the summer he was busy with military affairs, but still found time to enjoy some hunting and tennis. While he was occupied with such energetic pastimes, Mary and her ladies went for trips in the *trekschuyten*, gilded canal boats with colourful canopies and fluttering pennants. When she travelled on land, she rode in one of her husband's coaches, drawn by six dapple-grey horses, their harnesses decorated with orange plumes bearing the family crest.

Husband and wife were obliged to be prudent with their expenditure. William's coffers were much depleted by the war in Holland, as well as by the necessity of having to employ a large staff including pages, foot soldiers, gentlemen, kitchen servants and others. Mary's English maids of honour put an additional strain on his finances, as she had no independent income of her own, and King Charles II was in no hurry to pay her the promised dowry. As a bachelor, William had been good at shaking off his hated governors by being so rude to them that they were glad to leave his service as soon as possible. The English retainers proved more durable, though they resented his rudeness.

Among Mary's staff were her nurse Mrs Langford, her ladies-in-waiting, including Bentinck's first wife Anne, and Lady Inchiquin.

Her painting master Richard Gibsone had also accompanied her to Holland, where he helped her to develop her talent in miniature painting. She also had two chaplains, one for her household and one to supervise her personal devotions. The latter was Dr George Hooper, formerly Bishop of Bath and Wells. The English Church had saved her from the 'evil' of Catholicism, but did not wish her to become a Calvinist either. William was sometimes irritated to find her reading learned works on church history and ecclesiastical policy in her room. Though he might complain, he made no serious effort to stop her from devoting her time to such pursuits.

Throughout the early summer the French kept up the siege of the strategic town of Mons. William insisted that they must loosen their hold on the town and move out of the nearby fortresses, otherwise all peace talks and negotiations would prove futile. He was sure that King Louis did not intend to enter into serious discussion until Mons had fallen, and then he would be able to negotiate from a position of strength. The King ended the truce by publishing outrageous demands, and declaring that he would not give up any of the towns he had conquered in the Low Countries. As William marched on Mons with an army of 45,000 men, the French, fearing defeat, told the peace delegates at Nijmegen that King Louis would withdraw from the town if peace were negotiated at once, and a treaty was duly signed on 10 August.

By this time Mary believed she was with child for a second time. The weather was fine, and she stayed at Honselaardijk. Soon afterwards she became ill again, probably with a bout of malarial fever which was common in the Low Countries during summer. She was treated with asses' milk and physic, which left her feeling 'very low', and there were rumours of another miscarriage. Her spirits improved when Temple brought husband and wife the good news that King Charles had at last paid her promised dowry of £20,000. However, rumours of her ill-health continued to flourish. The Duke of York wrote to warn her of the dangers of too much standing while in her condition, and the duchess, who had always been fond of her stepdaughter, decided she would like to go and visit the girl herself.

On 13 October the duchess and her party, including Princess Anne and the Duchess of Monmouth, arrived at The Hague for a private visit. They were delighted to see one another again. On her departure from England, Mary had been very worried about her younger sister and, after the deaths of their siblings, had feared they might never meet again. But Anne had made a good recovery, and was as fond of her food as ever. The Duchess of York was equally pleased to find Mary, whom she had last seen in the depths of misery, now looking so well. Anne and her stepmother had found a nickname for Mary, who was now to be known as 'Lemon', as her husband was Prince of Orange. They stayed for a month, returning to England on 18 November to find the country in the grip of hysteria after Titus Oates's revelations of an alleged Popish plot in England and a wave of anti-Catholic hysteria.

While Mary began to furnish a nursery, William asked the States-General to stand as sponsors for their child. In February 1679 he was supervising alterations to his hunting lodge at Dieren, as they were sure she was soon going to bring a little prince into the world. Sadly, by the spring it was apparent that once again there would be no child. Some thought that she had miscarried again, while others believed that the sickness and fever she had suffered were symptoms of an on-going gynaecological infection, and that her miscarriage the previous year had brought on an infection that was mistaken for malarial fever, resulting in permanent infertility. Electress Sophie of Hanover told the family that the fever from which Mary had suffered could produce symptoms similar to being with child. Others suspected that the Prince's physicians had misdiagnosed the pregnancy, and did not have the heart to disillusion the would-be parents until all hopes of a child were long since past. William's foes throughout Europe accused him behind his back of inventing the pregnancy to disconcert his rivals and to try to lay spurious claim to the English succession, displacing his Catholic uncle and father-in-law. Even the Duchess of York, who had shown every sympathy to her stepdaughter, said she was convinced that the pregnancy had been entirely imaginary – an ironic judgement, in view of subsequent history. She also thought

William had too little patience with his young wife's emotional demands and constant ill-health.

Still only sixteen, Mary continued to hope to the end of her days that she would have that longed-for infant of her own, yet her health had been permanently damaged. Low spirits and physical prostration left her ill for some time, with a recurrence of the fever accompanied by agonizing pain in her hip, and not until summer was she really well again.

* * *

Meanwhile, during the winter Titus Oates's alleged Popish Plot and its aftermath had impacted particularly on the Catholic heir to the throne and his wife. When the new Parliament met in March 1679, Bishop Compton and several influential peers called upon the King to banish the duke from his counsels. It soon became clear that a large number of members wanted him excluded from the succession for his reactionary and religious views. King Charles tried to compromise, agreeing to limitations on the power of a Roman Catholic successor. This was not good enough for the Commons, who introduced the first Exclusion Bill, and the King was obliged to prorogue Parliament to prevent its passage. Various alternatives were discussed. At one point it looked as if the dynasty might be overthrown for the second time in thirty years, its only possible salvation being if the King were to divorce his childless and evidently infertile Queen Catherine and take another bride. Calls for Monmouth to be legitimized, or for the Princess of Orange to be declared Queen regnant if her father became sufficiently unpopular, were regarded as less practicable and possibly so divisive that civil war would again be the result. Monmouth was ambitious enough to regard himself as a king-in-waiting, while there were doubts that Mary would agree to assuming power during her father's lifetime. Her Dutch connections were suspect as Anglo-Dutch rivalry was still rife, in view of the recent war between both nations, while her husband William was seen as an incorrigible autocrat. Even worse, he was known to violate the Sabbath by hunting on Sundays, which made him unacceptable to the Presbyterians.

Though Parliament had been prorogued, political opinion was fiercely divided. Rather against his better judgement, the King was persuaded to send the duke and duchess out of the country for a time, until the hysteria subsided. They settled in Brussels, to be joined later by Princess Anne and her delicate younger half-sister Isabella. The duke visited his son-in-law and lectured him at length on the perils confronting the monarchy. In the autumn he learnt that King Charles had been taken ill, and was advised to return home at once in order to safeguard his interests, should the worst come to pass. Sailing from Holland as soon as he could, he returned to Windsor where he found his brother sitting up in bed, recovering from a mild stomach upset brought on by over-eating, though there were whispers that there had been a Catholic conspiracy to poison him.

Charles's recovery from what was evidently a mild, even self-inflicted, indisposition brought the duke's jealousy of the King's bastard son to a head. Evidently discomfited at finding the King looking so healthy after all, the duke said he was prepared to return to Europe, or anywhere else that he was required to go, but it was wrong to let the Duke of Monmouth remain in England at the same time and he should be sent into exile as well. Moreover, was His Majesty not doing the dynasty a disservice by showing his natural son so much favour? The King reluctantly sent Monmouth to Holland, but as he had been planning to go there anyway it was hardly a sentence of banishment.

Nevertheless it was something of an embarrassment for the Prince and Princess of Orange. One September evening they were at The Hague, preparing to receive their friends, when Monmouth arrived. Both of them gave him a cold reception and made stilted conversation with him. When he said he was planning to leave the next day, William unbent a little and asked if he was leaving before he had had a chance to dine at the palace. It was an invitation Monmouth gladly accepted, and as he left the table next day after dining, he told William in a low voice that he would like to have the honour of a private audience. Both men managed to shake off the rest of their company and went for a walk in the garden, where Monmouth confided in William that his father remained well-disposed to him, assuring him that he would not be exiled for long. Suspecting that the duke was setting his sights on his father's crown, the Prince of Orange offered him his friendship and support up to a point, but warned him that 'if you stick to your pretensions of legitimacy, I cannot be your friend'.[3]

All the same Monmouth stayed for several more days, and his charm reasserted itself. William and Mary found themselves warming once more to this delightful if indiscreet relative. But they knew that the longer he stayed, the greater an embarrassment he could become. It would not augur well for them, in the eyes of either English or Dutch ministers, let alone King Charles or the Duke of York, if rumours were to circulate that the Prince and Princess of Orange were being too hospitable towards the man who regarded himself as the rightful heir to the throne of England.

Mary was planning a trip to Brussels to visit her sister Anne and their half-sister Isabella, but in October she received a letter from the Duke of York asking her not to come, as the girls were returning to England and he was going to accompany them part of the way. However, he would like to meet her at Delft, to avoid attracting too great a crowd at one of the larger cities. William and Mary went to meet him and found him in a bad humour. He talked to William for half an hour without stopping. Not long after his arrival, a messenger came from King Charles to tell him that his banishment was over and he was being summoned back to England. Little did Mary realize that this was to be the last time she would ever see her father, her stepmother and her little stepsister. Her next meeting with Anne would take place under very altered circumstances.

It was clear to husband and wife that they had to be careful in any dealings with their English relatives. The aftermath of Monmouth's visit proved that the Duke of York did not really trust them. Moreover the French Ambassador, the Comte d'Avaux, was always ready to make mischief, never letting slip a chance to make capital out of the friendship between William and Monmouth, hoping to spoil William's good relationship with King Charles II and make him out to be unreliable. Though increasingly suspicious that his son planned to challenge the Duke of York for the crown after his death,

Charles was reassured by the knowledge that it would have been absurd for William to encourage Monmouth, as to do so would jeopardize his and his wife's place in the succession. In vain did Avaux try to explain this by suggesting that the Prince of Orange was attempting to ally himself with the Duke of Monmouth as part of an anti-Catholic conspiracy to exclude the Duke of York.

Until then William had been on good terms with his father-in-law. This did not suit the machinations of Avaux, who considered it would be as well if he could spread or encourage rumours that the Prince of Orange was mistreating his young wife, thus fomenting discord in the family and perhaps even breaking up what had been an important Protestant marriage. Excluding William and Mary from the succession would suit France, if it meant establishing a Catholic dynasty headed by the Duke of York and any children he might have by his second marriage, assuming that his wife would have at least one healthy infant who survived to maturity.

During these anxious times William took care to keep himself well informed, through the reports of friends, as to what was happening in England. One source warned him that King Charles might find his position untenable and be forced to abdicate, and as the Duke of York would be unacceptable as king to the Protestants, he or Mary, or both of them together, might be summoned to the throne.

In March 1680 Mary became seriously ill with a high fever, which might have been influenza or possibly (though less likely) another miscarriage. For a few days her life was said to be in danger, and William wrote to prepare his father-in-law for the worst. By the end of April she was out of danger, but she was in low spirits, suffering what in a later age would be diagnosed as chronic depression, for a long time.

This spell of ill-health indicated something of a crisis in Mary's life, if not a crisis in the marriage. On the threshold of her eighteenth birthday she must have realized that, whereas her stepmother might give birth to a succession of puny children, most of whom were destined to die in infancy, she might never produce an infant at all. Her husband was often tired and short-tempered after his military campaigns, frustrated at being unable to achieve anything. Returning home, he found his still very young wife rather childish, constantly suffering from ill-health, fretful and with tears never far away, surrounded by a protective entourage of doctors, chaplains and ladies-in-waiting ready to take her side if he showed any impatience with her. Though it is unlikely that he ever physically abused her, it must have been easy for him to take out some of his frustrations on her with a cross word here or there, particularly if he too had come to the conclusion that she would never give him a son and heir.

Mary's new chaplain Dr Thomas Ken, an exceptionally devout man who for all his religious fervour apparently lacked judgement and the ability to deal with people, had taken an instant dislike to William, who returned the ill-feeling. Ken was convinced that he was being unkind to Mary, mentally if not physically, and told Henry Sidney, who had just replaced Temple as ambassador at The Hague, that he intended to speak to the Prince about it, even if he should be kicked out of doors for presuming to do so. Mary's illness, he believed, was being prolonged by her husband's unkindness, and he felt she ought to be allowed to return to England to convalesce, though William would never give his consent. There is no record of Ken's having spoken to the Prince, and he may have realized that the Prince would never tolerate such interference from the household.

While Mary's failure to conceive weighed heavily on her, it was not the only cross she had to bear. Worse, perhaps, was the knowledge that her husband was said to be having an affair with one of her maids of honour. Elizabeth Villiers was one of the three sisters who had grown up with Mary and Anne at Richmond and had come to Holland with the former. An undistinguished-looking young woman with a cast in one eye, as a consequence of which she was known behind her back as Squinting Betty, she was highly intelligent, an accomplished conversationalist and a good listener. Attached to his wife as he was, the reserved William always found it hard to express his deepest feelings. After the heartbreaking disappointment of two if not three miscarriages within a few months, he probably found his emotional young wife hard to handle, seeking consolation in the sense of undemanding companionship – and perhaps nothing more – from a more level-headed woman in their entourage. There is nothing to substantiate the gossip that they were lovers, and it is said that the relationship was more cerebral than physical. One of William's more recent biographers, Nesca A. Robb, maintained that Elizabeth was never his *maîtresse en titre*, that she never obtruded on the public eye, was not unduly mercenary and that any presents he may have given her were not of the ostentatious kind which would have come to public notice. She may have been an unofficial counsellor whose opinions were valued, but she was never involved in making or unmaking ministers, and any political role was limited to minor diplomatic matters.[4]

Mary's father and uncle were shameless cuckolds who flaunted their infidelities and illegitimate offspring with scant consideration for their long-suffering, humiliated wives. Her more unassuming husband had the tact and grace to handle what was evidently a rare (if not unique) extra-marital relationship, if it was as intimate as that, with discretion. Some years earlier, in one of her first letters to Frances Apsley, she had remarked on how men always seemed to weary of their wives and looked for mistresses as soon as they could get them. Now she found herself in the same position, but there was nothing to be done but endure the situation. She had seen for herself that her place in her husband's life would be a limited one. William, she knew, saw politics and diplomacy as man's work.

Despite their differences in character, William and Mary shared a firm religious faith and high standards of personal conduct. She found much to occupy her time. In addition to religious duties, private prayer and meditation, she was involved in many charitable works and the supervision of her several households, namely Honselaardijk and the Binnenhof; Soestdijk between Amsterdam and Amersfoort, with good gardens, fine walks and rows of trees; Dieren, William's hunting lodge in Gelderland; Het Huis ten Bosch, an attractive summer palace near The Hague which he had inherited from his grandmother Amalia, and which was usually Mary's retreat when he was away; and later the splendid new building at Het Loo. There was always official entertaining, visiting, theatre-going, needlework, music and painting. Above all there was her favourite pastime of playing cards, and her old chaplain Dr Lake heard with trepidation that she was in the habit of playing on Sundays. She also enjoyed walking and making little journeys by barge along the canals. Husband and wife were both keenly interested in the furnishing of their homes and the layout of the gardens.

As a hostess and 'first lady' of such unimpeachable rectitude, even the censorious Dutch clergy could find little to criticize in Mary's behaviour, apart from her love of petty gambling and occasional theatre visits. She soon became as popular as her husband and fell in love with the Dutch people and countryside. She liked and respected the politeness, seriousness and piety which gave the Dutch a dignity free from pomp or affectation, and relished the lack of hypocrisy, sycophancy and backbiting so prevalent at the court at St James's. She also liked the houses which she found airy, well-proportioned and spotlessly clean, unlike Whitehall, with its endless jumble of corridors and apartments, its smoke, dirt, stench and confusion. Refuse and sewage often lay in the streets in England, whereas the Dutch burghers made great efforts to keep their towns clean and attractive.

The Stadholder's official residence, shared with the States-General, was the Binnenhof at The Hague, but both William and Mary preferred their country houses. Her favourite was Honselaardijk, 7 miles from The Hague, with forests at the rear and dunes and the sea at the front. Regarded as the finest house in the United Provinces, it contained some of William's finest pictures. The smaller House in the Wood, Soestdijk and Dieren were all improved and the two last had formal gardens added. William particularly liked Dieren as hunting in the forests of Gelderland was excellent, and the house was so small that he had to leave most of the court behind, so he could choose his guests.

Mary spent much of her time walking, enjoying boat-trips on the canals, sewing, playing cards and gossiping with her ladies. As a rule she and William dined separately, each with their own household. Their court was homely, relaxed and orderly, very different from the rough conviviality of Whitehall or the stultifying formality of Versailles.

* * *

In his thirtieth year, William's health was far from good. He still suffered badly from asthma, his complaint aggravated perhaps by anxiety about Mary, as well as by the sudden change from his active outdoor life to a more sedentary indoor existence, something which never suited him. During the summer he was particularly unwell and run-down, but proved to be no longer the good patient that he had been when suffering from smallpox. The more the doctors tried to persuade him to rest, the harder he drove himself. Going to Dieren for a few days to hunt, he was shattered by news of the death from fever of his lifelong friend Thomas, Earl of Ossory, who was in England where he had just been appointed governor and general of the English forces in Tangier. 'I have felt such grief that if he had been my own brother I could have felt no more,'[5] he wrote to Lord Arlington.

In this mood of desolation he proceeded to take up a long-standing invitation from George William, Duke of Celle. There was more to this than a social exchange, for he had hopes of drawing the duke, his brother Ernest Augustus, Elector of Hanover, and Frederick William, Elector of Brandenburg, into an alliance against France. Mary did not accompany him but stayed behind at Soestdijk, as she was still convalescent after the troubles of earlier that year. He spent three weeks at Celle, where the hospitality was lavish, hunting was pursued with dedication and he proved himself astonishingly energetic for one who had been so unwell only a few weeks before. His ill-health may have been partly psychosomatic, and when he was enjoying himself in sympathetic surroundings he seemed much better. Yet while he might spend some days in the saddle from dawn till dusk, and then the evening dancing or gambling or both, attend the theatre or make ceremonial calls and attend a state banquet, he never neglected his duties. Couriers arrived regularly from The Hague with official papers, which were conscientiously studied at any hour of the day or night.

After leaving Celle he also visited Hanover and Brandenburg, where he enjoyed himself rather less, but appreciated that in the interests of good political relations he had to be a conscientious guest. However, he was still sleeping badly, suffering from haemorrhoids and often had a poor appetite. The hours of hunting and travelling were borne stoically, though by the time he reached Soestdijk on 7 November it was apparent that the break had not really benefited him physically.

* * *

Since the end of the war in 1678 William had been arguing his case, with more passion than success, with the pacifist factions in the States-General, particularly the Amsterdammers, who would not acknowledge the continuing threat of French aggression. Encouraged by the French Ambassador, they repeatedly blocked his efforts to strengthen national defences and maintain the essential buffer of the Spanish Netherlands, suggesting it would be more to the States' advantage to live in peace with Louis 'without defiance or alarm', than to maintain armies which they could ill afford.

As the servant of the Republic, William found himself in the trying position of responsibility without power. Irritated beyond measure by his masters' apparently wilful blindness and paranoia, he also needed to watch the situation across the North Sea. The state of panic engendered by the Popish Plot had died down and it was increasingly evident that efforts by the Whigs, the opposition party, to exclude the Duke of York from the succession had failed. The Duke and Duchess of York therefore returned from their Scottish exile to a warm welcome at court. Louis XIV refused to pay William the revenues from his estates that were now in French hands, and French troops compounded the insult by overrunning and looting Orange, then persecuting the Protestants there. Louis's acts of aggression were carried out under the pretext of recovering French 'rights' over particular towns and territories. Most were in the Rhineland, where the local princes were too weak to resist, while their nominal overlord, the emperor, was preoccupied with defence against the Turks. More seriously, from the Dutch point of view, Louis tried to seize Luxembourg, which belonged to Spain. William did his best to persuade the English and Dutch to resist the French King, but Charles was now neutral, thanks to his French pension, and the States-General did not think the time right for a new war with France. They realized that if Louis resumed his encroachments on the Spanish Netherlands, the Dutch would eventually have to fight, but the Rhineland was far away and Louis had more men and money at his disposal than they did.

The States-General regarded William's call for war each time Louis embarked on another act of aggression as irresponsible. William, who was not required to pay the money himself, regarded the States-General and especially the men of Amsterdam as pusillanimous and unpatriotic, putting their own profits before the security of Europe. Some leading Amsterdam politicians, he declared, were in league with the untrustworthy Avaux. Despite all his persuasiveness, William could not get his way, and when Spain declared war on France in 1683 nobody came to her aid. Louis agreed to a twenty-year truce in 1684, whereby he kept all his ill-gotten gains, including Luxembourg and the key city of Strasbourg. Through a policy of intense but piecemeal aggression, he had strengthened and extended his frontiers without provoking a major coalition against him. William was never anti-French as such; he bought a wide variety of goods in France and imported French architects and landscape gardeners for his palaces. Nevertheless his dislike for Louis soon hardened into a fierce hatred.

Meanwhile, he was concerned at the pressure in England to exclude his father-in-law from the throne. In May 1680 the first Exclusion Bill was laid by the Whigs before the House of Commons, its provisions being for the crown to pass to the next Protestant in line to the throne, should the King die without issue. This should have been to William's advantage, as it would make Mary first in line to the throne. However, it soon became apparent that the Whigs saw the Duke of Monmouth as his father's successor instead. The King opposed the exclusion measure, seeing it as part of a much wider attempt to reduce the sovereign to a mere cipher. Later he admitted to confidants that he would have agreed to the bill's provisions if only Parliament had granted him more money and not tried to limit his prerogative in other ways, though he may not have been altogether serious in this. He could afford to adopt a pragmatic attitude, as he said at the same time that he did not believe an act of exclusion would have the power to prevent his brother James from succeeding to the throne. At any rate, he played for time; to reject it would risk open revolt from some quarters, while to pass it would be a gift to the republicans and Presbyterians. He allowed the bill to pass its second reading in the Commons, then prorogued Parliament at the end of the month and dissolved it in July.

Some statesmen had been ready to ask William to come over if the worst came to the worst. When rebellion broke out in Scotland in June, the King sent Monmouth to deal with the rebels. He acquitted himself well, first with a victory at Drumclog, and later by showing clemency towards the vanquished afterwards. Returning to England even more the popular idol than ever, he was acclaimed wherever he went and some of his admirers were ready to call him the genuine Prince of Wales. Rumours persisted of a 'black box' which apparently held a certificate proving a marriage in 1648 between the then Prince of Wales and Lucy Walter, thus confirming Monmouth's legitimacy.

William was less worried by the prospect of James's exclusion than by Charles's proposals of limitations on the powers of a future Catholic king, fearing that these might also weaken James's Protestant heirs. Some of the wilder Exclusionists, or Whigs as they became known, made no secret of their desire for the Duke of Monmouth to succeed instead of James, but William believed that this possibility need not be feared. Most of the Whigs supported Mary's claim rather than that of Monmouth, who had good looks, charm and charisma but was regarded as undependable. William refused to intervene, and events would vindicate his caution; demands for the Duke of York's removal from the succession proved to contain more noise than substance. The Commons passed a second Exclusion Bill which was sent to the Lords on 15 November, and King Charles made it clear that he wanted it rejected. After a debate lasting the whole day, his wish was granted and it was defeated by 63 votes to 30.

William had made an error of judgement by assuming that Charles would graciously accept the bill and then take steps to ensure that it would never be implemented. He had feared that the King's stand would lead to a major crisis or even renewed civil war, which would put England out of European affairs for some time. Fagel and Sidney drew up a memorandum from the States-General which urged Charles to come to terms with Parliament. William himself warned Charles of the dangers of offering to limit the prerogative, but his attempts to interfere in English affairs united Charles and James in irritation against their presumptuous young nephew.

As a result early in 1681 William was shocked to be told by Sidney that he had been recalled to England, and Bevil Skelton was to be sent to Holland in his place. Sidney, a good friend to William and Mary, had also befriended Monmouth. The Duke of York had urged the King to summon him home, as it would not do to have him in Holland to bring such influences to bear on the Prince and Princess of Orange. Convinced that the King was increasingly surrounded by troublemakers, William eventually decided that he had to go to England and see him in person.

At first King Charles put him off, so instead he went to stay with the Duke of Celle again for a week. Mary was well enough to travel, and she accompanied him. Both of them appreciated the short break and a change of scenery, though there was little respite from anxieties at home or abroad. In particular they were concerned at King Charles's latest suggestion to the Houses of Parliament, namely that after his death James should be banished and, during his lifetime, either William or Mary should rule as Regent. The Whigs wanted exclusion on their own terms and rejected the proposal. A week after its opening Parliament was dissolved, and never met again in the King's lifetime.

William was increasingly anxious that King Louis intended to devour the whole of the Spanish Netherlands, and pressed King Charles to seek a reconciliation with Parliament so that an Anglo-Dutch alliance could face the French threat head on before it was too late. Charles and James both thought he was meddling in matters which did not concern him, especially as he admitted he understood little of English domestic affairs and could not put forward any suggestions as to how King and Parliament could become reconciled. On 31 July William went to England and spoke to the King but achieved little, apart from persuading him not to send the unpopular Skelton to Holland; Edward Hales was chosen instead. William still hoped to persuade Charles to call Parliament and raise money for a war against France. Unless England could assist her allies, Holland and Flanders could be overrun by France and lost to the Protestant cause, and the English Parliament's support was needed in this venture. But Charles had no intention of recalling Parliament, saying the Whigs were obsessed with exclusion and not interested in what happened abroad, and that a new Parliament would be every bit as intractable as the previous one.

The meeting broke up with uncle and nephew both equally angry. Before his return to Holland, William was twice invited to dine in the City of London, a Whig stronghold. William considered that the Whigs could be valuable allies in his quest for an Anglo-Dutch alliance, but Charles was so annoyed at this display of apparent partisanship that he ordered his nephew to dine at Windsor, so that he could not accept the other invitations. William complied with reluctance, and afterwards complained of the poor quality of the food served. A former Speaker of the House of Commons, Edward Seymour, said angrily that the Prince of Orange had no right to grumble, as he had brought over such a low grade of champagne. King Charles and William parted with their differences unresolved. It was the last time they were to meet.

Until now, William and Mary had enjoyed a good, if slightly uneasy, relationship with the Duke of York. This was gradually replaced by a feeling of increasing mutual distrust. Mary suffered most from the division of loyalties, but her love for the Protestant religion and for her husband convinced her that they had to come first. Much as it distressed her to feel she was being disloyal, she realized that if she could not trust her father at the same time, that was how it had to be.

In the summer of 1682 she learned that Frances Apsley had married Sir Benjamin Bathurst, an important man of commerce. Though she was mildly hurt that her long-standing confidante had not told her before it became general knowledge, she immediately wrote to congratulate her. One year later she had a brother-in-law. In 1680 Prince George of Hanover had been sent to England to meet Anne and perhaps seek her hand in marriage. Neither of them cared for the other, but as Anne was only fifteen years of age at the time there was no urgency about the matter. In March 1683 a match was proposed between Anne and Prince George of Denmark, brother of King Christian V. Though he was Protestant, Denmark as a nation was an ally of France, and as part of the marriage settlement the Danes tried to have William excluded from the English succession. William was angry at what he saw as a major personal affront. Though this proviso was soon abandoned, William always regarded the Prince with suspicion.

George arrived in England on 19 July 1683, and they were married at St James's Palace ten days later. Stolid and placid, Anne accepted her husband without demur. Aged thirty, fair-haired, tall and good-looking, he created a better impression on the English than William had done. While he had had a distinguished military career fighting against the Swedes, he was prepared to spend the rest of his days as consort to the niece of a king, and possibly to a future Queen regnant, while he devoted himself to making model ships, eating and drinking too much. Easy-going and totally uninterested in politics, William was reassured to discover that George's presence at the English court was unlikely to prove any threat, unless he and Anne were to become the tool of unscrupulous politicians. Like William, George suffered from asthma, though wags said behind his back that these attacks were caused by his having to breathe hard lest he should be taken for dead and sent for burial.

In May 1684 the Duke of Monmouth turned up in Brabant. During June 1683 a conspiracy to seize and kill King Charles and the Duke of York at Rye House, on their return from Newmarket to London, had been thwarted when the brothers left earlier than expected. The two main ringleaders, the Whigs Lord Russell and Algernon Sidney, were executed and a third, Lord Essex, had also been sentenced to death but cut his throat in the Tower. The Duke of York was convinced that Monmouth had been aware of and maybe condoned the plans, if he was not actually involved, and he had been under suspicion ever since. Though not officially in disgrace, he had been advised that his absence from England would be prudent. Rather unwisely he took with him his companion Lord Brandon, who had been imprisoned in the Tower after the plot and only escaped execution because of insufficient evidence against him. King Charles asked William not to receive his son or to allow him any military honours.

But William and Mary liked and respected their charming if feckless cousin, for all his faults. William accepted the duke's admission that he had no ambition to be King of England, and as he was aware that most of the exclusionist group in England regarded Mary (and perhaps himself) as next in line to the throne, he did not regard him as a threat. Moreover he would not be dictated to in his own country, particularly as he was ill inclined to cooperate with his uncles while they showed signs of being ready to fall under the influence of France, no friend of Holland. In July William received Monmouth with all due hospitality at Dieren. When the King heard rumours that William was appointing officers recommended by Monmouth to English regiments in Holland, he was more angry still, suspecting that if these regiments came under the command of 'disaffected' persons they might later be used against him. William was perturbed that King Charles should think it a crime for him to receive Monmouth, and wrote to him in October saying how unhappy he would be to lose His Majesty's good graces 'though having received a person who has the honour to be your son and who may have displeased you . . . to find myself deprived of your friendship is the thing in all the world that touches me most sensibly'.[6]

The Duke of York reacted even more angrily than his brother, writing to Mary that 'it scandalises all loyal and monarchical people here to know how well the Prince lives with, and how civil he is' to the duke; 'let the Prince flatter himself as he pleases, the Duke of Monmouth will do his part to have a push with him for the crown'.[7]

William and Mary went out of their way to entertain him with a round of balls, parties, theatre-going and informal dances. Mary seemed several years younger in his presence, while Monmouth was perceptive enough to understand Mary's loneliness and depression. As a father twelve times over – five by his wife, and seven by two mistresses – he may have seen how empty his cousin's childless existence was. Shortly before Monmouth's arrival, when Mary was dining in public at Honselaardijk, a small boy escaped from his nurse and snatched some sweets from her table. When the horrified attendant tried to stop him, Mary laughed and kept the child beside her for some time. If she could not have children of her own, at least she could take pleasure in the company of other people's infants.

As for William, the ever-genial Monmouth managed to penetrate the austerity and reserve that chilled so many of the Prince's other associates. His almost reckless happy-go-lucky outlook, pleasure in simple gaieties and ability to cast aside worry and responsibility turned the normally dour and sedate William towards enjoyments he had long since disregarded. He was now seen learning English country dances from his irrepressible cousin, practising them with his wife's ladies and organizing balls and 'parties of pleasure'.

By the time Christmas 1684 had come and gone, there had been a remarkable change in the atmosphere at the court of The Hague. At the end of December Monmouth and his mistress Henrietta went briefly to England. He went to Whitehall to warn the King of another assassination plot, this time by a cabal founded in James's name though not with his knowledge, then returned to the Netherlands where he arrived at The Hague on the evening of 4 January 1685. Assured by King Charles of his continuing goodwill, or so he claimed, he was full of confidence for the future. He arrived late at night and Mary was already preparing for bed, but William summoned her, insisting on her getting dressed and coming down to receive their guest.

There was a severe frost at The Hague, and Mary, William, Henrietta and Monmouth were to be seen on sledges at Honselaardijk, and dancing, with Monmouth and Mary taking the floor together. Since her marriage and arrival in Holland Mary had never walked out in public. When she appeared, on foot, in the Lange Voorhout, accompanied by Monmouth, Avaux was astonished that the Prince of Orange, whom he called 'the most jealous of men living,' could 'suffer all those airs of gallantry' between the Princess and the Duke of Monmouth.[8] The duke was also given free access to William's cabinet at any hour, a privilege previously granted only to Bentinck, and was urged by the Prince to visit Mary each evening after dinner to teach her new dances. For a man usually so strict that he allowed his wife no private visits from men or women, this was remarkable.

Monmouth took the initiative in organizing private theatricals, which Avaux was expected to attend and did so under protest, complaining afterwards that he saw Her Highness act in roles not suitable for a princess and which he would consider ridiculous even for 'an ordinary woman'. He was equally dismissive of the sight of a princess of the blood royal learning to skate under the auspices of such a notorious 'heretical fugitive', with the permission – 'such is her complaisance to him' – of her husband. He claimed to have seen her on the ice with very short skirts tucked up halfway to her waist, with iron pattens on her feet, learning to skate with every appearance of enjoyment, and cast doubts as to her respectability.[9] Up to now, she had lived so regularly that from the hour she got up in the morning till 8 p.m. she never set foot outside her apartment, except maybe once a week in the summer for fresh air, and then always with two chamberwomen who had orders never to leave her side. However, Avaux usually obtained his information second-hand, and with his dislike of the English he was hardly an unbiased witness when it came to writing about the Princess second in succession to the English throne.

Within a few weeks this season of good cheer at the court of The Hague would come to a sudden end.

FOUR

Heir and Heiress Presumptive

On 2 February 1685 King Charles had a stroke. His doctors tried the traditional remedies of emetics, bleeding and blistering, and within two days he seemed better. After a relapse the next day, on the morning of 6 February he lost the power of speech and died just before midday. Later that day at Whitehall the former Duke of York, now King James II, wrote a short letter to his son-in-law:

> I only have time to tell you, that it has pleased God Almighty, to take out of this world the King my Brother, you will from others have an account of what distemper he died of, and thus all the usual ceremonys were performed this day in proclaiming me King in the City and other parts, I must end which I do with assuring you, you shall find me as kind to you as you can expect.[1]

Frost prevented ships from entering the Dutch harbours for several days, and news did not reach The Hague until the evening of 16 February. Mary was at cards when this and other letters announcing her uncle's death and her father's accession were brought to her husband. He sent for her and broke the news to her in person.

Despite his unpopularity at times during his brother's reign, with many Protestants – notably the Duke of Monmouth – averring that the country would never accept 'a Popish King', the first few weeks of the reign of King James II passed without incident. The muted reaction of those who shared Monmouth's belief showed that they were in a minority, and a moderate accession speech by the King to the Privy Council suggested he had no intention of any violent break with the past. He was rightly recognized as a more capable administrator than his brother; Protestants and Catholics alike, on the whole, believed that with his accession the country was in good hands.

With her father's accession Mary was heiress presumptive to the English throne, and in recognition of this her pages now knelt to serve her. The chances of her succeeding her father seemed much greater now than at the time of her marriage. Between 1674 and 1684 Mary Beatrice had had ten confinements. Five resulted in stillbirths, three daughters and a son died within a year, and only one daughter lived beyond the age of four.[2] She was unlikely to provide James with a son to take precedence in the succession over Mary and Anne. James was aged fifty-one, and though he had generally enjoyed good health nobody expected his reign or lifespan to be particularly long. It seemed only a matter of time before his death would enable William to gain control of the resources of England and bring them into the struggle against France. For the moment, the Prince of Orange was prepared to wait, his main concern being to see that nothing happened to jeopardize his and Mary's rights.

Under the circumstances Monmouth's presence in Holland was something of an embarrassment, if not a liability, to them both. Since the Popish Plot, a sector of the Protestant Whig party at Westminster had made no secret of their desire to see the Catholic Duke of York set aside in the succession and Monmouth become heir instead. It was rumoured that King Charles had intended to legitimize him, while some believed that Charles had been secretly yet legally married to Lucy Walter, and Monmouth was therefore already legitimate.

Charles had been devoted to his son and often treated him indulgently, but he had sufficient respect for the laws of succession to place his brother first. William knew it would be wise for them not to antagonize King James unduly, and he could hardly be seen giving tacit support to his rival. When he informed the duke of his father's death, the latter was overcome. Between him and the new King there had never been any love lost. Now he would have no more funds from his father and protector, only possibly from Lady Anna, the heiress and wife he had left, or from Henrietta his mistress, who might have rashly believed his hopes, dreams and vague promises that she would be a queen one day. It was said that his sobbing could be heard by passers-by in the street.

Within a few days of his accession, James sent William a message demanding that the duke should be arrested and sent as a prisoner to England. William refused, replying that he 'only took the Duke of Monmouth into his protection for the sake of maintaining the Protestant religion in England'.[3] Nevertheless he lent him funds and advised him to leave The Hague, warning him it would be in his best interests to return to England, be circumspect in his behaviour and avoid involvement in any rash conspiracies. If he did not go back voluntarily, he risked being kidnapped by French agents and sent back to his uncle as a prisoner. Alternatively, perhaps, he could consider staying in central Europe and joining the emperor's army, in which he would probably be swiftly promoted.

The combined persuasion of Henrietta and a flood of Protestant fugitives from England, acclaiming him as their leader, changed his mind. The Earl of Argyll came over, proposing a Scottish rebellion, while several gentlemen of power and influence in the West Country sent promises of support. Henrietta and her mother sold their jewels to help fit out a ship and buy ammunition, and a sympathetic merchant in Amsterdam volunteered his services. When he equipped his small invasion force and sailed for England unhindered, James's suspicions increased. William had little power in Amsterdam and, had it not been for the bungling of James's ambassador, the ships might have been stopped. The King was mollified when William sent Bentinck to England to warn him that the duke had sailed, and dispatched the three English regiments in the Dutch service to help suppress the rebellion.

William and Mary were alarmed by Monmouth's landing and initial good reception by some people in England. Their admiration and friendship for him did not extend to wishing him well in his efforts to claim the throne to which Mary was still heir and, given Queen Mary Beatrice's sad obstetrical history, would probably remain. Basically authoritarian in principle, William disliked rebels; he had no desire to see Monmouth seize the English throne, and therefore had no sympathy with the uprising. Their anxiety was short-lived. The rebellion of the 'quondam Duke', in the words of diarist John Evelyn, 'a favourite of the people, of an easy nature, debauch'd by lust, seduc'd by crafty knaves who would have set him up only to make a property, and took the opportunity of the King being of another religion, to gather a party of discontented men',[4] soon failed. In July his poorly led rabble attacked the King's troops at Sedgemoor in Somerset and he was defeated. Over 1,500 were killed. Monmouth himself was captured hiding in a ditch, sent to the Tower and beheaded a few days later.

While William had been relieved at the duke's defeat, he and Mary were shocked by the brutality with which King James and his Lord Chief Justice, George Jeffreys, put down the aftermath of the rebellion with their reprisals against Monmouth's followers. Nevertheless, his main intention was to safeguard his and his consort's position as heir and heiress presumptive. As yet he took little interest in English affairs; to him England was first and foremost a potential member of a future coalition against France. James's efforts to establish Catholicism did not alarm him unduly, and he had no objection to James's strengthening the monarchy, a measure from which he and his wife could only benefit.

Yet he was concerned that something might happen to displace him and Mary in the succession. Despite her protestations to the contrary, it was rumoured that Anne might turn Catholic and that she or another Papist might usurp Mary's place. King James was known to be more partial to Anne, whose husband was generally considered too stupid to be any threat to him, and his advisers still hoped to convert them both to Catholicism. Moreover, even if the succession were not altered to favour Anne and exclude Mary (and therefore William) altogether, there was still a remote chance that James's Queen might still have a son. William also feared that, like his father before him, James's headstrong behaviour might provoke rebellion, leading to another civil war and a Republic. Like most leaders on mainland Europe, William had a greatly exaggerated impression of republican strength in England, which by 1685 was a pale shadow of what it had been at the height of Cromwell's power.

In view of James's large and comparatively well-drilled standing army, and the English nobility and gentry's distaste for war, revolution was an unlikely scenario. Unlike their Scottish counterparts, the English aristocracy had never taken up arms against Charles I, and in 1642 had never considered fighting until he forced their hand by declaring war on Parliament. Habits of obedience to lawful authority were deeply engrained in the English, and the tale of foolish misguided Monmouth was a timely reminder of the fate of unsuccessful rebels.

Though she was not mercenary by nature, and gave generously to charity, Mary was unhappy when King James paid a generous allowance to Anne and Prince George of Denmark, much of which she suspected went on paying her sister's gambling debts, but refused to do likewise for her. When asked why he omitted to do so, the suspicious King retorted that it was because he could not be sure such money would not be used against him. William was likewise displeased that he also neglected to accord him the title of 'His Royal Highness'. With some reluctance, James made a half-hearted request to Louis XIV to respect William's authority as sovereign prince in the state of Orange, but received a withering refusal. He told Mary that his efforts had failed, adding that he could do no more unless he was to declare war on France, something he felt inappropriate for such a trivial concern. At the same time he informed Overkirke, who had come to London to send William's congratulations to the King in person on his accession, that the Prince of Orange would be expected to take a more friendly attitude towards France in future. Mary angrily thought this almost tanta-mount to an admission that her father was ready to ally himself with the arch-enemy, King Louis XIV, against her husband.

Later that summer it was reported at The Hague that King James of England was intending to kidnap his daughter and marry her to King Louis XIV of France. To most people in England this was beyond belief. Louis had secretly married his mistress Madame de Maintenon in 1684 after the death of Queen Marie Therese, but James may have cherished hopes of attempting to dissolve a partnership that he found increasingly threatening on both political and dynastic levels.

There was almost certainly more than wild rumour in talk of a deliberate attempt about this time, involving the ambassador Bevil Skelton and Mary's new chaplain Dr Covell, Dr Ken's successor, and presumably approved if not instigated by the court at London, to stir up trouble between the Prince and Princess of Orange. Some were prepared to believe that King James really thought he could persuade King Louis to annul his second marriage (which he may have regarded as about as binding as the supposed nuptials between his brother and Lucy Walter) in order to wed his elder daughter, once her marriage with the Prince of Orange was dissolved.

There was truth in the gossip that some of her household had been making efforts to inflame her jealousy of her husband's mistress, Betty Villiers. William was clearly attracted more by the wit and intelligence of 'squinting Betty' than by her beauty, or lack of it. Sometimes he came to bed late, his excuse being that he had been working at his correspondence. (Maybe the idea of 'working overtime at the office' is not new.) Stirred up by some of her household, one night Mary was persuaded to pretend to go to bed at her usual time, then to get up again quietly and wait on the back staircase leading to the maids of honour's apartments. Angry at either being caught out or not trusted, or perhaps both, William was furious and lost his temper. Mary retired to bed in tears, and there followed a period of noticeable marital coldness.

Knowing this was unlike his wife's usual good nature, William was sure someone had been causing trouble behind the scenes. He had the outgoing mail intercepted and, after obtaining the evidence he needed, summoned Mary to an interview in his private cabinet, locked the door and told her that her servants were doing their utmost to sow dissension between them. He swore that what had caused ill-feeling between them was simply a distraction, and his feelings for her remained the same as ever. Reassured, Mary burst into tears, threw herself into his arms and all was forgiven. So said Daniel de Bourdon, a character whose background was shrouded in some mystery. A French Roman Catholic who had begun his career fighting in the Spanish army some ten years earlier, he had arrived in The Hague around 1680, though in what capacity remains unknown. His only claim to posterity is as a hanger-on around the fringes of the court, a friend of Betty Villiers and later the author of some gossipy memoirs about the Dutch court. His version of events, particularly of a supposed private interview between husband and wife which would only have taken place behind closed doors, if at all, should be regarded with scepticism. This whole business would hardly be worth mentioning, but for the fact that the members of Mary's entourage who were more sympathetic to King James and the Roman Catholic cause used it to keep 'their' King in England informed, and to encourage him to try to stir up ill-feeling.

Whatever the truth of the matter, this incident evidently drew husband and wife closer together, by bringing the Villiers affair into the open. A purge of spies and troublemakers followed. Mary's mischief-making chaplain Dr Covell, her old nurse Mrs Langford and Anne Trelawney, another of the maids of honour, were all dismissed for their questionable role in the matter. Betty's position was now clearly untenable and she was dispatched to her family in England, but her father sent her back to Holland with a letter to William and Mary, begging for her to be reinstated. Though she was Bentinck's sister-in-law, he refused to see her again (as did Mary) and also ordered his wife not to receive her either. Eventually she made her home in Holland with her married sister, Katherine de Puissars, and William continued to see her occasionally over the next few years.

There were more pressing matters to be attended to outside their household. In October 1685 the Revocation of the Edict of Nantes, the culmination of several years of increasing persecution of the Huguenots in France, increased the flight of refugees to the United Provinces. William and Mary were concerned by tales of cruelty emanating from France, especially the persecution of the people of Orange, now swallowed up by King Louis. By the summer of 1686 events in England were causing the Protestant heiress and her husband further concern. Having easily seen off the Monmouth rebellion, James was now pushing ahead with his plans for restoring the Catholic religion in England. Mass was being openly celebrated in the capital, Catholic propaganda was freely disseminated,

Catholics were appointed to influential civil and military posts in open defiance of the law, and the force raised to meet the threat from the West Country was still under arms and camped on Hounslow Heath. King James had already begun to undermine the authority of the Church of England. The outspoken anti-Catholic Henry Compton, Bishop of London, was summarily suspended for refusing to take action against Dr Sharp, an Anglican clergyman who had preached an anti-Catholic sermon, while vacant sees were left empty or filled by men of suitably Roman inclinations.

Disturbed by the tone of her father's policy and aware of reports that he had not given up hope of finding some way of passing the crown to a Catholic successor, Mary broached the matter of her faith with Anne. Back came the reassurance that Princess George of Denmark deeply abhorred the principles of the Church of Rome, and intended to remain steadfast to her religion, come what may.

*   *   *

In just under eight years of marriage, Mary had matured considerably. In Holland she was now wielding considerable influence by setting a good example, with her industry and her simple way of life appealing to the frugal Dutch. She prompted her ladies to sew, do embroidery and read religious improving books at other times of the day. While still longing for a child, she was probably resigned by this time to the will of God and the fact that it could never be. Knowing better than to brood on it, she busied herself with furnishing their houses, enjoying the Dutch countryside and making friends with the men and women at court. She loved showing people around their houses, and was ever ready to take advice from craftsmen and others who knew more about furniture and decorative arts than she did. All the occupations and diversions of a great society lady kept her active, from religious observances and works of charity, the supervision of her household, visiting and receiving company, reading, writing and needlework, to dancing, painting and making music, art, poetry, theology, history and science, theatre-going, playing cards, walking, riding, driving and boating.

She and William generally spent the evening together, apart from occasions when his over-attention to Betty Villiers interrupted their routine, if the questionable Bourdon was to be believed. These precious times remained unsullied by any grave discussions about matters of state or government. William, she told her chaplain Ortwinius, insisted 'that I should not tire him more with multiplicity of Questions, but rather strive to re-create him, over-toil'd, and almost spent, with pleasing Jests, that might revive him with Innocent Mirth'.[5]

When her new chaplain Dr Stanley arrived at The Hague late in 1685, he was delighted to see a large congregation taking the sacrament on Christmas Day, and attributed this to her good influence. He reported to Compton that Her Highness was 'doubtless one of the best-tempered persons in the world and everyone must needs be happy in serving her'.[6] She was a contemplative young woman who probably had more in common with the Puritans of Cromwell's time than with the ladies of King Charles II's court, who saw the hand of God in everything. Naturally melancholy by disposition, a mood deepened by her sorrow at being childless, she filled her journal with references to God as the judge of everything she did and expressed a constant fear that he would find her wanting.[7]

At about this time the Prince and Princess of Orange first met Gilbert Burnet, a Scottish refugee clergyman who came to live at The Hague in 1686. An historian and courtier, Burnet had been a confidant of Charles II, but was forced to leave England after the Rye House plot, as a close friend of Russell and Essex, both of whom had been executed afterwards. He returned to England the following year but was exiled by King James, after publishing pamphlets attacking James's policies on religious and constitutional grounds, and an anti-Catholic sermon. The most prominent of the staunch Whigs who had left or been expelled from England to find sanctuary in the Dutch Republic, he came to their attention after discovering a plot, one of several hatched at the court of Versailles, to kidnap William while he was driving unattended along the beach at Scheveling. Out of consideration to his father-in-law, William was careful not to show any of these political refugees undue favours, saying it was up to the various towns or the States-General to expel them if necessary.

The talkative, kind-hearted and outspoken Burnet soon became devoted to Mary, whom he called 'the most wonderful person' he had ever known. 'She has a modesty, a sweetness, and a humility in her that cannot be enough admired. She has a vast understanding and knows a great deal.' Despite her limited education, he appreciated her intelligence, and took it upon himself to instruct her in English affairs. 'I began to lay before her the state of our Court, and the intrigues in it, ever since the Restoration, which she received with great satisfaction and shewed true judgement . . . in all the reflections that she made.'[8]

During one of their conversations, Burnet asked if she had given any thought to the position the Prince would fill when she became Queen of England. Mary had never discussed this with William, and apparently assumed that he would automatically become king as well. She was astonished to learn that he would simply become the Queen's husband, unless she was prepared just to be his wife and entrust him with the sovereign authority on her accession. He advised her to consider the matter carefully before coming to a decision, but she did not hesitate. The next day, in Burnet's presence, she told William that she had not realized the laws of England were so contrary to the laws of God. The husband, she said, should not be obedient to the wife; she promised him he should always bear rule; and she asked only that he would accept the command that husbands should always love their wives, just as wives should be obedient to their husbands in everything. Taciturn and unemotional as ever, William said nothing at the time, but he later told William Bentinck how pleased he was that Burnet had only taken a few minutes to settle a matter he had never managed to raise in nine years of married life.

William and Mary were fully prepared to take their place in the order of succession after James. Only in the event of a major crisis would direct intervention in England be likely. Since childhood William had been brought up to expect that he would probably inherit the English throne, especially as Parliament might rule that the Princesses of York were disqualified from the succession on account of their mother's humble birth. It had been some years before he had learnt that English law did not make the same distinctions as the dynasties of Europe over what was basically a morganatic marriage.

For the first two years of King James's reign, William was careful not to overstep the bounds of propriety, and limited his interests to keeping up and broadening his correspondence with English politicians of all allegiances. As he had hoped that his marriage to Mary would give him some influence, if not control, over English foreign policy, he made half-hearted attempts to try to bring some pressure to bear on James's foreign policy in particular areas, especially with regard to cultivating good relations with Sweden and Brandenburg, among the most influential of the German states. In September 1686 the Whig Lord Mordaunt urged William to invade England at once, assuring him there would be no opposition. Thinking Mordaunt was over-reacting, William answered that he would do so only if James tried to alter the succession or threatened the nation's religion. While King James respected his daughter's position as his heir presumptive, he was tactless (or pigheaded) enough to place her and William in an awkward position in November 1686 by sending over the Quaker William Penn to try to persuade them to promise their support for his campaign for the repeal of the penal laws and Test Acts. They answered that they fully endorsed such legislative matters, and were in no position to offer any support of the kind.

Undaunted, King James persisted in trying to get them to change their minds, and endeavoured to convince Mary of the merits of Catholicism by regularly sending her collections of papers, through the Marquis d'Albeville, to study. For the most part these were nothing less than thinly veiled propaganda. A long letter in French, setting out in detail his reasons for being a Catholic and urging her to do likewise for the good of her soul, was accompanied by a set of papers left by her mother and by Charles II on the same subject. A second letter followed, with a pamphlet by an anonymous writer titled *Reflections on the Differences in Religion*. Mary studied them dutifully, saddened to think her mother should have been so deluded. She wrote to thank her father, adding with perfect honesty that she had given much thought and prayer to the matter, apologizing for her lack of instruction and her weakness – as she saw it – in her reasoning, and for possibly wearying him with lengthy arguments and tedious disagreements, but as a result she only found her beliefs strengthened. 'I think it then my duty to have myself care of my own soul, and I praise God that by His grace I have seen myself so well instructed and satisfied that I am not Protestant simply because I have been educated as such, but because I am persuaded by my own proper judgment of being in the right way.'[9]

Although he must have realized his efforts were proving counter-productive, he would not give up and next he sent a Catholic priest, Father Morgan, to visit her with some more literature. She declined to receive him, on the perfectly justifiable grounds that her position as Princess of Orange made it impossible to grant an audience to a Jesuit priest in an unofficial capacity. Dutifully she braced herself to read some of the books, so that she could assure him she had done so, but they still did nothing to make her change her mind. The daughter could be just as obstinate as the father.

William's correspondence with the English had its limitations, especially as letters were always vulnerable to being opened in transit. In February 1687 he sent his friend Dijkvelt to England, ostensibly to give James general assurances of William's goodwill, but actually to sound out leading politicians, urging them to resist James's Catholicizing policies and assuring them that William would maintain the penal laws and Test Acts. He was visited by many leading figures, some of whom also wrote to William. Among them was John Churchill, who assured him there was nothing in the rumours that Anne had turned Catholic. While the King never made a great effort to convert her, she always feared that he might set his priests on her at any time. Adding to Protestant fears were Anne's domestic tragedies. That same February an epidemic of smallpox swept Whitehall, and she had barely recovered from a miscarriage when her two infant daughters Mary, aged twenty months, and

Anne, nine months, both died. George also fell ill and Catholics at court, convinced that he would follow his daughters to the grave, began actively canvassing a second marriage for her to a Roman Catholic prince. However, he frustrated their plans by making a full recovery.

In April 1687 King James issued a Declaration of Indulgence, giving freedom of worship to all Dissenters and Catholics, and suspending the laws that debarred them from holding public office. Anne wrote sadly to her sister that the priests now had so much power with the King 'as to make him do things so directly against the laws of the land', and it was 'a melancholy prospect that all we of the Church of England have'.[10] This was followed by rumours that King James was trying to have his daughters barred from the succession on the grounds that his marriage to their mother had not been valid, a move which the Earl of Rochester quashed by obtaining a statement from the clergyman who had performed the ceremony.

Even senior Catholics were disconcerted by King James's zeal. He now had four staunch Catholics on the Privy Council; Father Petre, the King's Jesuit confessor, was always close at hand and Catholic influence was being flaunted at court. The King was like a man possessed, convinced that he had only to act boldly and show the resolution his father and brother had lacked to succeed where they had failed and establish himself as an absolute monarch on the French pattern.

In August 1687 the Duchess of Modena, Queen Mary Beatrice's mother, died and William sent over Zuylenstein, to convey his condolences in person. At the same time he was charged with taking a closer look at the country and learning more about King James's relationship with an increasingly restive Parliament. With hindsight some historians have suggested that Zuylenstein had also gone to sound out leading Englishmen, especially army and naval officers, and to win them over to William's cause, with his unofficial lieutenant being his old friend Henry Sidney, former ambassador at The Hague. Whether William was seriously considering, or at least anticipating, the possibility of invasion by this time is debatable. While he was not yet fully committed, he looked at King James's increasingly self-destructive actions and was starting to anticipate the possible result. It has been argued that he already saw England as an important part of his design to save Europe from Roman Catholicism by using the country to break the French stranglehold on the continent, saying that it was from England that the salvation of Europe would come, as without her it would fall under the yoke of the King of France.[11]

Zuylenstein's mission opened up sources of information, enabling William to see where he might find the promises of support which would be necessary for a descent on England. According to a contemporary historian, the Revd Laurence Echard, writing only a generation later, 'King James might have kept the crown upon his head as easily as his hat in a high wind.'[12] Maybe the Prince and Princess of Orange had already surmised this for themselves.

By the end of the year the Queen was known to be pregnant. She had not been expecting a child since 1684. Isabella, her only child to survive babyhood, died at the age of four in March 1681. This had been followed by the birth of a daughter, Charlotte Marie, in August 1682, who lived for only six weeks, and two stillbirths. Though there was no reason to suppose that this next confinement would produce a healthy infant, the King and his supporters were as delighted as the Protestants were appalled. To the English people at large, the idea of another Catholic on the throne in the next reign, instead of the King's Protestant daughter, was anathema. The Protestants suspected that a Papist plot was in the process of being hatched, and even if the Queen did not have a son, her priests would obtain a baby boy and pass him off as hers.

Mary learnt the news initially from her stepmother, in very veiled terms, and then from the King. Her loyalty to her father had gradually been eroded over the years, and though she hated to think he could be capable of such underhand behaviour, she found it impossible not to have her doubts. His letter of 29 November confirming the pregnancy, she noted in her journal at the end of the year, mentioned it 'in a manner so assured and that in a time when no woman could know anything for certain that there was certainly cause enough to raise a small suspicion'.[13]

In March 1688 Danby wrote to warn William that, according to ladies at court, 'the Queen's great belly seems to grow faster than they have observed their own to do'.[14] An increasingly sceptical Mary asked Anne for details of their stepmother's condition. Anne's replies confirmed her view, saying that she thought the Queen's 'great belly' was as open to doubt as her insistence that the baby was going to be a son. The Catholics, she was sure, would stop at nothing to promote their interests. Mary was now convinced that James intended to trick her out of her inheritance and destroy the Church that she loved; fortified by her prayers, it gradually dawned on her that it might be necessary for him to be dethroned. Anne, who had ironically suffered a miscarriage that spring, told her sister that there were too many contradictory stories in circulation, and that whenever anybody talked to the Queen to her face about being with child, she looked as if she was apprehensive lest somebody should touch her to make sure. Whenever Anne herself was in the same room when the Queen was undressing, she always went into another room to put on her smock, as if she had something to hide. At one stage she was so resentful of Anne's inquisitive manner that it was said she struck her in the face with a glove, a reaction the stepdaughter never forgot nor forgave.

It was around this time that William realized it would probably be necessary for him to invade England. The possibility that the Queen might have a son, real or bogus, probably weighed less heavily with him than the fear that the increasing intensity of James's campaign to pack Parliament with staunch Catholics might goad his subjects to rebel. This impression was reinforced by a visit to him at Het Loo in May 1688 from Arthur Herbert and William and Edward Russell. According to Burnet, William told them that if he was invited by some men of the best interest to come and rescue the nation and the religion, he believed he could be ready to do so by the end of September. Yet he was still unsure of how the rest of Europe, particularly Holland's Roman Catholic allies, would react. While the German Protestant princes would applaud and cooperate in a successful invasion of England, powers such as Spain, the Holy Roman Emperor and the Pope might be less accommodating.

Historians have often disputed the actual date of William's decision to intervene, or, to put it bluntly, his plans to conspire to dethrone his father-in-law. The French Ambassador Avaux, hardly an objective witness, claimed that the Prince of Orange was one of those most responsible for the framing of the first Exclusion Act of 1679. Despite the lack of any evidence for this, others have seen William's intention in various events, meetings and conversations during 1685 or 1686, but this meeting with Herbert and the Russells is generally accepted as the defining moment. Alarmed by the reaction to the news of the Queen's pregnancy, James demanded the return of English and Scottish regiments serving in the Dutch Republic, to boost his army at home. William and the States-General refused to release them, saying that only the officers who wished to return to England of their own free will could go. At the same time the King requested the forcible repatriation of English exiles in Holland, notably Burnet, men who were obviously preparing propaganda to be used against him. When the Dutch declined to accede, the King insisted angrily that he was head of the family and must be obeyed, but he had no way of enforcing such edicts.

Matters in England were clearly approaching the point of no return. In April King James had issued a second Declaration of Indulgence suspending the penal laws, and ordered the Anglican clergy to read it from every church. On 18 May seven of the English bishops, headed by Sancroft, Archbishop of Canterbury, protested that this measure was founded on an illegal dispensing power and petitioned the King to withdraw it. They were sent to the Tower and charged with seditious libel.

On 10 June, Trinity Sunday, it was announced that the Queen had just been delivered of a healthy son at St James's Palace. Her confinement had not been expected for another month, and some at court said that she looked as if it was not due for several weeks. The lying-in chamber was filled with witnesses, but King James had foolishly given grounds for further suspicion by inviting only Roman Catholics, who could hardly be regarded as unbiased witnesses. The Archbishop of Canterbury was in the Tower, while the Hyde brothers, uncles of Mary and Anne, and the Dutch Ambassador, whose word could have been trusted, were not summoned. It added further fuel to the fire of those who were suspicious, and it was widely believed that the Jesuits had smuggled a baby boy into the Queen's bed in a warming-pan. On 12 June the King wrote to William that the Queen had been 'safely delivered of a sonne on Sunday morning a little before ten; she has been very well ever since, but the child was somewhat ill last night of the wind and some gripes, but is now, blessed be God, very well again, and like to have no returns of it, and is a very strong boy'.[15]

Anne had been taking the waters at Bath. On her return to London she was filled with remorse at not having stayed nearby to keep an eye on the situation, as she told Mary that now she would never be able to satisfy herself whether the child was her stepbrother or not. She could find no real evidence of fraud, but she and Mary still seemed to think their stepbrother was spurious. At first William and Mary ordered that prayers should be said in their chapel for the Prince of Wales. Notwithstanding their doubts, they did not want anybody to think that they had taken an unchristian aversion to the infant. James's ambassador at The Hague threw a party to celebrate the birth of the baby about to be christened James Francis Edward, but hardly anyone attended.

Once rumours had begun, there was no stopping them. After the initial doubts, nobody seriously disputed that the Queen had given birth. What was unclear was whether the baby had been either stillborn or another girl, and if so whether a baby in a warming-pan had really been substituted. The fact that this was not another ailing Stuart arrival was enough to sow suspicion in the minds of those who might otherwise have believed the King.* Even those who considered the warming-pan theory far-fetched felt obliged to lend it credence, in view of what this child's birth portended for the future.

---

* Ironically, the infant Prince of Wales lived to the age of seventy-seven, dying in January 1766. His younger sister Louisa was the longest-lived of his siblings, but she only attained the age of nineteen, dying in 1712. None of the others had lived beyond the age of four. That he was the only really healthy one among them alone gives some grounds for suspicion.

King James's wilful pro-Catholic policies and his treatment of the bishops were for most a step too far. Had he shown more religious tolerance, and been prepared to rule with the help of Parliament, rather than imposing his dogmatic policies on the country, he might have kept his throne. A tendency towards authoritarianism was his undoing. The Catholics owed their allegiance to a foreign power, namely Rome, and a Papist country was liable to fall under French domination. An increasingly Papist king with an infant son was unacceptable; and if the infant son truly were an impostor, the King would find it difficult to save himself. As William saw it from Holland, forty years earlier the King's father had destroyed the monarchy, albeit only temporarily. After his second son's reckless behaviour and wilful misgovernment, there was a risk that the destruction might be permanent. In his capacity as leader of the Protestant Stuarts in Europe, and as husband of the heir to the British throne, William saw it as his duty to intervene, but from a position of strength, not as another reckless, ill-supported Monmouth.

On 29 June the bishops were brought to trial, and the following day they were acquitted to widespread rejoicing. It was clear that their imprisonment and trial had been a foolish blunder, and that the King was responsible. That same evening Admiral Herbert, dressed as a common seaman, set sail for The Hague with a formal invitation, signed (with code numbers, as the document was technically treasonable) by the Earls of Devonshire, Danby and Shrewsbury, Richard Lumley, Edward Russell, Henry Sidney and Dr Compton, Bishop of London, requesting William of Orange to come over and save England for the Protestant religion, parliamentary government and the Whig party, and promising to be ready and waiting to support him as soon as he arrived. All signatories committed themselves to action on William's behalf; Danby, Devonshire and Lumley would play leading roles in the northern risings in the latter part of November, while Bishop Compton would escort Princess Anne to join the rebels at Nottingham. They advised him that they believed 'we shall be every day in a worse condition than we are, and less able to defend ourselves, and therefore we do earnestly wish we might be so happy as to find a remedy before it be too late for us to contribute to our own deliverance'. The majority of people, they said, were desperate for a change; not one in a thousand believed the Prince of Wales really was the King's son; and the army and navy, riddled with disaffection, would refuse to fight for the King.[16] As yet, no mention was made of any offer of the English crown; it merely invited him to come and help them to restore English liberties and the rule of law.[17]

When told of the new Prince's birth, Mary hoped for her father's sake that it was really his son, but the case against him was too overwhelming to be ignored. With some misgivings she gave orders that prayers should be said for the baby in their chapels, as to omit them would seem 'to show an aversion on my part against the poor innocent child', but in the first week of July she consulted William and 'we resolved to cease to pray for the child, but it was ceased by degrees'.[18] That month the infant was seriously ill, and Anne wrote that it would probably not be long before he was an Angel in Heaven. He recovered, but at the beginning of August he was very ill again for several days. Mary's former chaplain, Bishop William Lloyd, believed the true Prince had died a day or two after birth, that the Catholics had obtained a substitute boy which had also died and that there was a ready supply of 'divers children . . . laid out about this time to be in readiness',[19] provided by Catholic supporters of the King in order to keep up the pretence.

Much as Mary distrusted her father and longed to stand by her husband in answering the call of the signatories, she had to try to set her mind at rest on the matter of the Prince said to be her stepbrother. She wrote out a detailed obstetrical questionnaire for Anne to answer. The latter was more concerned with a forthcoming visit to Tunbridge Wells, as the doctors had told her that taking the waters there might prevent another miscarriage next time she was with child. She found Mary's questionnaire an effort, but she dutifully asked Mrs Dawson, one of the bedchamber women, who told her the Queen had gone into labour about 8 a.m. and had been delivered in the bed she lay in all night. Though the curtains at the foot of the bed were drawn, both sides were open and there had been no screen round it. She added that she had never seen any milk and that she 'never heard of anybody say they felt the child stir'. The Lord Chancellor and the rest of the council were all standing close by so that the Queen asked the King to hide her face with his periwig, as she did not wish to be brought to bed with so many men looking on her. Once the child was born and the cord cut, the midwife had given the baby to one of the Queen's attendants, who was about to carry it into the little bedchamber, but the King stopped her, telling the privy councillors that they were witnesses to a child being born, and that they must follow it into the next room to see what it was.

For most unprejudiced observers this would have been sufficient proof, but Mary was still unconvinced. By this time, however, perhaps she regarded her husband as so fully committed to an invasion of England that she needed to have her worst suspicions confirmed, in order to justify her support of the project. William was sufficiently sensitive to her plight to appreciate the torment she was going through, and perhaps his sympathy for her made him momentarily question his motives. But there was no escaping the fact that King James had probably tried to deceive his people, and that under the circumstances there was only one way of saving the English Church and state.

Nevertheless it was dreadful to contemplate the thought of her husband having to turn her father off his throne forcibly in order to save the English Church and state. A tearful Mary prayed hard for guidance, but in the last resort her duty to her husband was paramount. In July Zuylenstein returned from England with a negative report which reinforced their suspicions, and by the end of the month Mary's conscience was eased. The stepmother to whom she had once been close wrote to reproach her: 'Since I have been brought to bed, you have never once in your letters to me taken the least notice of my son, no more than if he had never been born, only in that which Mr Zuylenstein brought, that I look upon as compliment that you could not avoid, though I should not have taken it so, if ever you had named him afterwards.'[20] Mary replied coldly that all the King's children would find as much affection and kindness from her as could be expected of children of the same father.

William had always kept his views on the parentage of the new royal infant to himself. Like Mary he respected close family ties, and did not lightly contemplate heading a rising against the man who was his uncle and father-in-law. However, he was concerned lest England might drift into a second civil war, or become a satellite of Catholic France with James as the vassal of Louis XIV. Misguided, blundering King James might attempt to distract his subjects from the folly of his deeds by joining King Louis in another attack on the United Provinces, provoking another Anglo-Dutch war in which the odds would be heavily stacked against William's country. Despite the general feeling in Protestant England, it seemed most unlikely that the increasingly obstinate pro-Catholic James might change his policy in favour of the United Provinces.

All these factors made it practically impossible for him to avoid intervening to preserve the balance of power and safeguard his wife's inheritance. Three years previously Monmouth had chosen his moment to invade inadvisedly and paid the price; but to William, watching King James's repeated blunders and alienation of his subjects, it seemed the time was right. James's next mistake was to start bringing regiments of Irish Roman Catholics into England, but his subjects saw this as tacit acknowledgement that a foreign army was being installed to get ready to subdue the country, and French reinforcements might well join them.

It was still possible that events on the continent, or more specifically the behaviour of King Louis XIV, would frustrate his plans. In William's view it was vital for both English and Dutch to prevent France from overrunning the Spanish Netherlands. By the peace of Nymegen of 1678 Louis, having secured a defensible frontier in the Spanish Netherlands, now switched his attention to his eastern frontier. By 1684 he had strengthened his position in the Rhineland with piecemeal attacks which had not provoked an anti-French coalition, though their ferocity had crushed or discouraged opposition. Emperor Leopold, on the defensive against the Turks, recognized these gains in the truce of Ratisbon of 1684. Since then he had driven the Turks back through Hungary, and in August 1688 he took Belgrade. The European balance of power had shifted in his favour; the German princes were now more determined to resist Louis's aggression, and some of his former allies had turned against him. Unwilling to fight in 1683–4, the Dutch were now far more hostile to France, particularly in view of their anger at Louis's brutal persecution of the Huguenots. As a result Louis felt more strongly than ever a need to consolidate his position in the Rhineland and so strengthen his German frontier; and when he did so, he was likely to encounter more opposition than in 1683–4.

It seemed likely Louis might declare war in 1688 in the Rhineland. He had decided on several sudden, fierce preventive actions against various territories in Germany, aiming to strengthen his defensive position, relying on speed, diplomatic threats and bluster, and the deterrent effect of concentrated brutality, anticipating that his enemies would be unable to face a lengthy conflict. To him England was a lightweight, and after Charles II's separate peace with the Dutch in 1674, he had concentrated on buying his neutrality. When Louis tried to persuade James, soon after his accession, to enter into an alliance, he refused; France was so unpopular that a French alliance would have been a liability as regards securing an amenable Parliament. Now Louis, realizing sooner than James that William planned to invade England, warned him and sent details of William's preparations. Convinced that William would not undertake such a hazardous venture across the North Sea so late in the year, James refused to believe Louis and spurned his offers of naval help. Louis then miscalculated, assuming that though James could be of little positive use to him, he was still strong enough to defeat William or tie him up in a lengthy war in England. He also tried to persuade the States-General to withhold support for William's invasion, by getting Avaux to present the States with an address in which Louis declared that the bonds of friendship and alliance between him and King James would oblige him to assist the latter in the event of attempted invasion.

The effect was precisely the opposite of what was intended, seeming to confirm fears which had grown over the last couple of years that the Kings of France and England planned a joint attack on the United Provinces as they had in 1672. It made the States-General more willing to support William, though it embarrassed

James. His ambassador denied that any such alliance existed, but nobody believed him.

Louis had antagonized most of his Dutch allies by imposing restrictions on their herring trade and was succeeding, where William had often failed, in uniting most of the German princes against him by a threatened takeover of the Lower Palatinate. When the French army marched into the Rhineland at the end of September, thus removing any immediate danger to the United Provinces, the States-General finally gave William their blessing to go to England on 8 October. Confident there would be no attack on the Dutch Republic that year, William completed preparations for the invasion. He began a propaganda campaign to justify his coming actions before European opinion, not mentioning that the outcome would probably be James's abdication in his own favour, but told Leopold that he had no intention of dethroning James or harming the English Catholics. Fagel told the States-General that the Prince of Orange did not seek to conquer England, but simply to ensure that by the calling of a free Parliament the reformed religion would be secure and out of danger.

Respecting her difficult position as the daughter of the King whom he sought to threaten, he kept Mary fully informed, careful to do nothing without her knowledge or approval. During the summer of 1688 they spent as much time together as possible, both knowing that future events would have a significant impact on their future.

On 30 September William issued his declaration to the English people, consisting largely of a catalogue of grievances blamed on the King's evil advisers, rather than on the King himself, referring to the 'pretended' Prince of Wales and stating that the expedition was intended for no other purpose than to have a free and lawful Parliament in England assembled as soon as possible. While he had little interest in English laws and liberties as such, and his experiences in the United Provinces had not endeared him to representative institutions, he had little choice but to invade, as he feared that otherwise he would lose any chance of bringing England's wealth and manpower into his lifelong great struggle against France. He knew it would probably be necessary to dethrone or expel James and the Prince of Wales, as did Mary, who prayed for strength to carry out this dreadful act of disloyalty to her father.

Only the great prize of the crown could have justified the risks William was about to take. Undertaking a major naval expedition at the beginning of winter was not to be done lightly, especially when its path was blocked by a large well-organized fleet. William's army was less than half the size of James's, and he had to rely on the assurances of his English contacts that James's soldiers and sailors would not fight; however, their judgement was not to be put to the test. William's fleet managed to avoid the English naval force, and James's loss of nerve meant that his soldiers' loyalty was not tried in battle. Moreover, William had been taking a chance in making detailed and expensive plans for an invasion when the whole project would have been ruined if Louis had decided to strike against the Dutch Republic. But fortune favoured William.

Mary was saddened by letters from her father reproaching her for disloyalty. In the last he ever wrote her, dated 9 October, he told her that he could not believe it was in her nature to give her blessing to her husband's invasion. 'And though I know you are a good wife, and ought to be so, yet for the same reason I must believe you will be still as good a daughter to a father that has always loved you so tenderly, and that has ever done the least thing to make you doubt it. . . . You shall still find me kind to you, if you desire it.'[21] The Queen had added her appeal, saying she could not imagine that Mary would come over to England with her husband at the head of an invading force: 'I don't believe you could have such a thought against the worst of fathers, much less perform it against the best, that has always been kind to you, and I believe has loved you better than all the rest of his children.'[22]

However, it was too late to turn back. Mary tried to appear cheerful and confident, but as the moment of her husband's departure approached, it became harder. He told her firmly that if he did not return, she must marry again, but not to a Papist. Shocked, she assured him faithfully that she had never loved anyone but him, and could never love anyone else; and that she prayed to God that He would not let her survive him.

FIVE

'It is no small burden'

On 26 October William took his leave of the States-General. He thanked them for their support, assuring them that he had always served them faithfully and kept the welfare of the Republic constantly before him. 'What God intends for me I do not know, but if I should fall, take care of my adored wife who has always loved this country as if it were her own.'[1] That afternoon he and Mary dined together at Honselaardijk for the last time, and afterwards she accompanied him to the riverside, where he embarked in his yacht on his way to join the fleet. After he had gone, for a time she sat motionless in her carriage, fearing they might never see each other again. When his yacht had disappeared from view, she returned to The Hague to wait and pray.

The next day, 27 October, had been designated as an official day of prayer and fasting, and the Spanish envoy held a mass for the happy success of the venture, but the French Ambassador did not take part. The expedition set sail three days later, but a storm soon blew up and the ships had to return to port. On 9 November Mary received a message asking her to come to Brill the next day. There she had two precious hours with her husband, their last moments together on Dutch soil, but for her this second separation was even more heartrending than the first. When he left, she felt as if her heart had been torn out, and all she could do was commend him to God. On her way back to The Hague that night she met a large crowd at Maaslandsluys, and was overwhelmed, not to say frightened, at their enthusiasm.

Next morning William sailed from Helvoetsluys with over two hundred transport ships and an escort of about fifty warships. Mary attended public prayers in the town and then climbed to the top of the church tower to catch sight of the fleet, but by then only the masts were visible. By early afternoon all six hundred ships were well out to sea with a following wind and excellent weather, but next day the fleet was driven back again by a storm. At first some feared that William might have to abandon his enterprise, but little damage had been caused. After repairs the fleet waited for the wind to veer to the east, and on 11 November they tried again. For several days all contact was lost, and for Mary, as well as for everyone else in Holland, there was nothing to be done but wait for news and pray.

What William's force would eventually do depended on how the wind was blowing. Some things had to be left to chance, among them their point of disembarkation. The naval operation was something of a gamble, and it was not decided in advance whether they should make for the West Country or the north of England. The Earl of Danby, one of the signatories to the invitation sent to William, was based in Yorkshire, and this seemed an obvious target. However, supporters were said to be ready in both of these disaffected areas, which were equally far from the home counties where King James's army was concentrated.

After putting to sea, William decided the West Country would be more suitable. His strategy was to aim for a peaceful landing, leaving the outcome to chance if they should meet a British fleet on arrival. It was less than thirty years since the Anglo-Dutch wars had resulted in several naval skirmishes, notably the battle of the Medway, and a similar encounter, resulting in bloodshed, was best avoided if possible. However, William must have been aware that the home fleet would probably not be hostile. Several of the officers had been maintaining contact with him and his captains, and may have given him the encouraging news that a few days before some of the sailors had mutinied against attempts to introduce Catholic chaplains.

Good fortune was on his side, and for some years afterwards everyone talked about the 'Protestant wind'. It helped the invaders down the English Channel and at the same time prevented the

English naval commander, Lord Dartmouth, from attacking them. He and his ships were moored off the Essex coast, and their intelligence had advised them that the Dutch force was planning to land in the north. By the time he realized that this was not the case, bad weather prevented his ships from getting away in pursuit. When they did put to sea, they were becalmed for two days off Beachy Head. Once they could move again, a south-westerly gale drove them to seek shelter at Portsmouth. Meanwhile, favourable conditions carried William and his force past Dover; keeping clear of Portsmouth, with its large Catholic garrison, they headed further west. By the time the English fleet could make progress, the Dutch were well ahead.

On 4 November, William's birthday and wedding anniversary, divine service was held on board. That night the wind shifted to the west, and in a thick mist early next morning the captain mistook the sea-marks, and there were fears that they might end up at Plymouth off the south-west coast, where a potentially hostile English squadron was said to be ready to attack them. Next morning the fog cleared and a light breeze sprang up; they altered course eastwards for Torbay and landed at Brixham. Significantly 5 November was the anniversary of the Gunpowder Plot in 1605, an earlier deliverance for England from Popish perils. William Carstares, the Prince's Scottish chaplain, suggested that they should hold a short service of thanksgiving. The men were drawn up in their ranks, prayers were said and they sang Psalm 118 in as many languages as the soldiers of the camp spoke. As night fell they prepared a bivouac on rough ground just outside the village, although some of the men found billets in the cottages, and William himself made do with a mattress on the floor of a fisherman's hut.

On the next day orders were given to march for Exeter via Newton Abbot. The weather was wet and windy, with torrential rain causing floods along the lanes, and there was nowhere for the soldiers to sleep at night except in the thick red clay mud of the fields. William spent one night at Paignton, in rooms above an inn. Large numbers of troops fell ill in the unpleasant conditions, and as there was no hospital or almshouse in the area, they were sent back to Brixham where the cottagers were asked to take one or two men each and care for them until they recovered.*

The expected opposition from the Plymouth garrison failed to materialize, and everyone was in high spirits as they arrived at Exeter four days later, with full pomp and ceremony. The Bishop and Dean of Exeter had fled to London, and the remaining cathedral clergy clearly disliked having Burnet, who had organized a service of thanksgiving, in their pulpit. The common people gave William and his following a warm welcome, especially as he promised that all provisions would be paid for. In order to demonstrate his sense of discipline, he had two soldiers hanged for stealing a chicken. He waited for the nobility and gentry to come to him as promised; but became impatient when nobody wanted to be first. He was there at their invitation, he said; he had been obliged by his duty to God and his love for mankind to come and protect their religion, liberty and property.

A few figures of lesser rank joined his standard before Edward Seymour, perhaps the richest and most influential man in the west, came on 17 November; two days later the Marquis of Bath, commander of the Plymouth garrison, offered to place his troops at William's disposal. After that his following grew rapidly, and with it diminished the possibility that he might have to fight a pitched battle. A victory by foreign troops, even if led by the husband of the heir to the throne (assuming Mary was still officially recognized as heir in preference to her disputed half-brother), on English soil, would still throw his claim to the throne into doubt.

William now had with him the largest disciplined force of men that had ever landed in England. At the core of his armies were

---

* Requests for reimbursement from the government apparently fell on deaf ears. No Act of Parliament existed to compensate the people of Brixham for their nursing care and food given to the soldiers. Requests for compensation persisted, culminating in a petition in 1699 from the inhabitants of Brixham, Kingswear and Dartmouth, requesting the payment of debts of £1,500. Parliament answered that provision would be made, but no records exist to confirm that any sum was forthcoming.[2]

three English and three Scots regiments from Holland, together comprising some 4,000 men, with soldiers from Sweden and Brandenburg, plus Dutch guards, Württemberg cavalrymen, Swiss mercenaries and French Huguenot volunteers, totalling 11,000 foot and 4,000 horse.[3] This was no mere popular insurrection, simply hoping to dislodge an unloved sovereign, but a carefully planned military operation.

The standing army at the death of King Charles II had numbered about 9,000, but King James, believing in personal security and the ability to impose his wishes and policies on his subjects, had always been convinced that a strong force was essential. He had more than doubled the size of the army by the end of 1685, and by now it was about 34,000-strong. But James failed to take into consideration both the average freeborn Englishman's loathing of military government, compounded by the tyrannical rule of Cromwell, and the fear engendered by the encampments on Hounslow Heath formed each summer since the Monmouth rebellion. At the same time he was blind to the fact that most of the men in the army were loyal Protestants who resented the illegal commissions granted to Catholics and, in the absence of sufficient numbers of English Catholics to fill the ranks, the recruitment of Irishmen. Such moves had produced widespread disaffection among the men.

By the time he was ready to leave London and join his army near Salisbury, King James was a broken man. He had reversed all his policies, giving the Tories everything they wanted except a free Parliament, which he told them was not within his power as he could not hold free elections while a foreign army was in England. But his Protestant subjects were by now so suspicious of their Popish King that they greatly underestimated the value of these concessions. The situation would change dramatically if James were to defeat William in battle, but the embattled incumbent monarch had lost the will to fight. Before he even reached his army on 19 November his nephew Lord Cornbury had declared for William, and Lord Delamere had led a rising in Cheshire. Soon after, Danby and his cronies seized York, and Devonshire occupied Nottingham. James dithered at Salisbury, suffering from nosebleeds and insomnia.

On 21 November William began to march east from Exeter, but his army was still more than 60 miles away when, two days later, James decided to withdraw without giving battle. Several of his leading colonels, notably John Churchill, who had played a major role in the defeat of Monmouth and had recently been promoted to lieutenant-general, and significantly his other son-in-law Prince George of Denmark, all declared for William. James's army was still larger, but he felt he could trust nobody. On 28 November he accepted the recommendation of an assembly of Tory notables that he should negotiate.

On 7 December William received James's commissioners at The Bear, a roadside inn at Hungerford, and the next day he stated his terms. Among these were the dismissal of all Catholic officers and the revocation of all proclamations against William and his adherents; James was to pay William's army; William agreed that his army would halt 40 miles west of London, if the King withdrew his armies the same distance to the east; both James and William were to attend the next session of Parliament; and as a guarantee that James would not try to bring a French force to England, Portsmouth was to be placed under the guard of an officer who could be trusted by both. William was ready to leave the way open for reconciliation and compromise; he seemed prepared to leave James on the throne, though with greatly reduced powers, and was confident that a free Parliament would deal satisfactorily with the delicate question of the legitimacy of the Prince of Wales.

James received the letter from his commissioners the following evening, and told them he would give his answer next morning. He was in no mood to compromise. He had already sent his wife and son off to France, and as he felt himself deserted on all sides he believed he had no alternative but to follow them. In the small hours of 11 December, under cover of darkness, he slipped quietly down the back stairs from Whitehall Palace, accompanied only by two Catholics, Sir Edward Hales and Ralph Sheldon. After burning the writs for the new Parliament, they took a boat across the river to Vauxhall, James throwing the Great Seal into the Thames on the way. Horses were waiting, and he and his two companions rode eastwards where a boat was ready to take them to France.

The short reign of King James II was over, and for the next two months a state of interregnum existed; Britain was technically without sovereign or government. To William, his father-in-law's departure was a relief. The army officers agreed to submit to his authority and to keep their men together in order to preserve law and order. The London mob was out, sacking chapels, besieging and in some cases destroying the embassies of Roman Catholic powers. There were rumours that the Irish were coming to sack the city, and people prepared to arm themselves against the Papist enemy.

Just as the agitation was starting to die down, but before William could get there, James was back in the capital on 16 December, having been apprehended on his flight by Kentish fishermen and returned to Whitehall. Though he no longer commanded any respect, his sufferings had made him a figure of pity, and he was cheered by a waiting crowd as he forlornly entered the capital. William was less sympathetic; he knew his father-in-law had run away from responsibility, leaving his country in a state of anarchy, and could no longer be relied on. But in such a delicate matter he preferred the initiative to come from Englishmen; he called a council of twelve to consider what to do with the man who had to all intents and purposes abdicated, and it was agreed that he should be allowed to escape. The remainder of the royal army, which had been loyal to James until he was foolish enough to disband it without pay, was ordered to march out of London, to be replaced by the six English and Scottish regiments in Dutch service, and by William's own Dutch Blue Guards, which were sent to Whitehall.

James was asked to go to Ham House, Richmond, for his own safety. Fearing assassination at the hands of the Dutch soldiers guarding the property, he sought permission to go to Rochester instead, which was readily granted. He left London on 18 December, again under guard, and issued a proclamation declaring that he had left Whitehall because of the discourteous conduct of the Prince of Orange, but was prepared to return at the call of the nation, 'whenever it agreed to have liberty of conscience'.[4] This plea was to

106

no avail, and he sailed for France on 23 December. His return to London had been an embarrassment to William, who had to use more open pressure to get rid of him the second time; James's sufferings at the hands of the fishermen aroused further sympathy, and the Tories felt that William had driven him out.

Now James was gone, William had effectively conquered England by force of arms, though paradoxically without firing a shot. However, he was careful to avoid giving any gloating impression of armed victory or premature triumph, by delaying each move towards the crown until some form of authorization or invitation from Parliament would set the seal on his legitimacy. Maintaining that he was a sovereign prince merely come to save the English nation from tyranny, he took pains to avoid being seen as a rebel against the established order, or in this case against the incumbent sovereign. The Marquis of Halifax, who was shortly to be appointed Lord Privy Seal, was particularly impressed by William's character. Here was a man, he declared, who showed himself reluctant to pursue or punish political enemies, who was tolerant by nature and who openly expressed his regret at outbreaks of anti-Catholic violence throughout much of the country.

One small incident said much for William's magnanimity. On new year's eve he visited Charles II's widow Queen Catherine at Somerset House; he asked her how she was passing her time and whether she still played basset regularly. Smiling pointedly, she told him that she was unable to do so in the absence of the Chamberlain, Lord Feversham, who had also been James's Chief of Staff and was now under arrest in the Tower of London. Telling her that he did not wish to interrupt Her Majesty's diversions, William instantly gave orders that Feversham should be released.

Yet the vacuum left by James's unexpectedly precipitate flight made the immediate reimposition of order necessary; only the Prince of Orange really had the authority to do so. He was being pressed by several of his followers to assume the crown by right of conquest, and then to summon Parliament. In his manifesto, though, he had declared that it was not his intention to conquer England, and he intended to leave all disputed matters to the arbitration of Parliament. He accordingly summoned three leading members of the Lords to tell them how he saw his position. He made it clear that he had not come over to establish a commonwealth [Republic] or to be a duke of Venice, and refused to have any share in the government unless it was put in his person and that for the term of his life; he would not be 'his wife's gentleman usher', or a prince consort (a term not yet officially recognized). While he would not oppose the Princess's rights, and nobody respected her virtues more than he did, he would not hold any subordinate position. If the English offered him the crown, he would accept; otherwise, he would return to Holland. He would not accept being appointed regent for James, as this would place him in an impossible situation if he were to issue one governmental order and James a conflicting one. From his experience as Stadholder of Holland, he knew that a ruler could be acclaimed one moment and deeply unpopular the next. Enthusiasm for public figures waxed and waned, and if he were to become the governor or ruler of a nation which regarded him as a foreigner, he demanded a legally binding assurance of life tenure. If he became Queen Mary's king consort and she predeceased him, Anne might form an alliance with the French to depose him. He must be made king for life, and nothing else would do.

Nevertheless he would agree to Anne being designated as his heir if Mary remained childless, and to Anne and her children taking precedence in the succession over any children he might have by a second marriage, should Mary predecease him, leaving no issue, and if he took a second wife who produced any heirs. The Lords were prepared to accept this compromise; as he already exercised executive power, he was in a position to dictate terms. Parliament insisted that Mary should be made joint ruler, but it was clear that the real power would lie with William. On 6 February 1689 the Lords agreed that James had abdicated, and a week later William and Mary were formally offered the crown.

On 20 December William and the Lords came to an agreement whereby they took over the civil administration while he retained command of the armed forces. An assembly consisting of the surviving members of all King Charles II's parliaments and a substantial delegation from the City of London was assembled as a temporary House of Commons. This body asked him to take over the provisional government on 29 December and to send out writs for elections early the following month, after which a convention would meet. William withdrew all troops from the parliamentary boroughs, and the convention thus elected met on 22 January 1689.

Although his presence had been instrumental in restoring peace and order throughout the country, William's unanimous popularity could not be taken for granted. While his invasion had been broadly endorsed by most of the nation, such support had not envisaged driving James into exile and replacing him on the throne. The Whigs took it for granted that William would be grateful to them, to the extent of granting them a monopoly of power and helping them against the Tories, many of whom had accepted at face value William's promise of a free Parliament, which they had seen as a solution to all their problems. Their leaders had tried mediating between James and William on that basis, and James's flight left them mystified. William, they felt, had placed undue pressure on James after his return to London, and a belief soon grew that this was part of his plot from the outset to seize the crown and deliberately drive James out. The Tories felt they had been tricked into betraying their principles of non-resistance and passive obedience. On 30 January, the anniversary of Charles I's execution, Dr John Sharp, suspended under James II for his anti-Catholic preaching, delivered a sermon to the Commons pointedly condemning the deposing of kings as a Popish practice.

The main task of the convention was to resolve the issue. A proposal to recall James, who had twice deserted his followers, was supported by only a small Jacobite minority. For all their principles regarding the sanctity of the order of succession, hardly any of the Tories were enthusiastic about having him back, except on conditions which he would almost certainly find unacceptable. William favoured being made sole ruler, as did Bentinck, but the English emphatically did not. Arthur Herbert, commander of the invasion fleet, declared that he would never have drawn his sword in the Prince's favour if he could have suspected him of acting in such a way towards his wife. If the Prince of Wales was disregarded, Mary, not William, was James's heir and should still be seen as such. The majority intended preserving at least some degree of continuity.

Some of the High Tories were keen to avoid going so far as to depose James. They argued that his desertion and general behaviour had shown him to be incapable of ruling, and proposed that the next heir, Mary, should rule as regent on his behalf, as was then the case in the kingdoms of Sweden and Portugal, where the monarchs had been adjudged insane and incapable of ruling. This was rejected on the basis that James was clearly still in possession of his faculties, and the idea of separating the powers of the crown from the person of the king was disliked. As the proposal was narrowly defeated in the Lords, the Tories concentrated on a suggestion that Mary should be declared sole ruler, on the basis that James had abdicated and the crown had therefore passed by right to Mary as next heir. There was thus no need for Parliament to name a successor, and no need to introduce an elective element into the monarchy. Neither William nor Mary would accept this, so the convention finally accepted the fifth alternative, namely that James had abdicated, the throne was therefore vacant and the crown should be offered jointly to William and Mary. While the legal basis for such a solution was decidedly shaky, it met the circumstances as far as was compatible with all deeply held legal and constitutional beliefs and prejudices.

The controversy about the crown soon became a struggle between the largely Whig House of Commons and the predominantly Tory House of Lords. On 28 January a large majority in the Commons voted that James, 'having endeavoured to subvert the constitution of this kingdom, by breaking the original contract between King and people, and by the advice of Jesuits and other wicked persons, having violated the fundamental laws, and having withdrawn himself out of this kingdom, hath abdicated the government and that the throne is thereby vacant'.[5] Next day the Lords rejected the proposal for a regency by two votes, agreeing that James had broken the original contract, but deciding he had 'deserted' rather than 'abdicated'. On 31 January they voted against declaring the throne vacant, and proposed that William and Mary were to reign as joint sovereigns during their joint and separate lives, though the administration was vested in William during his lifetime. Should there be any children of the marriage between William and Mary, a prospect which everyone knew was unlikely, they would be next in the succession, though Princess Anne and her heirs would precede those of William by a second wife, in the event that Mary should predecease him and he married again. Anne would later refer bitterly to this measure as her 'abdication'.

The Tory majority in the Lords, led by Lord Danby, claimed that the crown had already passed automatically to Mary as legitimate heir, that it was not for Parliament to grant it to any other, and that she should be proclaimed Queen regnant at once. The Whig party in the Commons proposed William as king, in effect an elected sovereign, a measure which would finally bury the old principle of the Divine Right of Kings.

*   *   *

Since William's departure for England, Mary had had to exercise the utmost self-control. There was a total lack of news for several days, and she spent nearly all her waking hours in public and private prayer. After what must have seemed like an eternity, on 19 November she received a letter telling her that the expedition had landed safely in England. There was no news from William himself, as the ship he had sent to Holland with separate dispatches had been intercepted on the way. Now she knew that he had landed safely, she was able to relax a little and make a partial return to her old routine. Four days a week she entertained her ladies, though she still refrained from cards for the time being unless special guests were present. She was still haunted by the last words he had spoken to her, exhorting her to take a second husband in the event of his death, and in her darkest moments she wondered whether these had been a kind of prophecy. Not until the long-awaited letter from him arrived could she rest in the assurance that God had answered her prayers and brought about a happy ending.

On 30 December she heard the news of her father's flight to France. At around the same time she had a letter from William asking her to make preparations for her journey to England. Early in the new year she was visited by William's cousin and ally Frederick, Elector of Brandenburg, and his wife, Electress Sophie Charlotte. This raised her spirits, and she noted in her diary that she gave herself 'no time for any thing else. The circumstances of the time were such that we could have no publick entertainments, but onely treating them at my severall houses, which I did and played at cards'. She rarely retired to bed before 2 a.m. as a result. When there was dancing she did not take part, thinking it inappropriate while her father was in distress and her husband possibly in danger, but she was relieved to find she was not tempted, feeling 'that I believed I had overcome that which used to be one of my prettiest pleasures in the world, and that I feard might be a sin in me for loving it too well'.[6] After her guests left on 10 January, Mary returned briefly to her 'old solitary way of living'.

When the parliamentary proceedings were reported to her, she wrote to Danby that it had never been her intention to occupy the throne by herself, and she would not become queen unless William was made king. As the Prince's wife, she wrote, she would never be 'other than what she should be in conjunction with him and under him', and would take it very unkindly 'if any, under a pretence of their care of her, would set up a divided interest between her and the Prince'.[7]

Though elated at her husband's success she still felt sorry for her father, and knew she would far rather stay in Holland. On 1 February Admiral Herbert appeared at The Hague with a letter from William, summoning her to follow him across the North Sea as soon as possible. Though delayed for a while by contrary winds, she set sail on 20 February, the sea 'like a looking glass'.[8] As the English coast came into view, she looked behind her,

and saw vast seas between me and Holland that had been my country for more then 11 years. I saw with regret that I had left it and I believed it was for ever; that was a hard thought, and I had

112

need of much more constancy than I can bragg of, to bear with patience. Yet when I saw England, my native country, which long absence had made me a stranger to, I felt a secret joy . . . but that was soon checked with consideration of my fathers misfortunes which came immediately into my mind.[9]

William was waiting for her at Greenwich, and her delight at meeting him again was tempered by her finding him looking thinner, very pale and coughing blood. They fell into each other's arms, weeping tears of joy, 'both bewailing the loss of the liberty we had left behind and were sensible we should never enjoy here; and in that moment we found a beginning of the constraint we were to endure here after, for we durst not let owr selves go on with those reflections'.[10]

Everyone was eager for a glimpse of the new Queen. At twenty-six years of age Mary was a tall, elegant figure, handsome and good-natured, her face very agreeable, her shape graceful and fine. William and others had told her that it was important for her to appear as cheerful as possible in public; keen to please as ever, she overplayed her hand and was criticized for her apparent levity and lack of feeling towards her father. John Evelyn complained that she came into Whitehall 'laughing and jolly, as to a wedding', while Sarah Churchill (admittedly no admirer of Mary) remarked acidly that 'she wanted bowels', or sensitivity; the new Queen, she sniffed, ran about her apartments 'looking into every closet and conveniency, and turning up the quilts upon the bed, as people do when they come to an inn'. Such behaviour was 'strange and unbecoming' in the circumstances. 'For whatever necessity there was of deposing King James, he was still her father who had so lately been driven from that chamber and that bed; and, if she felt no tenderness, I thought she should at least have looked grave, or even pensively sad.'[11]

Mary was also criticized for taking up her cards again, and for smiling and talking to all, but as she admitted to her cousin Electress Sophie of Hanover she had 'to force myself to more mirth then became me at that time, and was by many interpreted as ill nature, pride, and the great delight I had to be a Queen. But alas they did little know me, who thought me guilty of that. . . . My heart is not made for a kingdom and my inclination leads me to a quiet life, so that I have need of all the resignation and self denial in the world to bear with such a condition as I am now in.'[12] To others she admitted readily that they were not to doubt the sincerity of her feelings when she said that she could not forget her father, and she still grieved for his misfortune. Yet although she had a duty to her father, she had even stronger obligations towards her husband and their religion. Burnet told her privately that she was being censured for what others regarded as her unnaturally cheerful demeanour, and she told him ruefully that she was merely 'obeying directions and acting a part which was not very natural to her'.[13]

On 13 February William and Mary received the Lords and Commons in the Banqueting House at Whitehall. The Declaration of Rights was read to them and they were asked to accept the crown. William replied that they both 'thankfully' accepted what they had been offered, promised to rule according to law and to be guided by Parliament. They were then proclaimed King and Queen. This Declaration, subsequently embodied in a Bill of Rights later in the year, dealt with James's 'abdication', William and Mary's elevation to the throne and the succession after their deaths. Their heirs would be Mary's children, if any, followed by Anne and her heirs, and then any children William might have by a later marriage. It declared that no Catholic, or spouse of a Catholic, could ascend the throne of England. A new oath of allegiance was to be taken by office-holders, MPs and clergymen, but in deference to Tory demands it avoided referring to William and Mary as 'rightful and lawful' monarchs.

Regarding the constitutional provisions, while clarifying certain disputed issues, the Declaration imposed only one new restriction on the prerogative: the assertion that the raising or keeping of a standing army within the kingdom in time of peace, unless with the consent of Parliament, was illegal. Previously the army's legal status had been undefined, though it was accepted that the King had sole direction of the army, navy and militia. Now his control of the army in peacetime was to be considerably restricted. It was not this new constraint that made the Declaration important to later generations, but the safeguards which it tried to provide for the rights and liberties of both Parliaments and subjects. It asserted that subjects had a right to petition the King, that parliamentary debates and elections should be free and that Parliament should meet regularly.

Through all the tribulations of these first few weeks, their simple religious faith sustained them above all else. In March William wrote to his aunt Albertina of Nassau-Dietz about his 'advancement' to the crown. 'It is the hand of God that has so disposed of it. I hope it will be to His glory, but it is no small burden that I have to carry.'[14]

*   *   *

The coronation of William and Mary in Westminster Abbey was set for 11 April, in what was British history's only coronation ceremony for two joint sovereigns. Ironically, on that same morning news was brought to London that James had landed in Ireland with an army commanded by French officers. Timed to have the worst effect possible on Mary, a letter from her father arrived as she was dressing for her progress from Whitehall to the Abbey, and was on the point of leaving her apartments. He wrote:

I have been willing to overlook what has been done, and thought your obedience to your husband and compliance to the nation might have prevailed. But your being crowned is in your own power; if you do it while I and the Prince of Wales are living, the curses of an angry father will fall on you, as well as those of a God who commands obedience to parents.[15]

The letter was destroyed, though a note of the contents was made by Lord Nottingham, who received it just before or just after delivery. William answered it, telling his father-in-law that 'all he had done was with his wife's advice and approbation'. In Mary's journals, no reference was made to it, so it was probably intercepted before she had a chance to read the contents. Anne received a similar note from

115

her father and asked her bedchamber woman, who had been present at the Prince of Wales's birth, whether he could really be her brother. The woman assured Anne that he was, and from that moment her loyalty to her sister and brother-in-law began to disintegrate.[16]

William was unwell at the time, and worries about both her closest male relatives for very different reasons did not help Mary approach this important day, about which she had been understandably nervous, with a lighter heart. She concealed her distress as best she could as she and William left the Palace of Whitehall soon afterwards, to go by barge the few hundred yards to Westminster where the nobility were assembled in the House of Lords, wearing their ermine-edged robes of state. Three hours later the whole procession emerged from the Palace of Westminster to walk to the west door of Westminster Abbey, the King wearing a crown topped with a pleated velvet bonnet to match his robes and the Queen a golden diadem. The King's crown was carried by the Earl of Grafton and the Queen's by the Duke of Somerset. Sancroft, the Archbishop of Canterbury, was prevented by ill-health from attending, and his place was taken by Dr Compton. The Bishop of Winchester and the Bishop of Bristol walked beside William and Mary.

As Queen regnant, Mary was inaugurated with the same ceremony as her husband. The Sword of State was girded round her as it was round him, and then she was raised into the throne and presented with the Bible, the spurs and the heavy jewelled orb. Instead of the usual light, elegant diadem of a queen consort which she had just been wearing, she was crowned with the massive, heavily bejewelled Coronation Crown, made specially for the occasion by Robert Vyner, who had also made her diadem and Crown of State. The total cost of these two crowns, an orb and two sceptres for the King and the Queen was £7,260. This excluded the price of the stones alone, part of the crown treasures; comprising 2,725 diamonds, 71 rubies, 59 sapphires, 40 emeralds and 1,591 large pearls, they were valued at £126,000. The most striking jewel in the Queen's crown was valued at £30,000. A diamond and ruby ring which William had given Mary, and which had been enlarged specially for the ceremony, was placed in error on William's finger.

The strain of wearing so much gold and jewellery throughout the long ceremony soon told visibly on both of them. 'I pity your fatigue, Madam,' Anne whispered sympathetically to Mary, who retorted irritably that 'a crown is not so heavy as it seems'.[17]

Another minor note of discord was struck towards the end of the ceremony. According to custom, the sovereigns' first offering was to be a roll of silk and twenty pieces of gold. The silk was laid on the altar, and Compton presented the King and Queen with a basin for their money. They had either forgotten or been unaware of this detail, and, heavily encumbered by their regalia, could do nothing but look helplessly at each other. Compton stood patiently until Danby chivalrously took out his purse and put some coins into the basin.

Whereas other monarchs of England had sworn to uphold the law made by their ancestors, William and Mary swore to rule according to 'the statutes in Parliament agreed upon and the laws and customs of the same', and promised to uphold the Protestant reformed religion. Burnet preached the Coronation Sermon, bidding them to 'reign long in your persons and much longer in a glorious posterity'. In view of the news which had struck terror into Mary's heart that morning, she must have pondered on the irony of his wishes for a peaceful reign: 'May your fleets be prosperous and your armies victorious. But may you soon have cause to use neither.'[18]

As they returned from the hall, the newly crowned sovereigns were acclaimed enthusiastically, though some observers could not refrain from making comparisons between the stooping King who walked so rapidly and the majestic carriage of his much taller Queen. Proceedings ended with a banquet in Westminster Hall lasting until 10 p.m. There were mutterings of discontent, especially from those who looked coldly at the Dutch soldiers being used to guard William and Mary as they were crowned King and Queen of England, and when their King refused to perform the traditional coronation ceremonies of the washing of the feet of the poor, and touching for scrofula, the King's Evil, dismissing them as mere superstition and empty ritual. Under protest, he consented to lay his hand on one patient, telling him, 'God give you better health and more sense,' and the man did indeed recover.[19]

William was relieved when it was all over. Later he remarked dismissively to an old friend, Burgemeester Witsen of Amsterdam, about 'the comedy of the Coronation' and 'those foolish old Popish ceremonies'.[20] As a Calvinist, he took his religion too seriously for the English. He found something utterly false in the spectacle of a mass of peers, who professed to believe in God even if they did not, swearing an allegiance to their sovereign they probably did not mean to keep; they had presumably done exactly the same for his father-in-law at the previous coronation, barely four years earlier.

As a devout Anglican, Mary likewise thought the day's proceedings savoured too much of worldly pomp and not enough of devotion. After eleven years in Holland she was out of sympathy with the English love of ceremony, and felt the coronation was 'all vanity'. It was only a few weeks since she had had to turn her back on a quiet life, leaving the country which she had come to love and all her friends there too. At 'home' their simple way of life had been respected. Now, in England, their routine would be circumscribed by pomp and ceremony, in a land pervaded by a general air of corruption and discontent everywhere they looked. They were surrounded by politicians evidently out to secure what power they could for themselves, reducing the prerogatives of the crown. Having been called to the throne in unusual circumstances, they both felt they were on trial, while over everything loomed the shadow of their predecessor.

SIX

'The title of King was only a pageant'

William and Mary both found adjustment to life in England a painful process. In the seventeenth century London was a byword for smog, its air polluted with smoke from domestic coal fires. Mary had been shocked to find how unwell William looked when she arrived in England, and Dutch envoys to England hardly recognized this thin, pale, pitiful-looking creature as the Stadholder with whom they had discussed affairs of state in Holland only months earlier. A cold he had caught at Salisbury before Christmas had settled on his chest, and sometimes he coughed helplessly for up to fifteen minutes at a time. Fighting for breath and trying to work while in a state of near-collapse weakened him further, though he tried to make light of his trouble, telling an aide after a coughing fit that he would 'soon blow to land'. His asthma had worsened, and he could not continue living in Whitehall, a depressing, dark collection of royal and state apartments and government offices stretching for half a mile along the Thames. The combination of overwork, anxiety and the stenches and fogs of London might prove fatal, and the doctors warned that at this rate he would not last another year.

Notwithstanding any inconvenience for ministers and courtiers, a move to somewhere more salubrious was essential. By the time of the coronation he and Mary had settled at Hampton Court, and only came to London on council days once or twice a week. This neglected palace, 'a great Tudor pile', was even damper than Whitehall, and in urgent need of modernization, but at least the air was more healthy there. William therefore decided to make it their headquarters, and he was prepared to disregard complaints that such a move would make them less accessible. Having been summoned by the great and the good to come to England and rescue the country from a disastrous neo-Papist regime, he was not going to sacrifice his health – if not his life – merely to save ministers and courtiers regular journeys of a few miles.

As these men had always lived in London, they had no idea how harmful to their King the atmosphere was, and thought he was being obstinate for the sake of it. They did not stop to consider that he spent several hours most days dealing with correspondence and other paperwork, and that when he emerged he was bound to be tired, taciturn and unresponsive. As talking made him cough, he avoided talking for its own sake. His asthma was exacerbated by close or overheated atmospheres, so he took care to avoid crowds and social functions when possible. All this was seen as characteristic of an apparent refusal to court his subjects' affection. Ladies at court, whom he generally ignored, called him 'the low Dutch bear' behind his back. Soon it was said that if only King James would change his religion, it would be impossible to keep him out. Nevertheless Mary knew that compromise was called for, and at length she persuaded William to acquire a country house nearer Whitehall. In June he bought Kensington House, on the edge of Hyde Park, from his Secretary of State the Earl of Nottingham, for £14,000.

William was irritated by English court etiquette. His days of going out alone for a ride on horseback on the spur of the moment, or calling on friends at a few minutes' notice, were now a thing of the past; all daily routines were subject to time-honoured ceremonial. In time he would arrange matters to suit himself. Ministers who complained that they sometimes had to wait for days at a time for an audience with him, and thought him lazy or unresponsive, would have done better to call him awkward. He might make the best use of the daylight hours by hunting, or might relax by chatting to old friends, often discussing nothing more weighty than art and architecture. Then he would realize that large batches of papers had accumulated, and sat up late at night signing them. Perhaps Mary soon learnt that it was not just clandestine assignations with Betty Villiers that stopped him from going to bed at a reasonable hour.

Both found the formal side of monarchy particularly irksome. The position of Stadholder had always been basically functional, and William wanted to bring the same attitude to the English monarchy, eschewing the ceremonial aspects of kingship which he disliked. In Holland he and Mary had been at the centre of a small, private court, where they had moved mostly within a circle of close friends and servants, with plenty of time to take a close interest in domestic details or planning improvements to their houses and gardens.

To add to his woes, William was extremely homesick. Sometimes on a fine day he would look out of the window, and sigh how he longed to be back at The Hague or at Dieren. His open partiality for the company of his Dutch friends irritated the English. Burnet remarked that the King loved and trusted the Dutch more, 'and the English, being of more lively temper than the Dutch, grew to express a contempt and an aversion for them, that went almost to a mutiny'.[1] The English did not take into account the personal sacrifices made by many of the Dutch. At the time of his accession William was in his thirty-ninth year. Some of his associates, such as Constantine Huygens, his faithful secretary for nearly twenty years, were much older, and it had been no mean effort for them to uproot themselves and come to a strange land in order to serve him. At any time they might find the country plunged into another war or counter-revolution, and even if England remained at peace they would still be blamed for anything that might go wrong. King James had been driven into exile after a very short reign and his father had been tried and executed, so the precedents were not hopeful. The Dutchmen and their wives had no love for England, which they thought dirty, shabby and sinful. King William's generous treatment of them was the least he could do to make amends for the inhospitable aspects of their new home.

However, there was a limit as to how long he could continue to disregard his advisers. Persuaded to conciliate his people, if only briefly, in early autumn he spent ten days at the Newmarket races, accompanied by his brother-in-law Prince George, plus various members of the nobility and the Dutch ambassadors. Like King Charles he mingled with the crowds, placed several bets with little success and accepted various invitations to dine. One evening he became quite drunk. On the following day he attended the races in a bad temper, and was provoked by an insolent (unnamed) Tory nobleman who deliberately rode under his horse's nose as he approached the course. The King lashed out at the man with his cane, provoking a wag to remark that it was the only blow he had yet struck for supremacy in all his kingdoms. Even so it was a good public relations exercise, and the crowds were pleased that their new King was starting to behave like a proper Englishman.

A few weeks later on Lord Mayor's Day he and the Queen were invited as guests of the City of London to the traditional show and dinner with the Lord Mayor, the two sheriffs and the aldermen, several of whom were rewarded with knighthoods afterwards. They dined for the first time in public at Whitehall, and a few days later the King was made a member of a City livery company. On his first birthday in England, 4 November, the shops were closed, bells rang and bonfires were lit in celebration. A special service was held at court that morning, at which the Bishop of St Asaph paid tribute to William as 'the Church's great deliverer', and in the evening a grand ball at Kensington House was so packed that one of the Queen's gentlemen-in-waiting was knocked down and accidentally trampled on.

The King made these gestures of goodwill with a degree of unease. Later he reverted to his old ways, spending more time hunting or busying himself with the troops at Hounslow – perhaps the only activities with which he really felt comfortable. The English nobility were irritated when he shirked their company in favour of his Dutch friends, with whom he would dine while the English were left angrily standing at his table. William Bentinck, created Earl of Portland at the coronation, was particularly unpopular and provoked much jealousy. Regarded as an unbending foreigner, he was nicknamed 'the Wooden Man', and the King continued to rely on his advice. The only Englishman at court who could compete with Portland was Henry Sidney, created Earl of Romney in the coronation honours list, and a faithful servant of the crown since restoration days. Now appointed Colonel of the King's Foot Guards, he enjoyed the monarch's full trust and confidence.

Mary's household was mainly English. She appointed the Duchess of Dorset her Lady of the Bedchamber, the Marquis of Winchester her Chamberlain, and John Howe, Member of Parliament for Cirencester, her Vice-Chamberlain. Only two of her ladies-in-waiting were Dutch. Neither was happy in London, and one of them complained to Huygens that they were treated with disdain by the English ladies and, worst of all, that Her Majesty was becoming 'too English'. Betty Villiers had followed King William to England and it was known that she saw him regularly. Unlike the two previous Stuart kings, William conducted his liaison with discretion, took pains never to flaunt her and refrained from showering her with honours and rewards. Mary accepted the matter with resignation; beside the example of her father, her husband's infidelities must have looked trifling.

Her daily routine began at 6 a.m. when she was served tea, and then spent two hours reading and writing. Prayers followed at 8 a.m., then business for about five hours until dinner. In the afternoon she played cards and gave public receptions, then at 7 p.m. there were evening prayers and supper. After that she dealt with private correspondence until midnight or later, and then retired to bed.

In most royal courts, kings and queens lived their lives with barely a moment of privacy, under the constant eye of nobility and even casual sightseers. This William and Mary did not find to their taste. William preferred to receive visitors privately, in his study or bedchamber, which they entered and left by the back stairs. Despite his efforts to be more accessible and sociable, he was always happier hunting at Windsor or Richmond.

At Hampton Court Sir Christopher Wren planned to demolish all the Tudor buildings except the Great Hall, replacing them with an elegant, symmetrical palace and formal gardens in the continental manner. He soon had to modify this plan, and restricted himself initially to adding a new wing. As it would not be ready for some time, Mary decided to convert a small pavilion that had been built at the water's edge to shelter those who had disembarked from the river. This became her favourite personal retreat, where she could read, gossip and enjoy the open air. Ever a gardening enthusiast, she took great pleasure in planning the alleys, flowerbeds and shaded walks. She and William spent much of their first summer in England together at Hampton Court, and she kept a careful eye on building operations, consulting with Wren who visited up to three times a week.

At Kensington Wren added new pavilions to each corner of the house, as well as designing a courtyard and entrance on the west side. These contained apartments for the King and Queen, and the council chamber. There was no attempt to create an air of grandeur, as at Hampton Court, and the essentially domestic nature of the dwelling was underlined by the fact that during their lifetimes it was known as Kensington House, not Kensington Palace.

As summer turned into autumn, William and Mary had to consider returning from Hampton to London. Kensington was not yet ready for them, but another winter of the fogs at Whitehall was out of the question for William. They were granted the loan of Holland House, and moved there on 16 October. The Queen found herself 'very ill-accommodated' there, and she was particularly unhappy at the thought that her father in Ireland might possibly declare war on them at any time, but they were persuaded to give a ball on William's birthday. The English nobility had been starved of royal occasions since the coronation, and came in great numbers, all keen for a sight of their sovereigns. Mary was particularly impatient for them to settle at Kensington, and with William's approval went there almost every day to urge Wren and his workmen on. As he was working at both properties simultaneously and was anxious to please his mistress, he took to cutting corners and experimenting with quick, untested methods of construction. It was perpetually on her conscience when an accident occurred in November; only hours after her inspection of progress, on the very spot where she had stood, a newly built roof at Kensington which had just been covered in lead collapsed, killing two workmen and injuring several more. A month later a similar fatal accident occurred at Hampton Court. Mary was horrified: 'All this as much as it was the fault of the workmen, humanly speaking, yet shewed me the hand of God plainly in it, and I was truly humbled.'[2] But Kensington was ready for the King and Queen to move in just before Christmas 1689, though the place was still covered with scaffolding.

In the gardens attached to their properties William supervised the waterworks and fountains while Mary chose the flowers, shrubs and trees. Their example naturally helped set new fashions for neat, well-proportioned redbrick houses, for geometrical gardens, for evergreen shrubs. William liked paintings by Raphael, Titian, Holbein and Van Dyck, all of whom were represented in the Royal Collection, and he had several such works moved to the walls of Kensington. Mary brought her collections of Chinese porcelain over from Holland, and her passion for blue and white china set a trend. She also owned a troop of Dutch mastiffs or pugs. One had once saved the life of William's sixteenth-century ancestor and namesake William the Silent, by barking to warn him of the approaching enemy. Ever since, they had been the mascots of the Orange family, and Mary's introduction of the breed to England started a craze for them.

One of her favourite activities was knotting, a primitive form of crochet which did not strain her weak eyes unduly. Before long she had set a trend in this as well, and fashionable society ladies took up knotting to pass the time on their coach journeys. Despite her eye trouble Mary was a voracious reader, and her library had a large collection of books in English, Dutch and French, with special emphasis on history. She enjoyed poetry, natural history and geography, occasionally read light novels, and in order to compensate for her lack of education tried studying philosophy and mathematics but soon abandoned them.

Much of her time was spent organizing and running the royal households. Royal menus had to be supervised, with up to ten meat dishes served at dinner and eight at supper, including roasted mutton, boiled beef, turkey, goose, quails and baked buck or hen pie, in addition to seasonal vegetables and fruits. On meat days, 18 pounds of butter were required in the King's kitchen, and on fish days 24. Beer, mead and Lambeth ale were always available, and eight bottles of ale, six of claret, two of Rhenish wine and three of Spanish were set aside for the King and Queen's dinner and supper, as well as safe drinking water 'from the best fountains'. Fortunately for the staff, both sovereigns were light eaters, and rarely ate from more than three or four dishes. Leftovers were a time-honoured perk for specific members of the household. Standing orders were maintained for generous supplies of wax lights, torches and candles, faggots and billets, as well as regular supplies of pit-coal and charcoal. The board wages of the household ranged from £1,360 per annum for the Lord Steward to £205 for the Chief Clerk of the King's Privy Kitchen, £108 for the Master Cook, £37 for the grooms and £10 for the chapel organ blower.

Much as Mary enjoyed absorbing herself in these domestic affairs, she was often unhappy. 'I must grin when my heart is ready to break,' she told William, 'and talk when my heart is so oppress'd I can scarce breathe.'[3] At twenty-seven, she had become old before her time. The upheaval of moving from Holland to England, the general change in circumstances and the increased responsibilities all told on her diminishing energy. Though born and raised in England, she had become a Dutchwoman through and through. Like her husband she was homesick, pining for the country and the way of life she had left behind. To friends in Holland, she wrote what a comfort it was 'to be regretted among people I think so much of, and in a country that I consider as much my own as if I were born there', and that 'the more I find myself harassed and overwhelmed with people here, the more I regret those happy days I passed in so much quiet in your country'.[4] Whenever she went out of London into a less busy part of the country, with cleaner and fresher air, she could not help comparing it unfavourably with the landscape and amenities at Dieren or Honselaardijk. She had left her beautiful Dutch buildings and friends behind, and tears came into her eyes as she realized that she would probably never see them again.

Yet at least she was grateful that she had to have nothing to do with politics, steadfastly believing that women should not 'meddle' in government. Soon after the coronation, the King tried to talk about matters of state with her, but she told him this was a matter of which she knew nothing. During the first parliamentary session of the reign, when the matter of administration in the event of the King's absence was put in her hands, she appeared to take no interest.

While William always remained a Dutchman at heart, he appreciated the niceties of respecting English sensibilities, even at the risk of upsetting his own countrymen. A Naval Agreement signed in April 1689 specified that, in the event of any joint Anglo-Dutch action at sea, the English admiral was always to take command. Five months later an Alliance Treaty bound England and Holland to make war jointly with France, and William declared an absolute embargo on any trade with France. Though this ran counter to the Dutch policy of free trade, it had to be accepted that England was now the senior partner.

Scotland also clamoured for attention, and to set his mind at rest William wanted to satisfy himself of Scottish loyalty by ordering elections to a Convention of Estates in the spring. Under the presidency of the Duke of Hamilton, this body formally offered him the Scottish crown in April. The Presbyterian majority north of the border were loyal, but Highland clans under Viscount Dundee still supported the former King James. Not content to abide by the Convention's policy, Dundee left the city with an army of horsemen to rouse the Highlands against the 'usurper'. In July his army of clansmen ambushed the government forces led by Hugh Mackay in the Pass of Killiecrankie, and Dundee himself was killed in battle.

Ill-health, homesickness and petty party differences were almost too much for William. The Whigs were intent on subordinating William's authority to Parliament, doubtless in recompense for their part in welcoming him as sovereign in his predecessor's place, and refused to make any alliance with the Tories, a number of whom were still in touch with the exiled James, ready to reap the benefits should the tables be turned in his favour.

William had been king for barely a year before he told some of his ministers that he was disgusted with English political life, that he could do nothing more for the country and that he had made a grave error in ever accepting the crown. As a result he proposed to leave affairs in the Queen's hands, and return to Holland for good. The animosity and inflexibility of the political parties in Parliament vexed him, and it was evident that they preferred the Queen with her charm; she was more popular than him, and might be better placed to govern. How much conviction his threat carried is open to question. Some ministers thought it was merely a wake-up call, a dramatic gesture intended to make the leaders of both parties think and come to terms. He did not tell Mary directly, and she only heard about it, much later than everyone else, from Burnet, so perhaps he was not being altogether serious.

Even so, several months of kingship had disillusioned him. Invited by a cross-party section to come and save England from an increasingly despotic sovereign, he considered his efforts had been rewarded with scant gratitude, particularly in view of the protracted discussions about who should wear the crown, and then the House of Commons' efforts to frustrate his wishes and limit his authority as sovereign. Till that had been done, he told Burnet angrily, he was not a king, and 'the title of King was only a pageant'.[5] Unlike King James, he had not been granted a revenue for life. His temper was not improved when Parliament put the Declaration of Rights on the statute book. To him it was at best an exasperating curb on his royal prerogative, at worst an insult.

His increasingly autocratic manner and ungracious behaviour did much to antagonize both parties in general. The Whigs regarded themselves as William's secret allies, and felt that they, more than the Tories, were responsible for placing him on the throne. With a majority of seats in Parliament, they hoped to translate this into exclusive power. To their disappointment they soon realized that their new King had summed them up as a party of republicans and exclusionists just as previous Stuart monarchs had, and that he looked more to the Tories for support. His first ministry was a predominantly Tory coalition, including Danby, now created Earl of Carmarthen, as President of the Council, Nottingham and Shrewsbury as Secretaries of State and Halifax as Lord Privy Seal and Speaker of the House of Lords.

Even within the family there was dissension. When Mary first arrived in England as queen in 1689 she had not seen Anne for ten years, and they were reunited in sisterly affection, but such harmony soon evaporated. Some at court blamed the cooling between them on the influence of the King, who no longer needed the support of the Prince and Princess of Denmark once he had become joint sovereign. William had taken a dislike to Anne, finding her heavy and dull, in sharp contrast to his wife, and he was revolted by her greed at table. To friends, he said that if he had had to marry the younger sister instead of the elder, he would have been the most miserable of men.

There was some competition between Anne's favourites, John and Sarah Churchill, created Earl and Countess of Marlborough after the coronation,* and the Villiers family, to whom they were distantly related. Rivalry at court was particularly acute between these factions. Hostility between the sovereigns and their heir was exacerbated by what some saw as William's jealousy of Anne's superior hereditary claim to the throne, whereas he was in effect only an elective monarch whose main claim rested on his marriage to the heiress. Gossips at court, not least the Marlboroughs, asserted that Mary was jealous of Anne's happy marriage and her ability to produce children, though as the latter proved so short-lived, and as the Queen's marriage could scarcely be regarded as unhappy, this need not be taken too seriously.

Much has been made of an occasion when William, Mary and Anne were dining together and he proceeded to eat an entire dish of green peas. Anne's defenders claimed that he did this solely out of spite, knowing her enormous appetite. Others suggested, more fairly, that at the time he was tired, absent-minded and simply did not realize what he was doing until they had all gone. Yet Anne apparently held a grudge against him because of this trifling incident for some time.

The personalities of both women accentuated the differences between them. Queen Mary loved conversation and was ill at ease with quiet people, while Princess Anne, taciturn and reserved by nature, was a woman of few words. Sarah, Duchess of Marlborough, urged her friend Anne to assert her rights as heir, and the first clash came in 1689 when Anne wanted to relinquish her

---

* They were raised to the rank of duke and duchess in 1702.

lodgings at the Cockpit for the larger, more luxurious apartments in Whitehall once occupied by the Duchess of Portsmouth, a mistress of Charles II. The King granted her request, but when she also asked for the adjoining apartments for her servants, he and the Queen pointed out gently that Lord Devonshire, head of the Royal Household, had been granted first refusal on them, and he would inform them whether he required them or not. Prompted by Sarah, Anne retorted angrily that she would sooner stay where she was, rather than have Lord Devonshire's 'leavings'.

More serious arguments arose over Anne's allowance. The Marlboroughs thought the Princess of Denmark's income should be settled by Parliament rather than left to her brother-in-law's generosity, or lack of it. They tried to raise the matter in the House of Commons without asking the King and Queen, and Mary angrily asked her sister what she thought she was doing. Anne muttered something about having heard that 'her friends had a mind to make her some settlement', to which Mary replied coldly, 'Pray what friends have you but the King and me?' This was promptly repeated to Sarah, who had never seen the Princess show 'so much resentment as she did at this usage' and hastened to fan the flames, 'for it was unjust in her sister not to allow her a decent provision without an entire dependence on the King'.[6]

Though William saw the advantages of keeping the heir to the throne financially dependent on him, he also appreciated the wisdom of avoiding family dissension. There was another more complicated financial matter in which William felt obliged to make some reparation to his sister-in-law and her husband. In July 1689 the Maritime Powers, as Britain and the Dutch Republic were collectively known, were mediating peace between Denmark and Sweden. As part of the peace settlement William asked George to surrender to the Duke of Holstein certain mortgages which he held on the Isle of Femern and the villages of Tremsbuttel and Steinhorst, as he (William) had agreed to procure settlement of the sums due or to pay them himself, and meanwhile to pay Prince George interest on them. In fact the King was unable to advance either principle or interest to George, because the Dutch States-

General would not vote enough to meet their part of the debt. George agreed as a compromise to lower the amount he was demanding, but William did not recommend payment of the debt to Parliament until 1699. George and Anne therefore found themselves without the Danish income which was theirs by right as it had been part of their marriage settlement, and the shortfall had to come from somewhere.

Irritated by the quarrel and this impediment to family harmony, the King asked the Earl of Shrewsbury to offer the Princess an annual allowance of £50,000 from the Privy Purse if she would agree to abandon her approach to Parliament. Shrewsbury was confident that His Majesty would keep his word; if he did not, he, Shrewsbury, would leave his service forthwith. The sceptical Countess of Marlborough knew it would not be of much use to the Princess if His Majesty did not stand by his promise. Having met with cold civility from King William, Anne was similarly uncooperative, preferring to see what her friends at court might be able to do for her instead. Always quick to resent any discourtesy to William, Mary angrily demanded an explanation from her sister on their next meeting. Anne chose to say little, which exasperated her sister as it had often done in the past. 'She could tell me no one thing in which the King had not been kind to her,' Queen Mary complained, 'and would not own herself in the wrong for not speacking to either of us, so that I found as I told her she had shewed as much want of kindness to me as respect to the King and I both. Upon this we parted ill friends.'[7]

Sarah found it easy to convince her friend that she had been deeply injured. It was unjust of the Queen, said Sarah, not to allow her a decent provision without an entire dependence on the King. Marlborough himself begged to be left out of the arguments. The duchess, he said, 'was like a mad woman', and the Secretary of State reluctantly called on Sarah herself, asking her to keep this family quarrel out of Parliament. Though Sarah seemed reluctant to cooperate, Anne still got her £50,000.

An anonymous Whig letter to William, published at the end of 1689, warned him that he had 'lost the hearts of a great part' of the people, and that 'your court and your councils are filled and guided by such men as most of all seek your ruin'.[8] Tory support was equivocal at the best of times. While most of them may have found King William an improvement on his predecessor, their fundamental loyalty to the principle of hereditary monarchy meant they still saw him as a usurper. A number, careful not to regard the revolution as irreversible, maintained secret contact with James and his court. William was well aware of this, and did not trust either party. When the conscientious Halifax left office, he lost his last illusions about party politics.

The ministers talked him out of giving up the government of England, but he was determined to leave for a while. At least he had an excuse with Parliament's vote of £2,000,000 for a campaign in Ireland against James. Relief at the prospect of taking part in military action, and the long-awaited move from Whitehall Palace into the more congenial Kensington just before Christmas, raised his spirits. New year's day was celebrated in splendour at Whitehall, where crowds of the nobility and gentry joined the Lord Mayor and the aldermen of the City, all turning up to wish the King and Queen a happy new year. They evidently appreciated this conviviality, and returned to town on 6 January to celebrate Twelfth Night at Whitehall, going after service in the chapel for dinner at Lord Shrewsbury's house, where Marlborough, Godolphin and other nobles were among the guests. The Queen retired to Kensington to play at cards and gamble with her sister Anne, while the formal dinner turned into a stag party. All the men became drunk to a greater or lesser degree, and the King's secretary, chasing his master with urgent papers for signatures, found him the following day ill-inclined to attend to serious business.

As King William intended to return to Holland or go to Ireland, if not both, it was fortuitous for him that James, with French support, chose to invade Ireland so early in the reign. For a sovereign to come from Holland, be declared King of England and then try to embroil his new kingdom in an expensive European war would have been an impossible task otherwise. Though Mary's position as queen was secure enough, that of William's as king was not. However, James had put himself beyond the pale by enlisting the support of King Louis XIV. The English saw his involvement as unwarranted interference in British affairs, and soon after the coronation the Commons turned its attention to French aggression in Ireland. In a parliamentary address they assured King William of their unequivocal support. They were helped by Emperor Leopold, who had been courted simultaneously by the States of Holland on one hand, and by King Louis XIV and James on the other, both the latter believing that Catholic monarchs should stick together. Angered by France's aggressive tactics in mainland Europe during the previous few years, Leopold declared war on France and recognized William as King, giving him the title of 'Majesty' – an honour he had never granted James.

In May 1689 King Louis XIV withdrew from the Palatinate, and the atrocities carried out by his troops as they left aroused English anger. England declared war on 7 May, and the Grand Alliance was signed. At Burnet's urging, Mary persuaded William to declare a day of public fasting. One summer evening a fisherman on the Thames caught in his net the Great Seal of England, which James had thrown into the river on his flight to France. Queen Mary regarded its recovery as a mark of God's favour, and when a live infant, a son, was born to Anne at Hampton Court she considered it a sign that the Stuart family was winning divine approval. She stayed with Anne throughout her labour (in view of her own sad obstetrical history this was an unselfish action indeed) and William arrived just before the child was born. The new arrival was named William in the King's honour, and the King agreed to be godfather. Five weeks later the baby suffered severe convulsive fits, and at one stage everybody came close to giving up hope. Thanks to their prayers as well as the doctors' efforts, he soon recovered.

In Holland William's absence had strengthened the anti-Orange party and the death in December 1688 of Gaspar Fagel, one of his most trusted supporters, had weakened his position and encouraged his rivals. Further acrimony between Whigs and Tories in January depressed him. He was afraid that Parliament would make an address condemning his plans to go to Ireland, and he was increasingly weary of the quarrels and intrigues that surrounded him. A heated exchange with his councillors convinced them that he was serious about returning to Holland, especially when he told them he had a convoy all ready to take him back to the country where he felt he belonged. After some persuasion he agreed not to return to Holland for good, as long as he was allowed to go to Ireland instead. A few days later, on 27 January, he came to Westminster, prorogued Parliament and announced that he was going to Ireland anyway. Members were taken by surprise, and though Queen Mary had known of his intentions for some time she hoped they might be able to dissuade him.

Low-spirited after a wet winter, she feared for his health as well as his safety in battle. She was also haunted by fears of a face-to-face encounter between her husband and her father, and was deeply upset by 'the sadness of such a business, to see my husband and my father personally engaged against each other'.[9] When she told William of her fears, he replied brusquely 'that he should go, if he saw the necessities of affairs required it'.[10] She accepted this, but when she broke down, overwhelmed by all her apprehensions and fears, he tried to soothe her by telling her that this was merely a continuation of the great work they had undertaken, which had to be finished.

As affairs in Scotland were in a chaotic state, it was suggested that the King should go there before departing for Holland, taking the Queen with him. But his indecisiveness on whether to go or not, and delays in preparations for the Irish campaign, meant there would be no time. Mary longed to be properly settled in London, and she dreaded the prospect of a journey to Scotland. To her relief, in January 1690 the idea was postponed indefinitely, and in the end neither of them ever saw Scotland. William continued with preparations for the European campaign, his health suffering under the strain of overwork and anxiety while he dismissed all pleas from friends, as well as his wife, to rest a little. He complained to Bentinck of the 'incorrigible slowness and negligence' he found everywhere he turned. 'One loses patience to see the slowness of the people here in everything that they do.'[11] Tired and overworked, at times he saw the Irish expedition as a duty for which he had little enthusiasm, saying he was in despair when he thought that he could be 'of no use to the common cause' while in Ireland. 'During that time you must count me as one dead and do the best you can.'[12]

Mary was equally concerned at the prospect of being left nominally in charge of the country during his forthcoming absence, even though she would be a figurehead without executive power. Anne's continued antagonism deepened her gloom further. Her fractious little sister, urged on by the poisonous Lady Marlborough, was continuing to defy her and the King. On the first Sunday in March she absented herself from communion at Whitehall and took the sacrament at her own chapel, contrary to normal practice. It was soon noticed by court gossips. She explained her actions by saying she had not been well, but attended a meal in public with the King and Queen later that day and, as usual, attacked her food with a hearty appetite which suggested a suspiciously swift recovery. At this time Anne was a magnet for the fanatical High Churchmen who still owed allegiance to ex-King James, were ready to criticize Mary at the least sign that she might have become 'tainted' by William's Calvinism and made fun of Mary's religious devotions, particularly her attendance at afternoon sermons. In despair, Mary said that they considered the revolutionary government was threatened by a republican party and a Jacobite party, and she had good reason to fear that her sister was forming a third.[13]

During the Lent season of 1690 she read all the way through the New Testament, prayed and meditated, but only exacerbated her melancholy until she became unaccountably morbid. Falling ill with a painfully sore throat on 7 April, she believed she was ready to meet her maker. Throughout the weekend she began to set her affairs in order, and by the following week she was all but convinced that her last hour was approaching. She had evidently willed herself into a state of passive acceptance.

Alarmed by her sister's plight, Anne came to ask forgiveness for all her transgressions, which the Queen readily granted, assuring her younger sister of her desire to help in any way she could. Even the slow-witted Anne knew better than to let slip a good opportunity of feathering her nest, and she promptly asked Mary to obtain her an additional £20,000 per annum, to be settled on the same terms as the original dowry from her father, from the Privy Purse, and without interference from Parliament. Though bitterly disappointed by Anne's greed, and suspecting the hand of the Duchess of Marlborough in this request, Mary agreed to see what she could do. However, the matter was overlooked as her condition worsened. Her trouble was partly a state of mind, for she recovered after being bled and taking physic. Those around her had the impression that she was disappointed to be well again, as eternal rest had been denied her and she would have to face her problems on earth again after all. She admitted ruefully a little later that, at her lowest ebb, she 'was really rather glad than sorry'[14] that she might be on the point of death.

The date of William's departure was repeatedly postponed, largely due to delaying tactics by Members of Parliament who resented his going. An Act of Parliament requiring powers to be transferred to the Queen had to be drafted, and enshrined in a Regency Bill, granting her the exercise of the administration during his absence. Anything that could be postponed had to be left until his return, though she had the power to call Parliament in case of emergency. Real power was delegated to a Council of nine, namely Carmarthen as Lord President, Lord Stewart as Lord Chamberlain, Lord Nottingham as Secretary of State, Lord Marlborough as First Commissioner of the Treasury, Lord Devonshire as Lord Steward, and the Earl of Peterborough (Monmouth), Earl of Dorset, Earl of Pembroke and Admiral Russell. On 2 June the King called these men together. Afterwards he admitted to Burnet that he felt very depressed, but he trusted in God and would go through with his business or else perish in it. He pitied the Queen, and his most fervent wish was that everyone should 'wait on her often' and give her their utmost support. Though he was fulfilling his duty, and was glad to escape from a deeply divided state and the chicanery of politicians to be setting out for a military campaign, it was particularly hard on her that her father and her husband should be 'opposed to each other in the field', and it would be very troublesome to the Queen if he were to be killed or taken prisoner.[15]

On 4 June he left London and his spirits rose almost at once. On Sunday 8 June he attended divine service at Chester Cathedral, and after dinner went to inspect the ships at Hoylake. The wind remained contrary for two days, but on 11 June he embarked, landing on the Irish coast near Carrickfergus three days later.

* * *

King James had been prepared to allow Irish Catholics religious freedom without antagonizing his Protestant subjects, as in England, but the Earl of Tyrconnel's aggressive administration soon made enemies of the Protestants. Tyrconnel was still in control when William invaded England, and in February 1689 the latter formally called on the Irish rebels to lay down their arms, offering religious liberty and security of property to those who did, and threatening to confiscate the estates of those who did not. It was to no avail, and by mid-March all of Ireland except Londonderry and Enniskillen was under Catholic control. That same month James arrived back in Ireland and held a Parliament in Dublin, which continued to alienate the Protestants by measures such as issuing an Act of Attainder bearing more than two thousand names, which would have dispossessed nearly all the Protestant landowners. James also urged the people of Derry to surrender, and laid siege to the town when they refused.

As Protestants controlled most of Ulster, King William had a firm base from which to act. Since the events of 1688, James was no longer the decisive leader of former days; his soldiers were often drunk and poorly disciplined, most of his officers lacked experience and the army was poorly equipped. King William's army also had its faults, and several mutinies in 1689 proved that loyalty could not be taken for granted. He kept his Dutch troops in England, sent the best English units to Flanders and then began raising new regiments for service in Ireland. The army sent across the Irish Sea that year included a high proportion of inexperienced officers and men, plus more seasoned Huguenots and Dutch, albeit with their share of defective equipment and provisions.

William did not intend to land in Ireland with inferior troops, and he paid considerable attention to detail. Those who worked with him noticed that while he often seemed cold and unresponsive towards his courtiers, he was a completely different man, cordial and warm-natured, when working with soldiers. His veteran commander the Duke of Schomberg was cautious; aware of the shortcomings of his forces, when he came face to face with James's army near Dundalk he avoided fighting, as he was unwilling to trust many of his troops in a major battle. Defeat at this stage would seriously jeopardize the Protestant cause. He therefore retreated to Lisburn where his army spent a wet and miserable winter, many of the men lacking proper warmth, food and medical supplies. Over seven thousand men, more than half the army, died of disease and exposure during the winter months. As the expedition and military administration clearly needed overhauling, William took charge himself. A full-scale military operation was needed if the Irish problem were to be speedily solved, and determined to leave nothing to chance William aimed to try to crush the Jacobites in a single campaign. His army, including Huguenots, Danes, Brandenburgers and Finns as well as some Irish Protestant regiments, would number around 44,000, with a large siege train and ample supplies including £200,000 in cash.

Mary had been left nominally in charge, but a Cabinet Council, made up of five senior Tories and four Whigs, was set up to advise her. Their enemies thought that this was because the King did not trust her. There was enough of the male chauvinist in him to believe that women should not meddle in politics, but he also wanted to protect her from unfair criticism in his absence. While he was away, she surprised everyone, not least herself, with her cheerful demeanour, although she was secretly terrified that her husband might never return, leaving her to face the twin dangers of a French invasion and a Jacobite rebellion. It was an experience she did not relish; she found herself 'now at Whitehall in a new world, deprived of all that was dear to me in the person of my husband, left among those that were perfect strangers to me: my sister of a humour so reserved that I could have little comfort from her', the Great Council of a strange composition, the Cabinet Council not much better'.[16] With restraint she waited until she had heard of William's sailing for Ireland before she began attending meetings of the Council. She found these occasions an ordeal, and at first attended only as an observer without taking part in any consultations. Almost every day they wrote to each other. She relied heavily on his support, particularly as the family gave her no comfort.

Prince George of Denmark wanted to follow in the footsteps of the Duke of York by serving as a naval volunteer, and told King William of his plans. The King said nothing but embraced the Prince, who took his silence as consent and made plans to sail in *St Andrew*. But the King had left Queen Mary orders that the Prince was not to be allowed to serve in any capacity. After asking Lady Marlborough, in vain, to intervene with Anne, Queen Mary was forced to send Lord Nottingham to the Prince with orders forbidding him to sail and advising him to recall his baggage. It was said that the sisters quarrelled fiercely over this, and that the Queen, alarmed by the growing influence of both Jacobites and republicans, took a dim view of her sister's political activities. Mary believed that the entire idea for George to go to sea had been concocted with the express purpose of embarrassing the government.

Anne was distant and unfriendly towards her sister, and the Catholic Dowager Queen Catherine also made her hostility evident, ordering Lord Feversham to forbid prayers to be said in the Protestant Chapel at Somerset House for the King's success. Queen Mary made clear her anger with Feversham, but she knew that the Queen Dowager was responsible, and as a result all outward show of friendship between the women ceased.

A visit to the theatre, her first since returning to England, brought her no comfort. She went to see John Dryden's *Spanish Friar*, a play that had been banned from public performance as it ridiculed the Catholic church. Unfortunately she had not previously read it, nor been advised of its contentious passages. In Act One, one character proclaims that the Queen 'usurps the throne: keeps the old King in prison: and at the same time is praying for a blessing'. At these words Mary put up her fan and looked the other way, aware that the audience were watching her. In Act Four, another character spoke of 'A crown usurped, a distaff on the throne', soon followed by 'What title has this Queen but lawless force? And force must pull her down.'[17] The Queen concealed her face behind her cloak and hood as best she could, but those patrons standing in the pit had turned their backs to the stage and were only looking up at her. The play was taken off the next day, but it was the talk of London society for some time afterwards.

There was a crisis on 22 June when Mary was informed that a French fleet had been seen off the coast of Devon and Cornwall. The English fleet, in poor shape, was commanded by Lord Torrington, known as much for his caution as a naval commander as for his idleness and love of the bottle. He successfully evaded the French fleet for a while, fearing defeat as the enemy forces were obviously superior in strength. Under the Queen's orders he reluctantly gave battle off Beachy Head on 30 June but was defeated. Two of the Dutch admirals under his command were killed, while ten Dutch ships and seven English ships were lost.

Though this was an unexpected setback, Mary took consolation from William's letter received that day, in which he reassured her that the life of an army commander agreed with him and that the Irish air was making him feel fitter than he had for a long time. She needed all the comfort she could find, for the naval defeat and the worry of having to preside at Council meetings were not the only crosses she had to bear in his absence. She was fearful that the French might take this opportunity to strike and invade England, and it was necessary to keep a careful watch on all major Catholic figures. These included the Queen Dowager, King Charles's widow Catherine, now living at Somerset House. She had recently omitted the prayer for King William's success in Ireland, though it seemed that it was the fault of the clergyman involved, on orders from Lord Feversham, a noted friend of ex-King James who was still in charge of the Queen Dowager's affairs. Mary expressed her anger to the Council, feeling that Feversham had been foolish rather than seditious, and asked Lord Nottingham to admonish him in person.

Feversham came to see her and apologized, but she felt there was something rather insincere in his attitude.

* * *

Meanwhile, in Ireland James had sent his army northwards, and when it reached Dundalk he heard of William's arrival. He fell back to defend the southern bank of the River Boyne, west of Drogheda. On 30 June William's army reached the northern bank. James's army of around 25,000 men, now including a French contingent, had one real advantage: an excellent defensive position. The river could be forded when the tide was right, but it would not be easy in the face of enemy fire. James drew up his army at Donore, on high ground commanding the most obvious crossing place at Oldbridge. On 30 June the armies faced each other across the river; it was said that William would not engage because he was superstitious about fighting on Mondays. There was some sporadic artillery fire on both sides and a cannonball grazed William's right shoulder. He slumped forward on to his horse's neck, and a cheer went up on the Jacobite side. News was sent to France that the usurper was dead and there was rejoicing at Paris, where people feasted, lit bonfires, let off fireworks and became riotously drunk. Some of them staged a mock funeral, while others made a wax dummy, christened it the Prince of Orange and subjected it to repeated mock executions.

In fact the ball had merely torn his jacket and shirt, and grazed his shoulder. The party retired to a sheltered spot so a dressing could be applied to the wounded area. When shocked officers gathered around him to enquire how he was, he told them brusquely to move on. To prove he had come to no harm, he rode the whole length of his army, waving his sword in his right hand.

James knew his chances of victory were slender. He would gladly have avoided battle, and had planned his retreat and sent off some of his artillery even before the fighting started. Full of confidence, knowing his numbers and firepower were superior to that of the enemy, William ignored Schomberg's pleas for caution and was intent on fighting. He decided to force a crossing at Oldbridge; to

141

create a diversion, he sent Count Meinhard Schomberg, his commander's son, upstream with about a third of the army. On the hot sunny morning of 1 July all went better than William could have hoped. When the younger Schomberg crossed the river James, obsessed with retreat, sent two-thirds of his army to prevent him blocking the way back to Dublin. The two forces, separated by deep ditches, were unable to fight. Only one-third of James's army, under Tyrconnel, was left to bear the brunt of William's attack. His Dutch Blue Guards were the first to cross, wading waist-deep under fierce fire. Once they were over, the Irish infantry turned and fled, but James's cavalry repeatedly charged the Dutch guards. They held their ground and were soon joined by the Danes who had crossed further downstream, and between them they beat off the cavalry attacks. A small force of Jacobites entered the river, and the Duke of Schomberg was killed. With complete disregard for his own safety, William led the cavalry across still further down; his arrival settled the issue and the Irish cavalry broke and fled. William probably had it in his power to order the capture of his father-in-law, but he had no intention of doing so. James was back in Dublin that evening, and hurried off to France the next day.

William lost about four hundred men, while the Jacobite losses were variously estimated at between a thousand and sixteen hundred, including some prisoners and wounded who had been butchered by the English. The King had fought fiercely, but suffered no further injury apart from a graze on his leg where part of his boot had been shot away.

Though it was little more than a skirmish, the Boyne was hailed as a great victory and it helped to offset two defeats. In the Netherlands the French routed the allies at Fleurus, where it was estimated that the Dutch lost up to thirteen thousand soldiers in a seven-hour conflict, while their naval victory over the English at Beachy Head raised fears that, now they had command of the English and Irish Channels, the French might invade England and also prevent William from returning. The Queen's advisers had suggested that she should allow Parliament to meet before he came back, and that she should send him a message asking him to sail for

England before the French could block his way. Nevertheless once the panic had died down, it was recognized that James had been driven out of Ireland for good; his last chance had gone and any plans King Louis XIV might have had for keeping a war alive in the country indefinitely collapsed. After two generations of success in war, the progress and prestige of France had been halted. William marched unopposed into Dublin, where the Protestants greeted him ecstatically. The news took about a week to reach Queen Mary; on 6 July a letter was brought to her confirming that the King was safe and sound, and another followed the next day containing news of his victory. At the same time she was reassured of her father's safety.

Though there was now no danger of a Jacobite conquest of Ireland, James's army, beaten but not destroyed, fell back on the Gaelic stronghold of Connaught. While it was one thing to win a battle in the field, William found it was quite another to take towns as strongly fortified as Limerick or Athlone. Moreover, with their backs to the wall, the Irish infantry fought with a determination they had not shown at the Boyne. In an effort to end the war quickly, on 7 July William issued a declaration at Finglas promising pardon to all common soldiers, labourers and artisans who surrendered by 1 August, but there would be no automatic pardon for the ringleaders without good reason. The declaration's uncompromising tone made the Jacobites more intransigent. William's efforts to take Limerick were frustrated; with about 14,000 Irish troops in the town, his force of 25,000 was insufficient for a full-scale siege. His siege train from Dublin was blown up in transit; more guns were brought and a breach was opened in the walls, but an attempt to storm it was repulsed. The inhabitants, including women and children, drove the besiegers back with great stones and broken bottles, and more than 2,300 of William's force were killed or wounded. After heavy rain on 28 August William feared his guns would sink in the mud and so raised the siege. He had hoped to end the conflict by taking Limerick that summer, and his failure to do so ensured the war would last for another year.

Reaching Waterford on 1 September he was delayed by storms. Despite a rough passage he landed safely at Bristol on 6 September, and later that week he and Mary were reunited at Hampton Court. Her delight at finding him looking so well and exhilarated after his success did much to compensate her for the strain of the previous few months, and she was touched by his approval of the way that she had managed her duties, such as they were, during his absence. She was happy to retire from a task she disliked, though she was flattered that from this time onwards he confided in her more readily on government affairs.

William III's reputation was secure among the Protestants of Northern Ireland. Yet to him the campaign had been a mere distraction, to be dealt with at once so that he could get back to what he saw as the more serious business of fighting the French on the continent.

During his absence in Ireland the allied campaign against France in Flanders had fared badly, and it was clear that his presence there would be required. A congress of allied powers to discuss the next year's campaign was deemed necessary, and the King suggested it should be held at The Hague. He wanted to attend partly for reasons of state and partly out of homesickness, the lure of his beloved Holland being too strong. However, there was business in England to occupy him for a few weeks during the end of the year. On 2 October he opened a new session of Parliament, and in his speech from the throne he asked for generous supplies, reminding them of the French threat to British security and the wider peace of Europe. In view of his success in Ireland there was general approval, and the Commons voted him £2,300,000 for the army and £1,800,000 for the navy.

By late 1690 King William's popularity was at its height. His fortieth birthday on 4 November was celebrated with salutes fired from the Tower of London and the shops closed all day. That evening the King and Queen dined in public, attending a celebration concert and play afterwards. Yet already his mind was on returning to Holland for the congress in February 1691. By the end of the year preparations were complete and he could hardly wait to embark on the journey.

SEVEN

'The consequences of such a breach'

Queen Mary dreaded the prospect of another few months of loneliness and responsibility without King William. Since his return from Ireland, she had cheerfully given up all involvement in government to pay visits to friends and live like a private person as far as possible. But according to gossip, there was a different reason for her unease this time. It was alleged that a rift had developed in the marriage, and William was said to be spending more time with Elizabeth Villiers, who was expecting his child. Mary had apparently taken this very badly, as well she might, and was said to have confided in a friend that girls who married at fifteen (as she had herself) had no idea what they were about, and that they might be tired of their partners before they were thirty.

For once, it seemed the Queen might not be totally blameless herself. The Earl of Shrewsbury was said to have caught her eye. It was beyond doubt that for a while at least she had definitely caught his, and that he seemed to walk around Whitehall as if in a dream. Queen Mary's Vice-Chamberlain, John Howe, maliciously described to a friend how Shrewsbury was evidently 'agitated' when in her presence. He maintained that Her Majesty was not as naive as everyone supposed, and he had felt how she trembled at the sight of Shrewsbury when he led her into chapel. Le Sieur Blancard, a French diplomat greatly respected by the King and Queen, faithfully reported this gossip to Dijkvelt in Holland. While convinced that the Queen was certainly 'virtue itself' and as faithful to the King as ever, he was concerned at her regular summons for Shrewsbury to keep her company or play cards, thus inadvertently encouraging gossip. Even worse, Shrewsbury had been told by a fortune-teller that his love would be lucky after the King's death.

With rumours of another possible Jacobite plot, it was an unfortunate time for a crisis in the marriage – if indeed crisis there was. Elizabeth Villiers was back in London, and the King seems to have been still attracted to her (though there was almost certainly no truth in the pregnancy rumour), particularly as Mary was still upset at having been without him during the Irish crisis and remained depressed at the thought of another long separation from him. Far from being sympathetic, William probably found her difficult to live with and sought feminine company, maybe more than platonic, elsewhere. That Blancard tried to suppress the gossip, while keeping Dijkvelt fully informed, suggests he was concerned that Jacobite agents, or others hostile to William and Mary, were pursuing their own agenda for endangering the entire revolution settlement, based as it was on Mary's willing submission to William's authority.

Mary still hoped she would be able to pay a return visit to Holland too, and had to resign herself to the possibility that it might happen sometime in the future, but not yet. To Mademoiselle d'Obdam, a former member of her Dutch household, she confided her hopes 'that the time will come when things will be in such a state that I can go with him. What a satisfaction for me, what a joy, to see once more a country so dear to me.'[1] When the King left on 6 January 1691, she was alarmed at the state of the seas and the dangerous voyage he faced. It was a relief when he was back in Kensington three days later, after adverse winds had prevented him from sailing. A week later he left London again, embarking on the yacht *Mary* at Gravesend and sailing the next day.

The ships ran into a violent storm almost at once. They were blown off course towards Dunkirk, then in the hands of French privateers, and Sijmen Janszoon Hartevelt, the same captain who had brought William to England in 1688, had to work hard to maintain the right course. When they arrived at the Dutch coast two weeks later, dense fog and thick ice made landing impossible at first. After two days of careful manoeuvring, they sent one of the crew to jump overboard in the darkness and scramble across the ice to the beach for help. A few hours later he reappeared with carriages and the rest of the half-frozen company could land at last.

The King was glad to be back in his own country, and to see his old friends again. To his amusement, a gamekeeper who had worked for him when he was Stadholder did not recognize him with his three-day growth of beard. On 5 February he made a grand ceremonial entrance into The Hague. Though he did not want the expense or fuss of a public entry, he was encouraged by the numbers of people already gathering despite the freezing cold, eager to welcome him home after an absence from Holland of more than two years, and by the sight of huge triumphal arches along the route, showing all the Princes of Orange since William the Silent, and illustrating the history of the House of Orange from 1572 to the Battle of the Boyne. A reception by the magistrates was followed by a firework display from a platform floating in the Vijver, but the rockets were swallowed up by fog before they could explode. On the next day he was formally received by the States-General, and in an emotional speech assured the Dutch that he would sacrifice all that he had in the world for the good of the State of Holland, without thought for his own personal safety or his life. He had accepted the English crown not out of personal ambition or greed, but to support and maintain the Protestant religion and peace in England, and in order to help assist Holland and her allies against France.

Apart from William and fourteen members of the House of Lords, those attending the Congress at The Hague included the Electors of Brandenburg and Bavaria; the Prince Regent of Württemberg; the Landgrave of Hesse-Cassel; the Prince of Brunswick; the Marquis de Castanaga, Governor of the Spanish Netherlands; thirty ambassadors; and various princesses and ladies. At the Congress's opening meeting William made a short speech calling for unity and strenuous action. Next came a series of formal and informal conferences on general strategy for the future, after which the Allies agreed to put an army of 220,000 men in the field against France, though it was not backed by any agreement on cooperating on diplomatic levels. Already jealousies and divisions were evident in the ranks.

The Congress broke up on 4 March and William retired to Het Loo, taking the Elector of Bavaria and a few of the other princes with him for a hunting holiday. It was overshadowed when Keppel, one of his favourite young Dutch Gentlemen of the Bedchamber, was thrown from his horse and broke his leg. Since coming to England with William in 1688, Keppel's rise in royal favour had been rapid, progressing from page to copying William's letters and now Gentleman of the Bedchamber and indispensable companion of the King's leisure hours. His secretaries became jealous, but William was oblivious to them, and paid no attention to the malicious gossip that his close friendship with the young man excited. These days he found Keppel better company than Portland, who was always so serious and increasingly preoccupied by affairs of state. After the riding accident he missed the young man's company, and paid several calls to the sickroom to see how he was recovering.

In England, everyone was expecting news of the King's return when in mid-March Louis XIV, with an army of 100,000 men commanded by Marshal Boufflers, appeared at the gates of Mons, a vital fortress in the south of the Spanish Netherlands. Not for the first time, he caught the Allies unawares. William went straight to the army rendezvous at Halle, south of Brussels, to find 50,000 soldiers assembled, but no sign of the promised Spanish reinforcements, and he had to look on helplessly while Mons capitulated. Louis XIV returned in glory to Versailles while William, furious with his Spanish allies, returned to England, escorted across the North Sea by a squadron of Dutch men-of-war.

Though he was still smarting after his recent humiliation, Queen Mary was delighted to see how well he looked. She was in good spirits as he had not been away so long this time, and her responsibilities had therefore been less onerous. She had been cheered at first by the news from The Hague, and proud of the figure her husband made there. On her sister Anne's birthday on 6 February, she had played cards publicly with Anne and Prince George at their apartments in the Cockpit, and afterwards gave a dance for them in her own drawing-room at Whitehall. However, it disturbed her that her husband's new-found popularity soon waned. She had expected him to return to England once the Congress had finished, and was disappointed to be told he had gone back to his military campaigning.

Mary, Princess Royal, and Prince William of Orange, at about the time of their betrothal in 1641, Sir Anthony Van Dyck. *(Rijksmuseum, Amsterdam)*

William, Prince of Orange, *c.* 1664, Adriaen Hanneman. *(The Royal Collection © 2003, Her Majesty Queen Elizabeth II)*

Charles II dances with his sister Mary, Princess of Orange, at a ball at The Hague, a few weeks before his restoration and return to England as King, 1660. From a painting by G. Janssens, drawn by G.F. Harding, engraved by W. Greatbach. *(Mary Evans Picture Library)*

James, Duke of York, with Anne Hyde and their daughters Mary (holding a wreath of flowers) and Anne. Begun by Peter Lely in 1669, it was completed by Benedetto Gennari about ten years later. *(The Royal Collection © 2003, Her Majesty Queen Elizabeth II)*

James Scott, Duke of Monmouth, son of King Charles II by his mistress Lucy Walter. From a painting by John Riley, drawn by William Hilton, engraved by W.T. Fry. *(Mary Evans Picture Library)*

'Arlequin Deodat, et Pamirge Hypochondriaques', Romeyne de Hooghe. A caricature illustrating the popular belief that the Prince of Wales, born 1688, was a warming-pan baby or impostor. The baby, in the right-hand corner, holds a toy windmill; his real father was said to be a miller's son. The King, in night attire, can be seen looking through the curtains, directly behind the Queen. *(British Museum)*

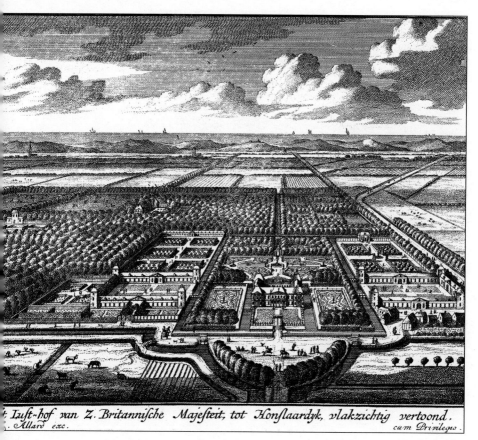

Honselaardijk, near The Hague, the palace which was always William's principal home in Holland. *(Rijksmuseum, Amsterdam)*

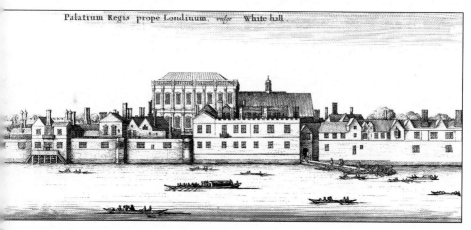

Whitehall Palace, the Stuarts' main London residence, from the River Thames. Engraving by John Webb after Inigo Jones, *c.* 1637–9. *(British Museum)*

Queen Mary Beatrice, consort of King James II, formerly Mary of Modena, *c.* 1685, the year of her husband's accession, William Wissing. *(National Portrait Gallery, London)*

Statue of William III, Brixham. The foundation stone was laid on the bicentenary of his landing at the harbour, 5 November 1888. The pedestal is 10ft high, the effigy 8ft, and shows him with his right foot on rock, his right hand holding a plumed hat and his left hand on his heart. It was unveiled exactly a year later. *(Private collection)*

Queen Mary, William Wissing. (The Royal Collection © 2003, Her Majesty Queen Elizabeth II)

William III, Peter Lely. (National Portrait Gallery, London)

William III at the Battle of the Boyne, engraved by J. Rogers after a painting by Benjami West. *(Mary Evans Picture Library)*

James II at the Battle of the Boyne, engraved by Barbant, fro Guizot's *Histoire d'Angleterre*. *(Mary Evans Picture Library)*

Hampton Court, *c.* 1700. *(Private collection)*

Kensington Palace, the south front. Originally Nottingham House, it was purchased by William III soon after his accession. The statue of him in front, by Baucke, was presented to King Edward VII by Kaiser Wilhelm II in 1907. *(Mary Evans Picture Library/Paul Barkshire)*

Princess Anne, William and Mary's heir, and his successor as Queen regnant, William Wissing and Jan Van der Vaart. *(Scottish National Portrait Gallery)*

Prince George of Denmark, engraving by R. Parr. *(Mary Evans Picture Library)*

HIS ROYAL HIGHNESS PRINCE GEORGE OF DENMARK

The BILL of RIGHTS *ratified at the* Revolution *by King* William, *and Queen* Mary *previous to their Coronation*

William and Mary at the ceremony at which the Bill of Rights was ratified at the revolution, prior to their coronation, engraving attributed to J. Cary, after Samuel Wale. *(National Portrait Gallery, London)*

The coronation of King William III and Queen Mary II, Westminster Abbey, April 1689. *(Bridgeman Art Library)*

William III on horseback, engraving by F.W. Van Hove. *(Mary Evans Picture Library)*

The Queene Leying in State who departed this life the 28 day of December 1694 to the great greefe of all good Subiects.

With mourning pen, and melting eyes, / Our loss is her eternal gain, / with bleeding heart, and sobbing Cries. / and yet we cannt but Complain, / here lament the loss of one, / as having lost the sweetest Queen. / who was the brightness of the throne. / as ever in the Realm was seen / Printed and sould by Joh: overton att the White horse without newgate

Queen Mary lying in state. *(The Royal Collection © 2003, Her Majesty Queen Elizabeth II)*

William Bentinck, 1st Earl of Portland, *c.* 1698–9, by an artist in the studio of Hyacinthe Rigaud. *(National Portrait Gallery, London)*

Arnold Joost van Keppel, 1st Earl of Albemarle, 1700, Sir Godfrey Kneller. *(National Portrait Gallery, London)*

'Maison Royalle d'Angleterre.' King William III, seated, with Prince George of Denmark on right, Princess Anne and Prince William, Duke of Gloucester, on his left, with a medallion file of Queen Mary above, from a French engraving sold by Mariette, Paris. *(Mary Evans ·ure Library)*

King William III on his deathbed at Kensington Palace, engraving by Pieter van den Berge. figures around his bed include the Earls of Portland and Bentinck; Dr Bidloo; Tenis Archbishop of Canterbury; and Burnet, Bishop of Salisbury; and have been assumed to inc his successor Queen Anne, though she was at St James's Palace at the time. *(Bridgeman Library)*

When news of the fall of Mons came through the English Jacobites were jubilant. One of the most persistently outspoken, Sir John Fenwick, dared to insult the Queen publicly; while she was driving in the Park one afternoon, he ostentatiously stepped up to her carriage but, instead of uncovering and bowing like any other gentleman, he stared directly at her and swept off his hat in her face. She ordered the park-keepers not to admit him again.

Just before Easter she learned of the King's imminent return, but her delight was overshadowed by an unfortunate accident. On the evening of 9 April a careless maid at Whitehall let a burning candle get out of control and the resulting fire blazed for about eight hours, destroying most of the Stone Gallery down to the waterside and the Duchess of Portsmouth's apartments. In a vain attempt to stop the flames from spreading, several buildings were blown up in its path, including Portland's lodgings; he lost several thousand pounds' worth of jewels. A terrified Mary was convinced it was another Jacobite threat on her life.

When he returned, William was less perturbed by news of the fire. He had never liked living at Whitehall, and had more pressing concerns at the time. Not intending to stay long in England, he had only returned in order to form a stable new government before going back to the continent for the summer campaign. Before leaving again, he had to deal with yet another conspiracy that came to light in his absence. The chief plotter was Lord Preston, whom the King personally examined in the presence of Lord Carmarthen. Preston confessed, and named among his Jacobite associates several whose loyalty was already suspect, such as Henry, Earl of Clarendon, James's Admiral Dartmouth, Penn the Quaker and five bishops who had always refused to recognize William. He implicated also the prominent Whig Leaders Dorset and Devonshire, the Duke of Ormonde and about a hundred MPs, mostly Whigs. The Tory Carmarthen was delighted, but a disgusted William stopped the hearing. Knowing he could never count on the wholehearted loyalty of his English subjects, he forgave Preston and released most of the other conspirators.

On the morning of 15 May he left Kensington with the Queen, who accompanied him to Ingatestone, and next day he sailed from

Harwich with a fair wind for Holland. After he had gone, Queen Mary wrote sadly to Electress Sophie that she had seen little of her husband in London, and that even during her last few hours with him, in the coach going to Ingatestone, their necessary discussion of 'business' left little time for more homely conversation.

It was the first time for over a century that a King of England had left his country to take command of his army in war. Both armies hovered within striking distance of each other throughout the summer, but Luxembourg refrained from attacking. In July the respected commander Louvois died suddenly in Paris, to be succeeded by his 23-year-old son the Marquis de Barbesieux. At the end of August William decided to leave the battlefield and everybody in England, especially Mary, expected his imminent return. Instead he decided to spend two months hunting at Loo with Portland and Romney, thus establishing a pattern he would follow for the next few years. From London Nottingham tried tactfully to remind the King of his duty, but William was enjoying himself too much to tear himself away.

While at Loo he was told of the surrender of Limerick, the last Jacobite stronghold in Ireland. Late the previous year Marlborough had led a short, victorious expedition against Cork and Kinsale. Sustained by hopes of French reinforcements (which eventually sailed too late), the people of Limerick had been defending the town against superior English forces under Godard van Reede van Ginckel for several months, and negotiations began only after Tyrconnel had died of a stroke and Sarsfield had taken over the command. A treaty was signed on 13 October 1691, allowing free passage for all Irish troops who wished to leave Ireland for France, paid for by the English government, while Roman Catholics were promised freedom to exercise their religion as they had under Charles II. To the Jacobites the surrender of Limerick, following Louis XIV's loss of interest in Ireland, was the greatest mistake the French could have made, as to them the Irish war was the 'best medium in the world for destroying the confederacy abroad'; the confederal armies could not prolong the war in Europe without the arms and money of England, which were distracted by war in

Ireland. King William would probably have agreed. Ginckel was rewarded with the titles Duke of Limerick and Baron of Aughrim.

The King returned to England, landing at Margate on 19 October. His coaches had been waiting in Harwich for two weeks, and he had to hire one, in which he drove off with Portland and Marlborough. Near Gravesend the coach overturned and both lords were thrown on top of the King, who wrenched his shoulder. Marlborough suffered minor concussion and thought his neck was broken, but the King reassured him that as he could still speak it was unlikely. Mary was waiting for her husband at Whitehall, and when he arrived William jumped out of the coach and ran upstairs to her room, calling out for her; courtiers were surprised to see their normally undemonstrative master kiss her twice.

In his absence Mary had had an unusually trying time. Since he went, she had been harassed by continual rumours of plots against them both, and she suspected her sister Anne was involved (or at least had prior knowledge of them, yet did not bother to tell her). In her troubled state of mind she made a start on looking over her diaries and written 'meditations', burning some of the more personal ones lest they should fall into the wrong hands after her death.

Constant anxiety about the state of the country in the King's absence added to her burdens. The treasury was heavily depleted, the High Church party – which had been antagonized by William's Calvinistic ways – was showing signs of growing disloyalty, the English fleet under Russell achieved nothing against the French and was almost destroyed by heavy storms, and the Tower of London, filled with prisoners, was almost blown up by accident when a floor collapsed under the weight of hundreds of barrels of gunpowder. Despite the differences with Anne, she was devoted to her only surviving nephew William Henry, Duke of Gloucester. She was so alarmed when the little boy, who was never strong, suddenly fell seriously ill, that she made a gift of a thousand guineas to the doctor who saved him.

In a meditation written that summer, she confessed her world-weariness and readiness to die. 'I do not know what will happen to me, but, life being so uncertain, I prepare myself for death. I bless

151

God that the only thing which makes death uneasy to me is that some might suffer for it.' She put this among the journals she kept always with her, adding a note for the King begging him to burn it as well as her other papers, 'and to preserve a tenderness for my memory, as for someone who has always been entirely his'.[2]

At the opening of Parliament on 22 October William asked for supplies for an army of 65,000 men to be voted. The Commons was in an amenable mood after Ginckel's victory at Limerick, but in his speech from the throne the King omitted the customary thanks for past generosity and several members took this affront badly. In turn they attacked the army estimates, arguing that England had no need for such an enormous army.

Despite this setback, his arrival home raised Mary's spirits, and she was hostess on his forty-first birthday and their fourteenth wedding anniversary in November. That night saw one of the brightest celebrations at Whitehall for years. William was particularly attentive, as if doing his best to make up for having been absent so much of the year.

Sadly another accident was about to disturb their equanimity. Whitehall was still partly in ashes when part of Kensington House was destroyed by fire early in November. Woken at 3 a.m. when the Earl of Essex burst into the King's bedroom to tell him that the Stone Gallery to the south of the courtyard was on fire, the King and Queen immediately flung on their nightrobes and came out to view the damage. The fire had begun in an empty room next to the porter's lodge, and lack of water hindered the firefighters. Portland sent for help to Whitehall, where the nearest pumps and ladders were kept. By the time they arrived all the newly built south wing, with its offices and apartments for court officials, was severely damaged. Fortunately everything deemed irreplaceable had been preserved intact, as the King's paintings and the Queen's porcelain had all been rescued and taken out into the garden for safety. William walked around to see what each member of the household had rescued and it amused him to find that most of them had brought out Dutch cheese, bottles and bread, as if they were about to begin a long siege. Despite the delay, the flames were eventually contained and extinguished two hours after help arrived. By the afternoon all the King's apartments, from which the hangings and furniture had been taken to safety, were back to normal. The doors of his office had been broken open, and a bundle of his papers had disappeared after being thrown out of the window in the panic, but it turned up that same day in a nearby house.

Mary took it philosophically, needing no reassurance that this had been another accident and not part of a plot on their lives. Neither her apartments nor those of the King had been touched, and Wren was soon at work on plans for a new gallery.

A few days later the King and Queen went to Hampton Court to inspect the new building work. The main block was well advanced, while the garden was also progressing well. Daniel Marot, a Huguenot who had fled from Paris to Holland and helped with the building of Het Loo, had accompanied them to England and helped design the new fountain garden at Hampton Court. William enjoyed helping to work out a system of pipes and canals to keep the fountains supplied with water.

Towards the end of the year William could turn his attention to more relaxing pursuits. He was keen to purchase the entire art collection of Queen Christina of Sweden, and planned to send an emissary to Rome for the purpose, but another buyer made a successful offer first. Nevertheless he had more success in other directions. The new approach road to Kensington House, paved and lighted, was now almost complete. He and Mary celebrated the new year of 1692 there in style, the climax of their festivities being the Twelfth Night ball with dancing that went on till after 1 a.m. The King allowed himself a little indulgence at the gaming tables with the Groom Porter, losing 200 guineas and then winning back £100.

Chelsea Hospital had just been completed, and William, sympathetic to the needs of old soldiers, personally ensured that they were kept well supplied with coal and the cellars fully stocked with beer. At around the same time he gave audience to the Governor of Christ's Hospital and his young mathematics students, and was so pleased with their performance that he requested some of them to be taken on board the fleet as fine new recruits.

One month later the King made what was probably his worst mistake in Britain. Since 1689 the Highland clans of Scotland, predominantly Jacobites, had resisted paying allegiance to William. Though his two Scottish secretaries, the Earl of Melville in Edinburgh and Sir John Dalrymple, Master of Stair, in London, constantly recommended a policy of severity towards them, William and Mary hoped to persuade the Highlanders to submit peacefully. During the summer they had sent John Campbell, Earl of Breadalbane, on a pacification mission to the chieftains, and in August 1691 the King had signed a general indemnity for all Highlanders who swore allegiance by 1 January 1692. Most of the Highland chieftains took the oath by 31 December, and only the stubbornly defiant MacIan, Chief of the MacDonalds of Glencoe, was too late. Determined to be the last to bend the knee, he arrived at Fort William to swear, and was sent another 40 miles through the mountains to Inveraray where he took the oath on 6 January. Proof of his submission, in the form of a certificate, was forwarded to Edinburgh, where it was suppressed, probably by order of Dalrymple's father. Though said to be a moderate man, Dalrymple had long nursed a bitter hatred of the Highlanders, and learned with delight that the most notorious of the Highland 'robbers', as he called them, had technically failed to sign before the appointed date.

On 16 January he obtained William's signature to orders that those chieftains who had not taken the oath should be proceeded against, adding that if MacIan and his clan could be separated from the others it would be a firm vindication of the public justice 'to extirpate that set of thieves'. When William signed the order, he imagined that punitive but not unreasonable measures would be taken, and he certainly had no knowledge of the form his minister's revenge would take. Dalrymple sent it to Edinburgh, adding that the MacDonalds were to be rooted out. Early in February the Campbells of Glenlyon, bitter enemies of the MacDonalds, arrived with a hundred men in Glencoe. For a week the MacDonalds granted them traditional Highland hospitality, then one night the Campbells rose and massacred their hosts in cold blood, men, women and children alike. Hardly any of the MacDonalds escaped.

The news took some weeks to reach Edinburgh, and another few months to filter down to London. Mary was horrified. Some thought that the battle-hardened William, who seemed less perturbed, saw the victims as merely rebels and casualties of war, and that in his scale of priorities the Scots counted less than the English, who in turn mattered less to him than the future of Europe and his beloved Holland in particular. Nevertheless it is hard to accept that he shrugged off the cold-blooded murder of women and children as no more than an unfortunate mistake. When he was advised of the rumours, he was preparing for another expedition to Holland, but he authorized Sir James Johnstone, his other Scottish secretary, to conduct a private enquiry into the matter.

Mary was much alarmed about William's health that cold winter, especially when he spat blood for a night and a day. For him it was an ideal excuse for leaving England again, which he did a week after the parliamentary session ended on 24 February. Mary went part of the way with him and returned sadly back to Kensington alone in the afternoon. This time she had hoped that he might take her with him, but it was not to be, and she resigned herself unhappily to another lonely spring and summer. To Electress Sophie she wrote that no sooner did the King return 'than there is only talk of his going away again, so that there is scarcely time to get over a horrid summer before one is dreading a sad spring'.[3] She was worried about the threat of invasion, and at times resigned herself to being ready to die, secure in the knowledge that her husband would take care of the Church. After Easter she was struck down with a feverish cold and felt so unwell that she was unable to attend church on the Sunday, the first time she had missed a service for twelve years.

In France Elisabeth Charlotte, Duchesse d'Orléans, was unimpressed with ex-King James, noting that the more she saw of him, 'the more excuses I find for the Prince of Orange, and the more admirable I think he is'.[4] After Louvois's death and the promotion of his son the Marquis de Barbesieux, an invasion of England became a possibility. Barbesieux readily accepted Jacobite accounts of a discontented England eager to get rid of William and Mary. Even if ex-King James was regarded as a lost cause, and too unpopular to be restored to the throne, putting his son on the throne instead under a regent was possible. Rumours persisted that King William and Queen Mary still considered accepting a proposal from some of their Catholic allies, among them Leopold, the Holy Roman Emperor, to adopt the Prince and raise him as a Protestant and their heir, and that they were only prevented from doing so by the unrelenting opposition of James and Mary Beatrice. If this was the case, it suggests that Mary may have had a change of heart about her half-brother and accepted that he was indeed her father's son.

Through the winter of 1691 James and the French worked at preparations for an invasion. By the new year a combined force of English, Irish and French, numbering nearly 20,000 men, was assembled in a camp at La Hogue on the Cherbourg peninsula and in April James himself arrived at the camp with a contingent of Irish soldiers.

The Jacobites in England were encouraged by news of these preparations, especially as William had left the country taking most of the army with him. James published a Declaration which made it clear that once restored he would continue to act as before, and it listed several hundred people on whom his revenge would fall. Queen Mary promptly published the Declaration, with the government's comments on it. Realizing that their leader had probably damaged their cause beyond repair, the Jacobites quickly drafted another, much milder document, but this was disregarded.

Papers found on a French vessel in April confirmed French plans for invasion, with a combined force intending to sail from Cherbourg and La Hogue, land in Sussex and march on London. Queen Mary had to take the threat seriously. She had little confidence in Russell, now in sole command of the fleet, and she and the Cabinet Council were alarmed by rumours of disaffection among the naval officers. Through Nottingham she sent a message to be read to all the officers, in which she dismissed rumours of their disloyalty as foul slanders, and expressed complete confidence in her navy. It had the right effect: the officers enthusiastically signed an address assuring her of their resolve to fight the French, and Russell himself, whose loyalties sometimes wavered back to James, swore to a Jacobite agent that if he met the French fleet he would fight, even though the King himself was on board.

Alerted to the dangers, the English began to prepare for the invasion, assembling the home fleet and bringing over Dutch reinforcements. The few troops available were dispatched to the coast, and preparations were made on shore. Some regiments that had been about to sail for Flanders to follow William were stopped at the ports, and along the south coast the militia was assembled and armed, Papists were ordered to leave London and Jacobite suspects were rounded up. Among those arrested were officers accused of a plot to seize the Queen immediately on King James's landing, and to place him back on the throne. Mary wrote with horror in her journal of 'dreadful designs' against her, and 'if their success answered their expectations, my life was certainly at an end'.[5]

She kept a brave face in public, and on 10 May came to inspect the six regiments at Hyde Park. There were now eight regiments of horse, two of dragoons and twelve of foot, all ready to fight, and Portland arrived from Flanders bringing William's promise to return himself should the worst come to the worst. It did not, as the French had found it impossible to assemble and equip their fleet, thanks to poor organization. By 13 May the Dutch fleet under Lt-Admiral Van Almonde, initially delayed by bad weather, had joined the English fleet at Spithead, and four days later the combined Anglo-Dutch fleet of eighty-eight ships sailed for the French coast. On the morning of 19 May they encountered the French fleet at La Hogue under Tourville, still waiting for reinforcements from the Mediterranean squadron, and with only half the number of ships. Nevertheless he still gave the signal to attack at 9 a.m., and battle raged for seven hours until a dense sea-mist halted the fighting. Yet it was clear that the retreating French had been heavily defeated. It was the end of any dreams James can have had of reclaiming his kingdom.

Any threat of a French invasion of England was now over. In London the bells rang all day long and the Queen ordered £30,000 to be distributed to all the seamen in the fleet with gold medals awarded to those officers who had particularly distinguished themselves. She expected that the Anglo-Dutch fleet would descend on the defenceless coast of France. Immediately after the victory the ships were all refitted, and 14,000 troops at Portsmouth under the command of the Duke of Leinster were put on alert, ready to embark for France and attack the key French naval bases of St Malo, Brest and Rochefort, in order to deflect the French war effort from Flanders. But there was no general agreement in London about how this plan should be carried out, and the instructions issued by the Queen and the Cabinet Council were ignored by Russell, who had been appointed to direct operations. In a stream of elaborate explanations about contrary winds and tides he justified his inaction, and when he heard of the resentment at his hesitation he threatened to resign. On 6 June the Queen ordered Russell to hunt down and destroy the thirty French warships sheltering in St Malo. He refused, on the grounds that it would be too risky, and in the end the French ships escaped to Brest. After waiting at Portsmouth all summer, the landing forces were finally embarked on 26 July and joined the fleet, but even then the landing at St Malo was not attempted. Mary was desperate for action and tried to encourage her commander. The Cabinet Council eventually decided to go to Portsmouth and resolve the issue directly, but Russell stood his ground.

* * *

Meanwhile, there had been a final rupture in relations between the Queen and Anne. Added to the sisters' differences over financial and other matters, and their contrasting personalities, was another grievance on Anne's part against William – his treatment of her husband, Prince George. The two men had nothing in common, and William never bothered to conceal his contempt for George, who was well-meaning and patriotic but stupid and lacking in leadership qualities. Under duress William took George in 1690 to Ireland with him, but never asked him to ride in his coach or join him at table, an affront that Anne never forgave. Nor did she take it any more kindly when he refused to let George serve as a humble naval officer the next year, on the grounds that it would not be commensurate with the dignity and standing of the husband of the heir to the throne. Anne's household was suspected of becoming a secret focus of Jacobite opposition to the government. Some ministers suggested privately to the King and Queen that Prince George's apparently well-meant but embarrassing behaviour was part of a campaign to gain popularity for his wife and for the Jacobites.

The Countess of Marlborough was quick to exploit any chance of strengthening her position and that of her husband. She shared with Anne the feeling that King William had 'used' their husbands. Anne considered he had slighted Prince George shamefully, while the countess had a similar grievance on behalf of her husband. Since the revolution, several chances of major command had passed Marlborough by. King William had employed him on the Irish campaign and admitted that he was a brilliant commander. Even so, he had appointed Ginckel to complete the war in Ireland, and had not chosen Marlborough as a commander for the Flanders campaign. In his frustration, the earl had made approaches to James at St Germain, and late in 1691 he had moved an address in the House of Lords to ask that the King should dismiss all foreigners from his and the Queen's service. From afar, James hoped this might be the start of a move to recall him. King William was kept informed by the Villiers family, particularly by Betty's sister Lady Fitzharding, who was in Anne's service and kept Betty up to date. The Villiers family had always hated the Churchills, and King William heard all the gossip which rebounded on Marlborough with a vengeance. Portland also kept him informed, and on 10 January 1692 Marlborough was dismissed. Reluctant to persist with petty arguments, King William gave no reason, merely telling one member that the earl had treated him in such a manner that he would have challenged him to a duel were he not king.

On the evening before Marlborough's dismissal, Mary had another confrontation with Anne, who was pregnant again, asking her bluntly if she was engaged in correspondence with their father at St Germain. When Anne indignantly denied it, Mary had no choice but to believe her, especially when Anne dismissed Sarah from her post as Groom of the Stole on 24 January. A few days later Anne attended the Queen's drawing-room, and drew attention to herself by ensuring that Sarah was prominently in attendance on her. Mary was angered by her sister's public discourtesy in bringing the wife of a disgraced officer to court, but said nothing at the time. However, later it became known that she had written almost immediately afterwards to insist that Anne should part with Lady Marlborough, 'since that gives her husband so just a pretence of being where he ought not'. She had 'all the reason imaginable to look upon your bringing her as the strangest thing that ever was done', she continued, reassuring her that 'I do love you as a sister . . . it shall never be my fault if we do not live kindly together.'6

On the next day, Anne's birthday, she refused to part with her favourite, writing to Queen Mary that an order from her to part with the duchess would be 'the greatest mortification in the world' to her. If she had a choice between a breach with her sister or dismissing Sarah, she would take the first; and henceforth she would retire to Sion House, Richmond, put at her disposal by the Duchess of Somerset, taking Sarah with her. As Anne and Sarah had been friends since childhood, she could not imagine life without the faithful companion who was now her Lady of the Bedchamber. To Sarah, she repeatedly declared that she would not 'truckle to that monster' who had 'used' them ever since he first arrived in England. The withdrawal of both women to Sion House made the breach public. William tried to talk Anne round, sending the Dukes of Ormonde and Somerset with a message to dismiss Sarah, but without success. In response Anne ordered the young Duke of Gloucester, who had been staying with the Queen at Kensington, to be brought back to her at Sion House forthwith.

Prince George was likewise unhappy that their differences should be made so public. As amenable and conciliatory as ever, he did what he could to keep up a show of normal relations, continuing to attend council meetings as usual and coming to kiss the King's hand on 3 March, the day before William left for Flanders. His personal guards had already been removed at the King's order, and when he arrived at Kensington the guards there took no notice of him when he went into the court. When he left, however, they sprang to their arms and beat their drums as usual. Two weeks later, after attending a Privy Council meeting at Whitehall, he led Mary back to her apartments where they dined together amicably. Either he was being extremely conciliatory, or else he was weary of the endless friction between them and irritated at the Duchess of Marlborough's part in exacerbating the family disagreements.

Yet both sisters had passed the point of no return. In April Anne, in labour, sent a message to Mary that she was having a particularly difficult confinement. The child died almost at once and only then did Mary, who had herself been seriously ill and confined to bed, appear at her sister's bedside. Rather tactlessly the Queen raised the highly contentious matter of Lady Marlborough's dismissal. Still recovering from her abortive pregnancy and deeply upset at such insensitivity, Anne refused to answer and Mary left soon afterwards. A few days later Anne sent the Bishop of Worcester to ask that she be allowed to visit the Queen, without having parted from Sarah. Mary replied brusquely that Anne was not to give herself any unnecessary trouble, 'for be assured it is not words can make us live together as we ought. You know what I required of you. . . . I cannot change my mind but expect to be complied with.'[7] Anne angrily sent this letter to Sarah, asking her to make the comments public: 'sure never anybody was used so by a sister!'[8]

Anne's guards were removed forthwith, and Mary ordered that in future no public honours should be paid to her. The minister of St James's Church, where Anne worshipped, was ordered not to lay the day's text on her cushion, and Mary forbade her own household to call on the Princess, making it known that anyone who did so risked her displeasure. During a visit of the Prince and Princess to Bath that summer, the mayor was forbidden to pay her any of the respect or honours normally shown to members of the royal family. Efforts made by others to heal the breach were in vain. As Burnet noted ruefully: 'Both had engaged themselves before they had well reflected on the consequences of such a breach.'[9]

General sympathy was on the Queen's side. Marlborough was arrested on 1 May, sent to the Tower and charged with treason.

Princess Anne wrote to the duchess of her fears that she and Prince George might also be sent to the Tower. It was rumoured that she planned to leave the country, though she would not desert the duchess while her husband was still in prison. The duke's accuser was soon exposed as an impostor, and Marlborough was released within six weeks. For the Jacobites it was proof that the Queen was devoid of all natural feelings towards her family: she had driven her father out of the country and into exile while she and her husband usurped his throne, and now she had turned her only sister out of her lodgings.

That autumn the Prince and Princess of Denmark came back to London. During a coach drive through Kensington, Queen Mary went the same way and passed them, but neither acknowledged the other. It was the last time Mary ever set eyes on her sister.

While dealing with these problems in May, Mary was alarmed by news of yet another plot against William's life. This time her father was almost certainly involved. Before his sudden death, Louvois had been behind a conspiracy against his country's greatest enemy, and his son Barbesieux saw it as a sacred trust to carry out his father's wishes, as well as to strike a blow to the cause of France's foes in general. He may even have thought that Orange agents were partly if not wholly responsible for Louvois's demise. Barthelemy Grandval, a young French officer, was to go to the Allied headquarters in Flanders and shoot King William while he was on a visit to his troops. He had two accomplices, a Catholic Dutch ex-officer, Leefdael, and a Walloon adventurer, Dumont. They were all to meet in Brabant. Before he left Paris, Grandval visited St Germain where he was presented to James, who had been kept informed and expressed his thanks for the mission they were about to undertake. Dumont and Leefdael both betrayed Grandval, who was arrested when he reached Flanders and court-martialled in August. William gave orders that he should not be racked when they questioned him, and that he should be silenced if he mentioned Louis XIV. Grandval made a full confession at his trial, alluding to ex-King James and King Louis as consenting parties to the scheme, and was executed soon afterwards.

In England the Cabinet urged Queen Mary to reveal the details of this trial in order to discredit the Jacobites, but she hesitated to 'publish her shame'. It was a source of bitterness to her that 'he who I dare no more name father was consenting to the barbarous murder of my husband', and that she should be 'pointed at as the daughter of one who was capable of such things'.[10] The only consolation she could find was that William showed her nothing but tenderness and understanding. In her darkest moments she feared that she might be bringing him nothing but misfortune, as if she was forever under a curse.

Alienated from her father and her sister, separated from many of her dearest friends, Mary had now only her husband to depend on emotionally, and her inability to give him the children they had both wanted was a perpetual grief to her, though she never completely abandoned hope. Sitting in her room at Kensington while William was away in Flanders, she read the New Testament and found the passage in St Luke's Gospel where Zachariah learned that his wife Elizabeth was with child after years of barrenness. It was a bitter reminder of her own condition, though she still struggled to persuade herself that it was the will of God.

Only William's presence could cheer her during these moods of intense misery and depression, but each time he went abroad the parting seemed harder to bear. More and more she was haunted by the feeling that everything that went wrong, like the quarrel with Anne, was God's punishment for the 'irregularity' of the revolution. It was because of her devotion to the Protestant faith that she had put her scruples as a loyal daughter on one side and consented to 'usurp' her father's throne.

Yet if her religion sometimes made her a prey to guilt, it was still her greatest comfort and her only support, and she was never happier than when she could retire to her study to read, write or meditate. She observed Sundays punctiliously, going to church three times a day and taking Communion once a month. As queen she saw it as her duty not merely to set an example, but also to do as much as possible for the church and for public standards of behaviour, matters which William gladly left in her hands. She always made careful enquiries into the private lives of candidates for ecclesiastical preferment, and if any had bad reputations she would refuse to confirm their appointment without suitable references from bishops or senior churchmen whom she could trust.

On her return to London in 1689 she had been horrified by the low moral tone of London society, which seemed to compare so unfavourably with the frugal, God-fearing Dutch. Her campaign for moral improvement reached a crescendo in the summer of 1692, reflecting her own morbid preoccupation with the sins of the nation. In William's absence, and with the wholehearted support of John Tillotson, the recently appointed Archbishop of Canterbury, she issued royal proclamations for the more reverent observation of the Sabbath and against swearing and profanity. She sent directives to magistrates throughout the country to use particular severity with regard to drunkenness, and had circular letters urging the general reform of manners read from pulpits everywhere. It included several puritanical regulations for observing the Sabbath in London, including an order that hackney coaches could not drive that day, and that constables had to take away pies and puddings from anybody they met carrying them in the streets. She was determined that the royal household should also uphold the example. Her officers of the Guards were told that they should strictly enjoin all the soldiers under them to refrain from swearing and drunkenness, and that it was their duty to attend divine service every Sunday. Thanks to the over-zealous activities of some informers, the measures were soon brought into disrepute. However, several charitable societies were formed as a result of the Queen's lead.

In May 1692 Louis XIV conquered the fortress of Namur on the Meuse, and a month later at Steenkerk the French army defeated the English and Scottish battalions of William's army, the latter suffering 6,000 casualties. An attack on the French privateers' raiding-base at Dunkirk proved a failure. William's main relaxation away from these disasters, and an increasingly difficult Parliament at Westminster, was to take himself back to Holland to hunt at Het Loo. That autumn he was about to return to England when the French swooped on Charleroi, another of the great Meuse fortresses, and he had to hurry back to rejoin his army in Flanders and beat off the attack.

Each time he left England Mary was increasingly impatient to welcome him home, and whenever she received news of his landing at Margate or Harwich she would set out to meet him on the road. Usually they spent the night at Ingatestone, then travelled back together through London to Kensington House. Their welcome from the London crowds who turned out to cheer them was as ever a reminder of their solid popularity with the common people, however much politicians and nobles might stand aloof, and this enthusiasm was not diminished by any military defeat.

EIGHT

'Two or three small strugglings of nature'

Mary particularly welcomed her husband's return in October 1692 as it meant she was again 'freed from care and business'. Though he looked ill, and was clearly disappointed by the failure of his summer campaign, he was relieved to be home. A few days later she accompanied him to see progress in the building at Hampton Court; then he went to Windsor to hunt and they both attended the Lord Mayor's show.

Meanwhile in the United Provinces, every Allied disaster and defeat provoked criticism and a leading regent, Simon van Halewijn, the son-in-law of Johan de Witt, had started peace talks with the French on his own initiative. Arrested for high treason and thrown into Loevestein prison, at his trial he spoke for many when he said he would rather be dead than look on any longer at the Dutch making sacrifices in order to serve the King of England.

The English themselves also reacted with anger. After the Steenkerk disaster there had been bitter attacks on William's Dutch commanders in both Houses, and the King was accused of giving English troops in Flanders all the unpleasant tasks. In the following year a Private Member's Bill brought in by a Whig MP for the naturalization of foreign Protestants was the signal for another session of strife between King and ministers. Though this was intended for the benefit of refugees from religious persecution, principally the Huguenots, every opponent in the House of Dutch influence at court at once declared that it was obviously designed for the benefit of the Dutch who would come over and take the best jobs, and the Bill was quietly dropped. These attacks irritated him, but the King took them in his stride.

Before leaving for Flanders towards the end of March 1693, William appointed the Whig Sir John Somers as Lord Keeper, and gave the vacant Secretaryship of State to another Whig, Sir John Trenchard. Thanks to this new understanding between William and the Whigs, the new parliamentary session which opened early that year went smoothly enough. Nevertheless Queen Mary's months of administration got off to a bad start. She fully shared the conviction of her husband and her father that the Tories were the crown's natural allies and the Whigs its natural opponents, and was displeased by the King's promotion of Somers and Trenchard. She knew that the Tory Nottingham, the King's most faithful servant, was on his way out, and she felt it deeply when he resigned. The two new Whig members of her Cabinet Council, outnumbered by the Tories, were aware of her sympathies and as a result the atmosphere at Council meetings was strained. She found the Council more divided than ever, with the old members plainly dissatisfied with the new and all of them aware of her political inclinations.

Another problem calling for her intervention came in June 1693, when a convoy of Dutch and English merchant ships, loaded with valuable cargoes from the Levant, was attacked by the French and suffered losses estimated at more than a million pounds. This touched off painful recriminations within the Cabinet, and Mary made her anger plain at Council meetings. When a deputation of City merchants came to report their vast losses and their sense of grievance, Mary commanded Somers to give them a binding assurance that a Committee of the Privy Council would be immediately appointed to enquire into the whole business. It was a relief when the Lord Mayor assured her of the City's continuing loyalty.

More than usual this year, she had found the burden of government almost intolerable. Electress Sophie had written urging her not to neglect her health, and Mary took her advice, escaping as often as possible from Whitehall, sometimes going to Hampton Court to see how the new buildings and the gardens were coming on. Occasionally she walked all the way from Whitehall to Kensington, and during a weekend visit to Hampton Court that wet summer she caught a severe cold which she found hard to shake off.

When they met on the King's return on 30 October 1693 at Ingatestone, both were tired and strained after a difficult few months. She still had a cold, while he was in exceptionally bad humour. Omitting his customary praise for her handling of state affairs in his absence, he showed her none of his usual tenderness and seemed to disapprove of almost everything she had done. In her diary at the end of the year, she noted in a philosophically pious frame of mind, 'I continue still in an earnest desire of doing good, but alas! I do not find I have made any great progress therein.'[1]

For William, 1693 ended on a note of triumph when his increased army estimates were passed with a huge majority. Early the next year he made it known that he would withdraw his opposition to the Triennial Bill, a Whig measure laying down that Parliament must be called by the king at least once every three years, and that it should not have a life longer than three years. It had been introduced in Parliament the previous year and passed both Houses but William, who had regarded it as an attack on the royal prerogative, exercised his royal veto. The Bill was almost a matter of principle to the Whigs, and William's refusal to consider it had alienated Shrewsbury, the one Whig he really trusted. William wanted him back in office and hoped that by conceding on the issue, Shrewsbury might be induced to accept the vacant Secretaryship of State.

When weather permitted, he enjoyed going with Mary to look at their houses and gardens, inspecting work in progress and making plans for the future. The Queen's main preoccupation at around this time was a new hospital at Greenwich, which she planned to fund for the benefit of veteran seamen, the relief and maintenance of their widows and the education of the orphans of those who had died while defending the nation at sea. Wren had cheerfully agreed to undertake the work of his own free goodwill, and he frequently consulted her over the plans. Another scheme close to her heart was a plan for starting a college in Virginia, proposed by James Blair, a New England clergyman, to give English settlers the educational opportunities yet denied to them. She supported the idea and the William & Mary College, founded by royal charter, was built to a design drawn up by Wren.

The King and Queen continued to take an interest in the welfare of the sickly Duke of Gloucester, who suffered from hydrocephalus, had to be helped to his feet if he fell over and needed to be carried upstairs. They had a premonition that he would not live long, and despite their differences with his mother they tried to help make his short life on earth a happy one. True to his heritage, he had developed a boyhood passion for games connected with soldiers and the army. With some help from the older generation, he had 'created' two companies of boys in Kensington as a miniature army. On several occasions, the King and Queen were summoned to watch them march past, the little duke at their head, and afterwards the 'troops' would receive a present of 20 guineas from the King to be shared among them.

Another favourite of theirs was Lord Buckhurst, the two-year-old son of Lady Dorset, a beloved lady-in-waiting to the Queen who had died tragically young. He was sometimes brought to play at Kensington. One day he heard the Queen mutter impatiently because the King was working in his study and would not come to tea. Eager to help, he went and banged on the study door. When the King asked irritably who was there, the child ordered him to come to tea at once. Without a further word the monarch put his pen down, helped the boy into his cart and pulled him into the drawing room to join the Queen. The effort proved a little too much for him and he had a severe attack of coughing. A lady-in-waiting threatened to take the boy away as a punishment, but the King begged her not to.

By now everyone around the King had noticed that he seemed to be tiring of Portland. Their old friendship was showing signs of strain and the Wooden Man, they said triumphantly, was on his way out. His old friend's bluntness, which the King had once found refreshing, was beginning to get on his nerves, as did his ponderous manner, and Portland increasingly found himself the butt of William's bad temper. Courtiers jealous of his monopoly of William listened delightedly when the King, out hunting one day, failed to find and began to abuse Portland, who was responsible for the royal parks, in the most violent terms.

Keppel's rapid rise in the King's favour was not lost on a bitterly resentful Portland. Genuinely anxious not to upset his much-valued but increasingly irritating old friend, William tried to soothe his ruffled feelings, sending him little notes after angry scenes between them. And when Portland, convalescing from an illness, was left behind in England at the beginning of the 1693 campaign, William made a special visit to his friend's estates at Sorghvliet so that he could report to their owner that he found everything in good order.

But when Portland finally arrived in Flanders in May, he was upset to discover how indispensable to the King Keppel had clearly become, travelling in the King's carriage and constantly at headquarters with him. Nor was Portland much better pleased when the King's 'third favourite', Romney, was summoned from England to become Lieutenant-General of the English armies in place of Solms, killed at the Battle of Neerwinden. Like everybody else, Portland could never understand William's attachment to this agreeable but incompetent drunk, who had had to be recalled from Ireland only a few months after being appointed Lord Lieutenant and Governor as there were such loud complaints about his administration. Keppel and Romney, as well as other agreeable courtiers like Ossory's son the young Duke of Ormonde and the Earl of Essex, made up a merry party at Het Loo that autumn, while Portland sadly felt there was no longer a place for him.

The conquest of Charleroi in October 1693, which left the French solidly established along the Meuse, was the climax of another disastrous campaign for the Allies. At the start William had written gloomily from Flanders of the enemy's superiority in numbers. He had nevertheless foiled a French attempt to conquer Liege, the gateway to the Republic, but was beaten at the one major confrontation of the summer at Neerwinden. While the French suffered heavy casualties, the Allied armies were completely broken and fled. William himself had fought bravely, narrowly escaping death three times when bullets went through his wig and his sleeve, but his forces were outnumbered by the French under the Duc de Luxembourg. In Catalonia the French defeated the Duke of Savoy at

Massaglia, while on the Rhine they overran and devastated the Palatinate, razing Heidelberg to the ground.

* * *

Mary longed for an end to the war which took William away for months at a time every year, and in the winter of 1693–4 they both followed with interest the informal peace talks at Maastricht between the King's personal envoy Dijkvelt and various French agents. The French also seemed eager for an end to hostilities. The Allied blockade of the French Baltic trade with Sweden, Hamburg and Denmark was beginning to bite, and disastrous harvests for three years in a row brought famine to many parts of France.

Now there were genuine hopes for peace and, knowing his old enemies well enough to warn the imperial envoy against optimism, William had allowed himself a little post-war planning. Early in March 1693 he travelled to Winchester with his new Whig friends to inspect the palace there that Charles II had started in 1683. It had been planned by Wren as the finest palace in England and part of the main building was completed when Charles died. William was very impressed. The idea of completing the first great modern palace to be built in England in decades appealed to him, and during winter 1693–4 he and Wren discussed the plans together. They could only remain dreams as long as the wars continued, for Hampton Court and Kensington were still being altered and Whitehall was being restored at further expense.

Meanwhile the French at the Maastricht talks were as stubborn as ever. They refused to give up the strongholds of Luxembourg and Strasbourg, and insisted that William and Mary should declare the Prince of Wales as their successor if they died without children, in which case he would be sent to England to be brought up as a Protestant. In exchange Louis would undertake to pay James and his family an annual pension. Dijkvelt argued that the question of succession could not possibly be a matter for negotiation with a foreign power, and demanded French recognition for William, but the French said that this could not be dealt with in a treaty any more than could succession matters.

One measure which received the royal assent in the parliamentary session finishing in April 1694 was very far-reaching. This was the act which established the Bank of England, proposed by another Whig addition to the King's ministry, Charles Montagu. It freed William from the problem of finding credit for his wars, since one of its statutes laid down that it should at any time lend the State £1,200,000 on a credit of 8 per cent. Yet for once William was free of financial worries, as Parliament had voted him supplies of £5,000,000 for the war – the largest sum ever.

Bad winds delayed his next departure for Holland, keeping him travelling for days between London and Gravesend or Harwich in the hope of a favourable wind. Mary was delighted, as for the first time in years William was with her to celebrate her birthday – her thirty-second – on 30 April. When he went to Gravesend on 4 May to embark she accompanied him, but as she was on her way back to London she heard that he had been delayed by gales. She turned round for a last glimpse of him before he left, and they went to Canterbury to stay the night. The following day he went to Margate and embarked for Holland while she returned to Whitehall.

In June 1694 the English landed 400 troops under General Talmash at the French base of Brest. Expecting no opposition, they were surprised to find a well-prepared French force ready for them. They were driven back into the sea with heavy losses, and Talmash died from his wounds. The Allies compensated for this defeat later when an Anglo-Dutch fleet commanded by Russell appeared in the Mediterranean and the French abandoned Barcelona. In Flanders the Allies held the French at bay, and William himself retook the fortress of Huy. The States-General were in an amenable frame of mind, although they resented Holland's apparent subservience to the English King when news of his secret peace initiative at Maastricht leaked out. When he appeared before them in the autumn they thanked him for his care of the State, and a few weeks later, to his delight, unanimously voted the army estimates for 1695 that he had laid before them.

*   *   *

At home, the Queen was increasingly ill and weary. The state responsibilities which she had dutifully if reluctantly shouldered, the unpleasantness of argumentative politicians and the increasingly long separations from her husband and her fears for his life and health while he was away had all taken their toll. In the spring she had suffered from a feverish chill, and at thirty-two she was old beyond her years. No longer the good-looking woman of younger days, she had lost some of her earlier good looks. She had put on weight with lack of exercise, was plump and double-chinned, with a constant high colour. Her eyes, which often gave her trouble, were usually red-rimmed and inflamed.

With William gone during the summer, she took up her responsibilities with even less enthusiasm than before. Though not unkindly meant, his criticisms of her efforts the last year had been taken to heart, and this year she attended only a few meetings of the Cabinet Council. On the social side she made few if any public appearances at the theatre, musical evenings on the Thames or dinners in public at Whitehall. Now she was becoming more reclusive, sometimes shutting herself up completely. Ladies and friends at court found her more abrupt and withdrawn than formerly. In May, on her doctors' advice, she went on a course of asses' milk. Her personal accounts revealed that she was purchasing plenty of new clothes, probably her only consolation in life. In addition to buying new dresses, nightgowns, fans and other accessories, she had a standing order for two dozen pairs of white gloves a month, and from one favourite shoemaker alone she purchased seven pairs each month.

Early in September she went through her personal jewel-caskets and wrote out a complete inventory of them in her own hand, starting with the necklace of pearls that William had inherited from his grandmother Amalia and which she was often painted wearing. She kept her descriptions of each item brief, adding a detail to one, William's engagement present to her: 'the ruby ring with which I have been crowned'. At her coronation she had had a larger stone put in it, and by accident it was confused with William's coronation ring. That summer she had considered it a very bad omen when the stone fell out during dinner and was lost, though it was soon replaced. The most spectacular item of all was the Little Sancy, one of the most famous diamonds in Europe, a faceted stone of thirty-seven carats, framed in gold. For centuries it had been prized by the French royal family, but in 1642 the exiled Marie de Medici sold it to William's grandfather Frederick Henry. William's mother Mary Stuart had pawned it to raise funds for her brother Charles II while he was banished from England. After his restoration and her death in England in 1660 William, who was greatly attached to it, begged his uncle Charles to help him retrieve it, but he still had to wait a few years before he could buy it back himself. Among Mary's other jewels were rings of pearls, diamonds and emeralds, necklaces, bracelets and numbers of jewelled buttons, a fashion of the times. She possessed £13,000-worth of pearls and her diamonds were valued at about £9,000.

One reason for making this inventory was a love of organization and a sense of pride in her possessions, like any keen collector. But she had a premonition that her days were numbered and she owed it to posterity, as well as to William and everyone else who would be dealing with her estate, to tidy affairs up as well as she could while she still had time. It was not the first occasion on which she had felt, perhaps even wished, the end was near. She indicated how she wanted some pieces to be disposed of after her death. At the same time she listed her debts in detail, and in another paper she calmly wrote directions for her own funeral.

Worn out by the strain of the summer, she touched on her own feelings about death in a letter – probably the last she ever wrote – to a friend whose mother had just died. Commenting on what a great loss it was for her children, she added tenderly that the woman was surely 'happy to have been delivered by God from so much misery'. She prayed to God, she added, 'to make us all ready [for death] as we ought to be'.[2] Long since reconciled to her inability to bear a child, she wrote in her journal that if she had had children, 'I should have been in pain for them, that is why I regard the lack of children as a mark that the Lord wills that I be more detached from this world and readier when it pleases Him to call me to Himself.'[3]

While she was God-fearing and sometimes censorious to the point of primness, her gossipy letters to women friends and her enjoyment of jokes and the occasional fragment of scandal were ample evidence of a sense of humour. For years she loved going to the theatre and giving balls, though she no longer danced herself, and sometimes she went on little shopping excursions and sightseeing trips as she had often done in Holland. Some of the visits she made invited comment and speculation. It was said that she called upon a fortune-teller, a Mrs Wise, who would not tell her anything though she had freely said to others that King James would return one day. Afterwards she had dined with the disreputable Mrs Granden, and the King scolded her in public for dining 'in a bawdy house'. When Mary defended herself spiritedly on the grounds that she had done nothing Mary Beatrice had not, he asked her if she meant to follow the example of her stepmother. Members of her household were annoyed by his treatment of her, but she was used to his cutting manner and knew it meant nothing. She remained devoted to him. That year she commiserated in a letter with the recently widowed Duchess of Hamilton, offering the condolences of one who believed 'the loss of a good husband the dreadfullest thing that can happen in ye world'.[4]

* * *

William landed at Margate on 9 November and London welcomed him with delight. By now the British seemed less disposed to peace than he was, and seemed sure that another year or so of military campaigning would bring the French to defeat or reason. He was losing his appetite for the interminable conflict, writing to Heinsius that 'there are few men who have more cause to desire a good peace than I have, and even one that was in any way tolerable I should prefer to the continuation of the war'.[5] Weary in spirit, he looked haggard and strained, and suffered from severe headaches. The war and the seemingly futile quest for peace abroad, the struggle with different political factions at home and various subsequent anxieties were taking their toll more and more. His House of Commons, where he now enjoyed the support of the Whigs, seemed almost too cooperative to be true and he was thankful for their support, but it was the only consolation he had at what was the start of the unhappiest few months of his life.

Within days of setting foot on English soil he had caught a chill and took to his bed on 20 November, dosing himself with quinine and living on a diet of apples and milk. Mary nursed him for the first few days, until she fell ill at the beginning of December. Smallpox was raging through London that winter, and everyone feared the Queen might be suffering from it. She had never had the disease, and they guessed that in her weakened state she probably would not have the resistance to survive it. For a few days she stayed in bed and at first her household feared the worst, but she was soon up and about once more. Yet she was probably not strong enough for the next shock. During the Sunday service at Whitehall John Tillotson, Archbishop of Canterbury, a gentle tolerant man who had become a much-respected friend of the King and Queen, began to feel unwell. As he did not wish to interrupt the service he said nothing, but from the expression on his face everyone noticed he was not himself. Soon afterwards he suffered a stroke and within five days he was dead. On being given the news the Queen wept, and Burnet broke down at his funeral while preaching the address. Mary wanted Stillingfleet, Bishop of Worcester, a learned man and an admirable preacher, as his successor, but William considered him too High Church and appointed Thomas Tenison, Bishop of Lincoln, instead.

William caught another chill while out hunting but still sat up until late at night working in his study, sometimes not coming back to Kensington but staying overnight at Whitehall. Worry about his ill-health and grief at Tillotson's death broke down Mary's resistance to the virulent strain of the contagion which was sweeping London. She woke up one morning feeling unwell and noticed a rash had broken out on her arms. She dosed herself and said nothing to anyone else. Aware that this was probably the beginning of the end, that night she locked herself in her study and went through her papers, burning some and putting others in order, as she had done on two previous occasions – once when she was about to leave

Holland – and again in 1691, when she had feared the possibility of a French invasion.

In years past William's return every autumn and the knowledge that she would have a few months of his company had raised her spirits. This time she had been anxious about his poor health since his arrival in England, and he was still not well in the middle of December when he told her that he would soon be leaving again. She accepted it submissively as God's will, but by 22 December everyone knew he was making active preparations for a resumption of the Flanders campaign. Instinctively she knew she would not live to bid him farewell the next time he sailed away. As another prematurely aged royal personage, Albert, Prince Consort, would tell Queen Victoria some one hundred and fifty years hence, she did not cling to life.

On that same day he went in state to Parliament to give his assent to the Triennial Bill. Had matters been otherwise, he would probably have exercised the royal veto, but his mind was not on business and instead of dining in Whitehall he hurried back to Kensington afterwards. It was common knowledge that the Queen probably had smallpox. Superstitious Londoners heard that the eldest of the lions in the Tower, which had been there for twenty years, had suddenly sickened and died. The same had happened just before the death of Charles II.

The doctors confirmed William's worst fears; the disease he had survived but which had carried off both his parents had now attacked his wife. She accepted it with a resignation which astonished all her household. Her first reaction was to order everyone who had not yet had the disease to be sent away for fear of infection. William had a bed put in her room and saw to it that she took all the medicines offered.

Everyone around him was amazed at how his wife's illness had transformed this previously cold, undemonstrative man. When Burnet came to enquire after her, William took him into the privacy of his closet and at once burst into tears, crying 'that there was no hope of the Queen, and that from being the happiest, he was now going to be the miserablest creature upon earth. He said that during

177

the whole course of their marriage, he had never known one single fault in her.'⁶ To his old confidant Antonius Heinsius, Pensionary of Delft, he wrote poignantly: 'You know what it is to have a good wife. If I were so unhappy as to lose mine, I should have to withdraw from the world, and though we have no monasteries in our religion, one can always find somewhere to go and spend the rest of one's days in prayer to God.'⁷

On Christmas Day special prayers for her were said in all the churches and her physicians were hopeful again as she had rested well and said she felt better. The spots had disappeared and they thought it might be measles after all. The King shared their optimism, but everyone's hopes were dashed when the doctors examined her again that evening. Far from disappearing, the spots had turned inwards and sunk in – the most ominous sign of all. She passed an uncomfortable night, and was haemorrhaging in her throat. In desperation all nine doctors attending her tried every remedy; she was bled, hot irons were applied to her forehead, to give her blisters and draw off the effects of St Anthony's fire, and various draughts and potions were administered.

At the same time they told her (rather unnecessarily) that she should prepare for death. Archbishop Tenison was chosen as their spokesman to tell her what she already knew, and she told him gently that 'I thank God I have from my youth learned a true doctrine that repentance is not to be put off to a deathbed.'⁸ She asked for the Collect of the Communion for the Sick, 'That when the soul shall leave the body it may be presented without stain before Thee', to be repeated twice a day at her bed.

William refused to undertake any business or to see anyone except Burnet or Portland. When he broke down again and burst into tears, Mary begged him to control himself and not to make her suffer the pangs of death twice, reminding him that he owed it to his country to take care of himself. She asked him why he was crying, as she was 'not so bad'. He replied in tears that if God caused this blow to fall, it would be all over for him. At length he was persuaded to leave the room and a camp-bed was put up for him in the anteroom, where he occasionally rested for a few minutes.

On the morning of 27 December London's most renowned physician, Dr Radcliffe, was called to Mary's bedside. Surrounded by his nine colleagues, he examined her and confirmed that her case was hopeless and nothing further could be done for her. While she had had a fairly restful night, her husband's condition alarmed everyone; he could not sleep and refused to eat. That day she called for the archbishop and received Communion again. She tried to pray but was too weak, and whispered that others should do so for her, as she was 'so little able' to do so for herself; she refused her medicine, saying she had but a little time to live and would rather spend it a better way. All she had was a last request to make of the archbishop concerning the papers she had sorted out and preserved in the small escritoire in her study, and which were to be given to the King after her death. There was also a last letter to her husband in the little desk by her bed.

Again pregnant, Princess Anne, now living at Campden House, had taken medical advice and spent the last few weeks resting on a couch in order to avoid yet another miscarriage. When Mary's illness took a turn for the worse, Anne was sent daily messages on her sister's health. Hearing that she was on the point of death, she sent one of her ladies to say that she was prepared to run any hazard if the Queen would consent to see her again. The Queen's Groom of the Stole, the Countess of Derby, replied in a letter to Sarah that Her Majesty could not be disturbed as it was necessary to keep her as quiet as possible, and hoped she would defer the visit. Lady Marlborough remarked acidly that, if she was well enough to receive the sacrament, surely she could see her sister.

It was now too late. Towards the evening of 27 December Mary was evidently weaker, listening while Tenison read some of her favourite psalms. He had been standing at her bedside for most of two days now, and with a faint gesture she told him to sit down. Once or twice she tried to say something to William but the effort was too much for her. When he approached her in tears again she motioned him away and soon afterwards she slipped into unconsciousness. Three-quarters of an hour after the clocks had chimed midnight, on the morning of Friday 28 December, there were, in Tenison's words, 'two or three small strugglings of nature',[9] and Mary drifted peacefully into eternal rest. Throughout a snowbound London bells tolled to announce that the reign of William and Mary was over.

It was a merciful release for the frail, weary woman. Unable to share her husband's detachment, Queen Mary had been eternally haunted by guilt for her part in her father's downfall. As her friend the Earl of Ailesbury noted later, 'God knows what she suffered inwardly and to a high degree.'[10] Yet she had been too loyal to her husband and her religion to make her doubts public, and she threw herself wholeheartedly into her role as consort. Her Stuart blood and close claim to the throne were crucial in persuading many of those who might otherwise have opposed the revolution settlement; her charm, dignity and goodness of heart helped reconcile the entire English nation to the change. During her husband's absences she overcame her natural diffidence to display an assurance and an instinct for rule which, it was often said, would have made her one of England's great queens if she had survived her husband to reign alone.

Though the marriage had not always been happy for them both, there is no reason to suppose that it was any less successful on a personal level than most similarly arranged matrimonial alliances of the time. Assertions that it 'came near to shipwreck'[11] can be regarded as largely the product of Jacobite gossip. William was always reserved by nature, and inclined to be boorish at worst, particularly to those who did not know him well. However, it suited their political foes to make the most of any apparent outward disharmony between husband and wife.

* * *

The bereaved William was prostrated with grief. For a few days it was feared that the nation might lose the King as well as the Queen. Immediately after her death he collapsed at her bedside and Portland had to carry him, almost insensible, to another room in the house.

As long as there was a possibility of his following her to the grave, Britain's role in the war against Louis XIV was in danger of collapse.

Though Anne was his heir, Parliament had begun to suspect her Jacobite sympathies and her general attitude towards France. Nobody would have countenanced any overtures towards her ageing father, but her loyalty to the Allied cause was open to question. Tenison stayed at Kensington for several days, to be on hand and provide what comfort he could. At first the King lay on his bed in a state of numbed depression, motionless and silent. He even stopped coughing for a while – an ominous sign as he needed to cough constantly in order to clear his lungs. For several days he could only bear to see a few close friends and acquaintances, like the archbishop, Portland, Keppel and Shrewsbury, and kept breaking down in tears while he talked to them. He found relief in long talks with Tenison about Mary and religion, telling him that if he could believe any mortal being could be born without the contamination of sin he would believe it of the Queen. Seeing Mary's death as a punishment from God for his sins, he went to prayers twice daily and Burnet was pleased to hear that he had 'entered upon very solemn and serious resolutions of becoming in all things a true christian, and of breaking off all bad practices whatever'.[12]

Tenison brought up the subject of Betty Villiers, telling the King that he had wronged his wife by committing adultery. Penitently William promised the archbishop he would have no more to do with her. The initiative may have come from a letter which Mary was said to have left for her husband. Lord Hardwick claimed he saw a testament in which she admonished the King 'for some irregularity in his conduct', though he added cautiously that it was written in such general terms 'that one can neither make out the fact nor the person alluded to'. It has been suggested that a tired, harassed William had resumed his old relationship, or alternatively that the ever-devout Mary, foreseeing his loneliness after she was dead, was afraid he might stray into temptation again, either with Betty or with a younger woman.[13] All the same William kept his promise to Tenison and broke with his mistress.

He kept himself locked up in his room for a while, and when he was persuaded to go into the garden to get a little fresh air he was so weak that Keppel had to have him carried out in a chair. Others spared him the ordeal of any practical arrangements following the death of his Queen. A few hours after her death her body was embalmed; her heart was put in a small violet velvet-covered box and placed in an urn next to that of Charles II in the Henry VII Chapel. The withdrawing room was hung with mourning and on 29 December the Queen's body was taken there while preparations were made for her lying-in-state. In the evening an order was published by the Earl Marshal of England requesting that as from 13 January the Lords, the Councillors and all members of the Royal Household should have their coaches, carriages and chaises draped in black, any shiny ornaments on them painted black and their servants attired in black liveries.

Both Houses of Parliament sat on the day of Mary's death. It was standard practice for Parliament to be dissolved after the death of a monarch, but for nearly six years England had had a king and a queen reigning jointly, and now all that was necessary to signify the change in power was to break the Great Seal of William and Mary and issue a new one for William alone. Both sessions were brief and many of those present had their handkerchiefs to their eyes. The Lords and Commons both sat for some time in silence, and then moved to present the King with an address of condolence, delivered the next day. After expressing their grief at His Majesty's loss they begged him most humbly not to indulge in grief 'to the Prejudice of the Health of Your Royal Person; in whose Preservation, not only the Welfare of Your own Subjects, but of all Christendom is so nearly concerned'.[14]

The King broke down as he replied that he was very much obliged to them for their solicitude, though at that moment he could think of nothing else apart from the great loss they had all just suffered. The poet Matthew Prior wrote from the English embassy at The Hague of the great sorrow in Holland, where a normally cold and unemotional people were deeply touched. By the new year the King was seen outdoors once more, walking in the snow-covered gardens of Kensington without leaning on Keppel's arm.

One of the first people he agreed to see was Prince George, who came on his own. Though George may have been widely regarded as a fool, he had always been wise enough to distance himself from unpleasantness. There had been no last-minute reconciliation between the sisters, but the Prussian resident, Friedrich Bonet, reported that on her deathbed Queen Mary 'had nothing in her heart against her sister and that she loved the Duke of Gloucester very much'.[15]

Anne wrote respectfully to her widowed brother-in-law on 29 December, asking him to accept her 'sincere and hearty sorrow' for his great affliction in the loss of the Queen, admitting she was 'sensibly touched with this sad misfortune, as if I had never been soe unhappy as to have fall'n into her displeasure'.[16] He had been touched by her simple words and sent the Archbishop of Canterbury to see her on new year's day. William was eager to make a new start and, as his advisers – thought to include John, Lord Somers, the Lord Chancellor, and Archbishop Tenison – pointed out, he could no longer remain estranged from the heiress apparent, especially as she possessed a stronger hereditary claim to the throne than he did. He restored her guards, granted her the use of St James's Palace again and passed her all the Queen's jewellery.

Anne came to visit him in person at Kensington on 13 January, though she was so lame that she had to be carried upstairs in her chair. They talked amicably, all ill-feeling swept away by their shared sadness, compounded in Anne's case by the thought that she and her sister, the only survivors from that ill-fated brood of eight, had never managed to swallow their pride and bury the hatchet between them. It was said that they could scarcely refrain from tears or speak distinctly, as they talked for three-quarters of an hour behind closed doors. Despite all the differences that had arisen between them, they recognized the importance of securing the Duke of Gloucester's rights as second in succession to the throne after his mother, against the ambitions and pretensions of the Jacobites, who hoped that Queen Mary's death would remove any semblance of legality for King William's presence on the throne and thus would make a Catholic Stuart restoration possible.

At St Germain James may have seen a glimmer of hope in his daughter's death. If he felt any grief he never showed it, and not only did he omit to wear mourning for her but also forbade his court to show any sign of respect to her memory. According to his minister Charles, Earl of Middleton, 'The King my Master does not consider her his daughter, because she had renounced her being so in such an open manner.'[17]

To the annoyance of his ministers William was not ready yet to face anyone outside his close circle of friends. Huygens went several times to Kensington with papers requiring the King's urgent attention, without success. Keppel found him waiting once and told him bluntly that the King did not want to see anybody and was not doing anything. If he wanted to consult people, he would send for them. The turning-point came on 22 January, when the King dictated a letter to Heinsius, whom he thanked for his condolences. For the first time since Mary's death, he spoke of the war with France and his wish for peace, adding in confidence that he no longer considered himself 'capable of waging war'. In a letter to Vaudemont that same day, he repeated these doubts about his strength, and said he hoped to be able to discuss various matters with him in person, should he live long enough to return to Holland.

Kensington House was being put into mourning and to spare the King the sight of black velvet being hung in every state room, Portland stepped in and took him to stay at Richmond Park on 23 January, so he would be well away from the noise and activity. While he found it 'cruelly cold', at least he was able to venture out into the park and find solace in a little hunting. The change of scene lifted his spirits and gave him strength to begin facing the future alone. On the first Sunday after his return to Kensington, Huygens saw him receiving people again, seeing four or five people at a time. In the evening he dined in public and appeared more outwardly cheerful than he had for several weeks.

Privately he was still unsure of himself. He admitted to Vaudemont that it was an effort to turn his mind to the necessary business of kingship: 'though my loss renders me insensible to all the concerns of this world, I am none the less abandoned to them'. When the question of a return to campaigning abroad arose, he

184

admitted that he shuddered to think of it. 'God grant that I may be enabled to go overseas and take action sooner than I dare to hope, for I confess that I am more than ever unfit to command.'[18] Nevertheless that week he called an extraordinary session of the Privy Council. He had asked the Lords of the Admiralty to be present, and he gave instructions to equip with all expedition all men-of-war in the English ports that were fit for battle.

Anne's first visit to him after Mary's death was soon followed by others and the announcement that Anne would hold court again at Berkeley House and that, once the King appeared in public, he intended to entertain Anne and her husband at dinner. While relations between the King and his sister-in-law never became very cordial, William understood the importance of at least an appearance of understanding with the princess next in line to the throne. The return of Anne's favourites followed soon after, and on 29 March Marlborough kissed hands at an audience with William.

Jacobite sympathizers from London flocked to St Germain to report gleefully – and rather inaccurately – that without his wife beside him the Prince of Orange had become 'a stranger to the nation'. He would henceforth need the support of Dutch armies to maintain himself in power, and this would make an English uprising inevitable to prevent the nation from being overrun by foreigners. No more would the King be able to take the field against France in person, as in future he could no longer entrust the government to anyone in his absence. They spoke more for their own aspirations than for the nation, and had reckoned without the general sympathy for William, who might still be unpopular with some but was generally respected as a hardworking and conscientious monarch as well as a husband who had just unexpectedly lost his wife.

Even at St Germain and Versailles there were those who genuinely mourned Mary, with several of the gentlemen appearing at court in black on the grounds that they were mourning a relative. Liselotte was indignant that James had not merely forbidden his court to go into mourning for his daughter but also seemed quite unmoved by her death. She made no secret where her own sympathies lay, writing in March with relief to her aunt Sophie that King William was in good health again and that his grief would certainly lessen with time.

In London Mary's body was now lying in state in the Banqueting Hall at Whitehall Palace, where thousands of yards of black cloth and purple velvet had been used to cover the walls. Despite the bitter cold, large crowds were queueing by 6 a.m. each day, though they were admitted only between noon and 5 p.m. to see their Queen lying in a bed of purple, while round the bed was a balustrade covered in black velvet and thousands of candles burning. At the four corners of her bed her heavily veiled Ladies of Honour kept vigil, relieved every half-hour. Outside the streets echoed to the sound of hammering as Sir Christopher Wren supervised preparations for the funeral. He had orders to prepare rails from Whitehall to Westminster Abbey, with the walks between them to be gravelled and the rails to be covered with black cloth.

The King had already made generous provision for the Queen's personal staff and ordered all her debts to be paid as soon as possible. The furniture of the room she died in and all the rich velvet hangings in Whitehall became a bone of contention between her ladies-in-waiting. Her favourite, the Countess of Derby, wanted to be chief mourner, and also claimed this furniture as her due in her office of Groom of the Stole to the Queen. The King had given in to her demands but protests arose from all sides, and in the end the Privy Council had to intervene, giving the Duchess of Somerset the honour of being chief mourner. Lady Derby was reluctant to give up her claims to the furniture and hangings, and on 28 February a royal warrant had to be issued to ensure that no goods of the late Queen were removed or otherwise disposed of without the King's direction. The row was settled at the beginning of May, when the countess was pacified with a pair of diamond earrings which had been worn and used by the late Queen.

On 5 March the long funeral procession set out from Whitehall to travel the short distance to Westminster Abbey in a driving snowstorm. According to custom the King was absent, but for the first time the funeral of a monarch was attended by both Houses of Parliament, 500 members clad in black. Next came the Lord Mayor, the City aldermen, judges, officers of the household and guards, with the banners of England, Scotland, Ireland and France. Then came Sir Edward Villiers, the Queen's Master of the Horse, leading her favourite mount covered with purple velvet, and finally the hearse itself, drawn by six of the Queen's horses and escorted by the six first dukes of the realm. At the head of the hearse lay the crown and sceptre on a cushion, and behind walked the Duchess of Somerset as chief mourner, supported by Lord Carmarthen and Lord Pembroke. Lady Somerset's train, 6 yards long, was borne by another duchess and four young ladies, and after them came the lords, ladies and clergy in their long mourning cloaks. Inside the abbey the Queen's body was laid under a silver-fringed black velvet canopy.

The crowds in the streets heard the great guns at the Tower firing every minute, while in the church, blazing with wax candles, sounded the sad music of the funeral anthem composed for the occasion by Henry Purcell. After Tenison's lengthy funeral sermon, the coffin was lowered into the crypt. This was the signal for the household officers to break their white staves and fling them, together with their keys of office, into the tomb, which was then sealed and the long procession wound slowly out of the abbey. Not until later was a letter from Mary discovered, requesting that her funeral ceremonies should be kept simple and inexpensive.

After her death the King lost interest in the rebuilding and furnishing at Hampton Court, which was too full of memories of her, and in the improvements they had planned together and discussed with Wren. Her personal library was broken up and dispersed among various friends, while the porcelain was given to Keppel who later took it back to Holland.

Nevertheless the woman who had never wanted to be a queen, yet filled the position with a quiet dignity, left a permanent memorial after her. The City of London had asked if they might commemorate the unique joint reign by raising a statue to both William and Mary in front of the Stock Exchange. Flattered as he was, the King had other ideas for honouring her memory. In 1691 she had asked Christopher Wren to convert the palace at Greenwich, begun by

Charles II in 1662, into a seamen's hospital. Her enthusiasm for the project had delayed the work considerably, as she would not allow the original elegant Queen's House, designed by Inigo Jones, to be pulled down, or the buildings erected for Charles, which fitted so well into the garden-designs of Monsieur Le Notre, to be demolished. When she died her design was still unfinished, and William decided that its completion would be the greatest tribute to her memory. Wren brought out his old designs and work on Greenwich Naval Hospital was begun anew.

William was never quite the same man after his bereavement. His friends at court and his ministers felt he had aged considerably and that something had died in him. Though he still spoke of Mary, after the spring of 1695 he never mentioned her name in his letters, as if he could not bring himself to write it without breaking down and returning to the state of grief which some had feared would precipitate a final collapse. For the last few years of his life he observed 28 December as a day of personal retreat, for private meditation and prayer, and he always wore a lock of her hair next to his heart.

Yet by the spring he was clearly getting over the worst of his grief and shock after the Queen's death. While Kensington remained his home, with all its poignant memories of her, he had been encouraged to establish a routine for visiting Richmond and Windsor every weekend to hunt and shoot. He had also resumed control of state affairs and was engaged in preparations for what he imagined would probably be his last military campaign abroad.

NINE

'This pernicious resolution'

Once King William III was a widower, the Jacobites thought he would never dare leave England again without having Mary to stay behind and rule the country, nominally at least. However, the matter of appointing a regency in such an event was easily settled and after proroguing Parliament on 3 May 1695 he appointed a council of seven, namely Shrewsbury, Devonshire, Dorset, Pembroke, Godolphin, Somers and the Archbishop of Canterbury. On 12 May William left for Flanders, where he found a French army of 100,000 men under the command of François de Neufville, Marshal Villeroi. After a siege of several weeks Namur surrendered in September, in what would be one of William's few undisputed military victories. The garrison was captained by Marshal Boufflers, who was shown every respect after giving himself up and was allowed to return to Versailles. Louis XIV conferred a dukedom on his crestfallen commander for services rendered, but even in France the conquering William III was unquestionably the hero of the day. To Electress Sophie, Liselotte wrote approvingly in October that he was now spoken of 'in quite a different tone', with remarks like 'A great man, as great a King as he deserves to be.'[1]

The recapture of Namur marked a turning-point in allied fortunes, and William sent a messenger to England with the good news. Next he went to Holland for a short break at Het Loo, then to The Hague to request funds for the next year's campaign. His victory, he found, had silenced the pacifists and given fresh impetus to the Dutch war effort, and the necessary finances were readily voted.

He hoped that England would give credit where it was due for his triumph, and was anxious to get back home before enthusiasm had subsided. Landing on 10 October, he spent a night in Canterbury at the Dean's house and then returned to Kensington where he held a council meeting that same evening. It was decided that a general election should be held at once, while the English were still in a good temper. He was persuaded to do some electioneering himself, and welcomed the prospect of a progress through the country to see areas which he had not yet visited. The weather was mild that autumn and he was in better health than he had been for a long time. On 17 October he left Kensington, arriving that same night at Newmarket. For four days he hunted and attended the races before continuing his journey to Althorp in Northamptonshire, the home of his political adviser Sunderland. He stayed a week, then continued to Stamford, Lincoln and Welbeck, reaching Warwick on his forty-fifth birthday in November, then on to Burford and Woodstock, ending up at Oxford.

Constantly in the best of moods, he hunted wherever he went, but never forgot that he was campaigning for the election. He tactfully told the foxhunting nobles of Northamptonshire that their countryside was the finest in England, if not the whole world. At Sherwood Forest, where he hunted with 400 horsemen, he was appalled to see the open saw-pits, and to the huntsmen's delight gave orders that they were to be filled up. Only one or two individuals did not extend a welcome, notably the Earl of Exeter, a fervent Jacobite who closed up Burghley House and went to London in order to avoid his sovereign. Yet others more than made up for such discourtesy, and he was wined and dined by old friends like the Earl of Northampton at Castle Abbey, the Duke of Newcastle and Lord Montagu at Boughton, who eagerly showed him his collection of paintings.

Wherever the King went, huge crowds were waiting to give him an enthusiastic reception. They cheered him at Stamford, at Lincoln and at Welbeck, and above all at Warwick where his host, Lord Brooke, had organized a magnificent firework display to mark his birthday, the festivities including 'a bowl of punch for the townspeople of one hundred and twenty gallons, made in a vessel call'd Guy Earl of Warwick's Pot'.[2] He arrived late in the evening at Burford to find an assembly waiting for him outside the town with lighted torches, while in the town there were bonfires and illuminated windows in his honour, and his host Shrewsbury presented him with two examples of work from the well-known local saddlery.

Though he had asked that his visit to the normally Jacobite Oxford on 9 November should be brief and simple, with neither entertainment nor dinner, the City fathers intended to mark his appearance as if it were a state visit. After his reception in the theatre, where he was presented with a Bible, a Common Prayer Book and a pair of golden-fringed gloves, he was led to a dinner table – but he refused to sit down. It was rumoured he had been warned of a conspiracy to poison him.

By now his ministers were anxious for him to return home, none more so than his Under-Secretary of State, James Vernon, who found it difficult maintaining proper communications between London and the travelling court, and William had already agreed to make the 50-mile journey from Woodstock to Windsor in one day. He arrived back that same evening, tired but content, and touched by the unexpectedly enthusiastic hospitality he had met almost everywhere. Two days later he returned to Kensington House. To mark his return his friend the Earl of Romney, as Master of the Ordnance, organized the most spectacular display of fireworks in St James's Square that London had seen for many years, in celebration of both his birthday and the victory of Namur.

The new House of Commons that assembled on 22 November was at first ready to give him all the support he needed that year. After his tactful opening speech, in which he attributed the summer's military successes largely to the extraordinary courage and spirit of the English troops, they voted him more than £3,000,000 to carry on the war. Less popular was his decision to make substantial grants of land in Wales, the domains of Denbigh, Bromfield, Yale and others, to Portland. In December Parliament, led by the Welsh MPs, queried a gift of nearly five-sixths of the ancient demesnes of the Prince of Wales (had there been one), with all its copper mines and a yearly income of £6,000, to a foreigner whom they regarded as no more than a mighty favourite. One of the most outspoken attacks came from the Welsh MP Robert Price, whose speech against a 'Dutch Prince of Wales', predicting that Wales would be turned into a Dutch colony, was later published in pamphlet form. On 22 January 1696 the Commons passed a Bill laying down that the lands could only be given away by Act of Parliament, and the King withdrew his gift. Instead, three months later, Portland received a grant of lands from eight different English counties.

After the massacre at Glencoe Queen Mary had pressed for an enquiry in the hope of saving the King's reputation. A commission had been appointed, but little had been done by the time of her death. Bowing to the pressure of Scottish opinion, in April 1695 the King had appointed a new commission, which laid most of the blame on Viscount Dalrymple, the Master of Stair. The Scottish Parliament had sent an address to the King asking him to punish those responsible but he was slow to answer, and by December 1695 it was apparent that he proposed to take no action. Dalrymple had been suspended during the enquiry and, though not reinstated, was virtually exonerated by a statement from the King that the viscount had been in London, several hundred miles away, could therefore have hardly been aware of the impending executions and was accordingly pardoned. Some saw it as a tacit admission of royal responsibility, and thought they detected a sense of guilt for his treatment of Scotland. Certainly in June he gave Royal Assent to an Act recognizing the newly founded Company of Scotland, through which a group of Scottish traders hoped to make their country's fortune by trade with the New World, and to establish a Scottish colony on the Darien peninsula. However, the House of Commons objected to this Scottish threat to their overseas trade, and as William could not afford to antagonize the strong City interests behind this protest he had to yield, demanding resignations from those responsible for the Act. English subscribers to the Company withdrew their money at once, but the Scots refused to give up their project and within six months they had raised £400,000, two-thirds of the capital needed.

In January 1696 William was advised of more invasion scares. From Holland, and then from Brussels, came stories of preparations being made in France for a descent on at least one of the three kingdoms. He was reluctant to take such rumours seriously until news came the following month of a plot in which his assassination would be the signal for a general Jacobite rising, backed by invading forces from France. According to the Duke of Württemberg, French preparations at Dunkirk had reached an advanced stage. The plan was for James's illegitimate son the Duke of Berwick, who had slipped into the country, to mastermind everything from London. The assassination, to be carried out by the Scotsman Sir George Barclay, was planned for 15 February. At the eleventh hour one of the conspirators, Fisher, lost his nerve and revealed everything to Portland. The plan was for the King, on his way back from hunting at Richmond with an escort of twenty-four men, to be ambushed and slain at Turnham Green by a body of forty-six men led by Barclay. Portland had heard of several earlier plots and was sceptical but did tell the King about this one. William dismissed the revelations as nonsense and refused to give up his precious weekend hunting. The day before his departure, Captain Pendergrass, an Irishman and another of the conspirators, came to Portland late at night with the same story and provided further details, namely that the moment the fatal blow was given there would be a general insurrection, and James was ready to embark at Calais with a French army to invade England.

There was an element of farce about the scheme. James was waiting for his supporters to rise up in rebellion in England, while blissfully unaware that King Louis was increasingly weary of his hopes and dreams. Prudently, the French King had privately ordered his generals not to put to sea until they heard that a rising had started. Now convinced that the conspiracy was no idle rumour, Portland warned William, and it was announced that due to bad weather the King would not go hunting that weekend, but that another hunt was planned for the next week. The conspirators took fright, and two more of them turned informer, coming to tell Portland that the attempt was delayed for the following weekend. On 23 February William went riding in Kensington Park with a heavy guard of nobles, who had not been told why they were invited, though many knew of the threat to their master. An alternative plot had been devised whereby the King was to be seized and killed as he returned from church at St James's on the morning of 24 February. Fourteen Jacobite ringleaders were duly rounded up in London, Barclay and Berwick fled the country and the plot collapsed. William was reluctant to believe that Berwick had been a party to the plot until his valet was captured and admitted as much. This, and the fact that Berwick had been in London associating with known Jacobites, confirmed his guilt.

At the first alarm the trained bands in England had been raised and armed, and the fleet under Russell was sent to cruise the Channel to intercept the French. James waited in vain at Calais for the prearranged signal, a bonfire blazing on the Kentish coast, to launch the French armies across the Channel. When it failed to materialize, the troops were disbanded and James returned to St Germain. Though a little crestfallen, he took this ignominious defeat with Job-like patience. Having said at the outset that it would only succeed if God wished it to, he now told his supporters calmly that the good Lord did not wish to restore him after all.[3]

In England the emergency was declared at an end, and on 7 March William, who had not been allowed to go out of doors for days without a strong guard, was able to go hunting again in apparent safety. James later told a Frenchman that he considered the murder of the Prince of Orange at Richmond or Kensington would have been no more heinous a deed than if an ambush had been prepared for him in Flanders. Louis XIV was indignant at being regarded as a possible co-conspirator, and no more was heard from him of the slightest interest in any efforts to help restore James to his throne by force.

No matter what resentment he may have felt against James or the French court as a result of this threat to his life, the King remained silent on the subject. On the contrary, it had brought in its wake a new explosion of loyalty and patriotic fervour throughout the country, and William might even have been grateful. Less pleasant, however, was the additional security that would surround him for the rest of his life. Extra guards were posted at Kensington, and more rigorous searches of carriages entering the courtyard were undertaken as a matter of routine. The price of their monarch's safety, it was recognized, had to be perpetual vigilance.

While some from the governing classes still felt pity for the former King James, this plot to assassinate his son-in-law and bring over a foreign army had alienated many of his less fervent supporters. In Parliament Sir Roland Gwyn spontaneously proposed an Association for the defence of their sovereign and country, which was signed by 420 of the 530 MPs, while another member, William Blaythwayt, referred to the would-be assassins as parricides. Their example was followed by tens of thousands of Englishmen all over the country and in the colonies. In a surge of anti-Jacobite feeling, on 27 April Parliament itself passed an Act 'for the better security of His Majesty's person', by which all MPs and all holders of office solemnly recognized William as their rightful and lawful king, and pledged themselves 'to assist each other in the defence of His Majesty and his government'.[4]

This new upsurge of loyalty to William was motivated less by love for him in particular than by a new national mood which had been growing since the revolution. Under this Dutch King, Parliament had been allowed to assert its independence as never before, and the Francophobe House of Commons of this time represented the interests of a business community with a vested interest in William's well-being. Substantial sums had been lent to the state in his name, and a return of James II would have resulted in the cancellation of these loans. Politically it was clear to all that the restoration of King James would entail subordination to France and would provoke the enmity of the rest of Europe; and in the seven years since the revolution England had developed a proud awareness of her importance in European affairs.

As soon as the six-year-old Duke of Gloucester heard about the Association, he decided to present his own address to the King. The little duke had always admired his uncle, and followed his military exploits in Flanders with keen interest. William and Mary had likewise always adored him, spoiling him as though he was their own child and giving him magnificent presents. Though Anne had never really warmed to her brother-in-law, she never did anything to dissuade her son from worshipping his uncle. It was increasingly unlikely that either the King or Anne would produce another heir, and Gloucester was seen as the sole future of the dynasty, assuming that he lived to maturity. At the beginning of 1696 William had paid a new year visit to Anne during which he promised that the duke would be given the Order of the Garter for his seventh birthday, and the installation took place on 25 July in great splendour at Windsor.

By this time William had left England on 14 May for the Republic. He was preoccupied by the shortage of ready money in England, caused by the poor state of the coinage following years of the practice of clipping surplus silver from the coins' irregular edges. With wartime inflation the intrinsic value of English silver coins had overtaken their face value, and they were disappearing from circulation to be melted down. Before William left London he had given orders that the coinage should be reminted in a form immune to this abuse, and from 4 May the old coins were withdrawn from circulation. Mints throughout the country were put to work producing new coins and commercial life in England came to a standstill. William himself had difficulty in obtaining sufficient funds to go to war, and the financial situation was not much better in the United Provinces. Long years of war had drained the treasury of the States-General, and they had been forced to raise taxes, leading to rioting and disorder in Amsterdam later in the year.

By the time he arrived the hated law had been annulled and calm restored. But William saw that throughout Europe people were sick of war and high taxes, especially in Holland and England where the main burden of the war effort fell. Though the Emperor and the Queen of Spain made difficulties about possible terms, William himself was determined to try to achieve a peaceful settlement. The French seemed equally eager to end the war, and had shown that there would be no more difficulties about recognizing William as King of England. James inadvertently helped Louis XIV by publishing a document stating that he could never come to terms with William or recognize the slightest diminution of his rights. He had been offered the throne of Poland, made vacant by the death of John Sobieski, but refused, and Louis felt he had done all he reasonably could for his tiresome guest.

Hopes of peace in Europe were shattered in August, when Victor Amadeus, Duke of Savoy, signed a peace treaty with France. Peace talks came to a halt, and a disappointed William retired to Het Loo. More preparations, diplomacy and endless arguments with Parliament awaited him, destroying the fond illusion of Liselotte, sister-in-law of Louis XIV, who herself had once been considered as a possible bride for William of Orange. She had proposed her only daughter, the twenty-year-old Elisabeth Charlotte, as the second wife of Europe's most eligible widower, and instructed her Danish lady-in-waiting Christina de Meyercrone to write discreetly to Portland on the subject, only to receive a polite but discouraging reply.

Apart from the matter of religious differences, William had no intention of marrying again. He had now been a widower for two years, and had faithfully kept his promise to Archbishop Tenison to break with Betty Villiers. It was said that after the death of the Queen, Betty had pulled a lock of hair from Mary's head, presumably at her lying-in-state. This may have been malicious gossip, but the furious King was apparently among those who believed it. Even so, in 1695 he settled on Betty the Irish properties that had belonged to his father-in-law, whose daughter ironically had signed the patents in October 1693 when William was on the continent. Anne was angry with him, especially as the money due to Prince George for the surrender of his mortgages in Holstein had not yet been paid.

In November 1695 a match was arranged for Betty with George, fifth son of the Duke of Hamilton, a soldier who had distinguished himself in almost every great battle of William's reign, from the Boyne to the conquest of Namur, where he was wounded. The King had promoted him to brigadier-general and in January 1696 created him Earl of Orkney. Their marriage was a happy one, although some members of the Hamilton family were outraged by the connection, and Betty's new sister-in-law the Duchess of Hamilton would never speak to her. Even after her liaison with the King was broken off, Betty remained a force in politics, and kept up her friendship with several of the Whig leaders. William had enjoyed talking to her and must have missed her amusing and entertaining company as he missed the love and tenderness of Mary, but he showed no eagerness to replace either mistress or wife.

The English and Dutch were keen that their King and Stadholder should consider marrying again, and Portland was asked to produce a list of eligible Protestant or Lutheran princesses. He came up with six: the Princess Royal of Sweden, Hedwig Sophie, then fifteen years old; the Princess Royal of Denmark, Sophie Hedwig, eighteen years old, with a good figure, a nice character, beautifully brought up and a sound Lutheran; Sophie Charlotte of Hesse-Cassel, sixteen years old; Marie-Elisabeth of Saxe-Eisenach, aged twenty-five; Marie-Elisabeth of Holstein-Gottorp, twenty years old; the last was the daughter of William's old ally and cousin Frederick of Brandenburg, the fourteen-year-old Louise Dorothea Sophia. From a political point of view the last named was easily the most eligible; there was much to be said for a marriage alliance between Germany's most important state on one side and England and the Dutch Republic on the other. Even though William was disinclined to remarry, he did not totally rule out the idea of trying to give England a prince to secure the succession after Anne and the Duke of Gloucester, and the United Provinces a future Orange Stadholder. Reluctantly he acceded to everyone's expectations and agreed to meet the Princess. The first reports he heard of her were not encouraging; she was said to be a lean bony girl with a gauche and unappealing manner, well-read but not very amusing.

In September 1696 William travelled to Tolhuis on the Rhine, where Friedrich was waiting to greet him. At Moylandt they were received by the Electress in her own apartments. For about an hour they stood around talking; according to their own interpretation of protocol, both men had an equal claim to the only great armchair in the room but they were polite enough not to insist on it. Then Frederick left the room and everyone sat down to five hours of cards, the King in the great armchair, the Duke of Celle who had travelled with him in an ordinary one, the Electress on her bed and

Portland and Keppel on stools. The rest stood watching, among them Princess Louise, until Keppel broke protocol by gallantly pulling forward another stool for her and inviting her to sit down.

The Elector's court was dull and dowdy, though the Electress herself bore a faint resemblance to Queen Mary in her looks and was full of chat and civility. Matthew Prior reported to Shrewsbury that the prospective bride was 'not ugly, but disagreeable; a tall miss at a boarding school, with a straggy lean neck, very pale, and a great lover, I fancy, of chalk and tobacco-pipes'.[5] William was kind and polite to the girl; that evening he dined with her and her mother and Keppel for male company, while Portland made polite conversation with their host the Elector in the next room. Nevertheless, despite William's initial plan to stay for twelve days, he left next day for Het Loo.

The English and Dutch had considered his second marriage almost a foregone conclusion, and were disappointed. When told of their expectations, he asked coldly whether the people had forgotten the Queen so soon.

* * *

William arrived back in London in October 1696 to find that Shrewsbury had resigned as Secretary of State. Sir John Fenwick, long known to the government as a notorious Jacobite sympathizer, had been arrested in June on a charge of high treason for his complicity in the assassination plot of the previous March. He had offered to reveal everything about the conspiracy, but when his account was read it proved to be less a confession than an inventory of damaging assertions of Jacobite sympathies against leading Whig members of the government, including Godolphin, Marlborough, Russell and Shrewsbury. William was not surprised to read it, as he had always been aware that many of his subjects were playing safe and maintaining contact with St Germain. Determined to frustrate this attempt to tarnish his government's standing, he assured Shrewsbury of his full confidence in his loyalty, and realized that Fenwick was intent on causing mischief. The latter's friends and colleagues pointed out that the panic-stricken Shrewsbury's sudden flight from London could be taken as an admission of guilt. The King refused to accept Shrewsbury's resignation and he remained Secretary of State in name alone, while Under-Secretary James Vernon gradually took on all the responsibilities.

Fenwick had never been forgiven by the King for once behaving insultingly to Mary in public, while Whigs and Tories alike felt that the sooner this tiresome individual was out of the way the better. Since one of the two witnesses necessary for a conviction of high treason by the ordinary process of law had fled the country, Parliament voted a Bill of Attainder against him, the last successful such action in English history, and William gave his assent on 11 January 1697. Seventeen days later Sir John was beheaded on Tower Hill.

The King was in low spirits that winter, and it was particularly noticeable at the ball that Anne gave for his birthday in November. Since the death of Queen Mary, Anne had acted as his hostess on court and ceremonial occasions in her sister's place, though by now she was so lame that she had to be pushed around in her chair all the time. She invariably presided at entertainments for his birthday each year, and he repaid the compliment to her every February. This superficial reconciliation had done little to diminish the personal antipathy they still felt, due partly to the Duchess of Marlborough's incessant attempts to stir Anne up against the King, and partly, it is said, to his persistent jealousy of her superior hereditary claim to the throne.

At around the time of his birthday, and for several weeks afterwards, it was evident to all that he was tired, unhappy and missing Mary more than ever. On the second anniversary of her death he shut himself up all day and saw no one, and began drinking more heavily to drive away his melancholy. Only late at night, sitting for hours over the table with his friends, did his gloom sometimes lift. An English friend once asked Keppel if he ever heard the King utter a word to anyone. Keppel, who had long been the sovereign's indispensable companion at these drinking sessions, answered that he talked plenty at night over his bottle, when he had nobody around but his Dutch friends.

Huygens, now aged sixty-eight, knew that Keppel disliked him and wanted him replaced as secretary by d'Allonne. He reported disapprovingly from time to time in his journal that the King seemed to be working less by day, and drinking more by night. Increasingly preoccupied with the troubles of his own family in Holland, Huygens had seemed strangely unsympathetic when the Queen died. William could not bring himself to dismiss him after so many years of faithful service, but merely gave him less work to do. In October 1696 he retired with a generous salary, but both men had drifted apart and their close friendship was a thing of the past. Returning to Holland, Huygens died a year later.

The mutual antipathy between Keppel and Portland was common knowledge at court. Portland, who seemed too serious, too greedy for wealth and too possessive about the King, had never been liked, and few were sorry to see him fall from favour. Middle-aged and devout, he cut an uninspiring figure beside the more amusing, carefree and instantly likeable Keppel. He had one or two supporters who regarded the pleasure-loving Keppel as boisterous, shallow and dissipated, but they were in the minority. Having found the younger man a great comfort after Mary's death, the King accepted his little faults without question and found him a useful secretary as well as agreeable company. In January 1697 he decided to make Keppel an English earl, and conferred on him the titles Earl of Albemarle, Baron of Ashford and Viscount of St Edmondsbury, in addition to the rank of Major-General. The English did not readily welcome another Dutchman to the ranks of their aristocracy.

William and Portland went back a long way. The latter had become a page to the adolescent Prince of Orange in 1664, and for much of his life the King regarded his friend as the only man in whom he could confide anything. Both men had married in 1677, though Portland's first wife had died in 1688, ironically at the time of her husband's friend's greatest triumph. During the next few years in England he was given several titles and honours, including Groom of the Stole, Gentleman of the Bedchamber and Treasurer of the Privy Purse; he also obtained membership of the Privy Council and was made a Knight of the Garter. The appearance of Keppel (henceforth referred to as Albemarle), in looks and personality very like a younger version of Portland, made all the difference to Portland's position of superiority. Keppel's family background was similar to Portland's and William enjoyed his friendship as well as respecting his abilities as servant and secretary. Being relatively poor, he could be expected to work much harder than the ageing and increasingly indolent Portland was prepared to. For this William could overlook Albemarle's dalliances, his mistresses and his scandalous behaviour. He once allegedly tried to seduce a mistress belonging to the Elector of Bavaria, and had an affair with Madame de Richelieu which resulted in the birth of an illegitimate child. Rumours abounded that he had contracted gonorrhoea in the course of his liaisons.

Portland found it hard to accept his loss of position as the King's main confidant. Recognizing that the old bond was irretrievably broken, in March 1697 he wrote to resign all his posts at court. In his distress William wrote begging him 'to change this pernicious resolution, and I feel sure that if you retain the least affection for me you will not refuse this prayer, however hard it may seem to you. I ask you only for another year's trial.'[6] Largely out of concern for the King's health, Portland relented, although he had some misgivings. His old friend and master had been suffering all winter from dizzy spells, sleeplessness and lack of appetite, and was beginning to worry about the swelling in his feet and legs.

After a few days' hunting at Het Loo he felt much better. Portland had accompanied him, and was glad to see his recovery, though disappointed to note that the King and Albemarle were as intimate as ever. At an interview with the King on 28 May, Portland reiterated that he still planned to leave his service. William was about to leave for the army headquarters at Iseringen, while Portland was going to Brussels as the guest of William's friend the Prince de Vaudemont. The King wrote to him sadly asking him 'not to take any desperate resolution'. Portland replied with his reasons: 'it is your honour that I have at heart, and the kindnesses which Your Majesty shows to a young man and the manner in which you appear to authorize his liberties and impertinences, make the world say things which I am ashamed to hear, and from which I believe you to be as far removed as any man in the world.'[7]

Astonished, William replied in hurt tones, saying that it seemed 'a most extraordinary thing that one may not feel regard and affection for a young man without its being criminal'.[8] Portland apologized if he had given any offence, saying that if his remaining in the King's service would put a stop to the hurtful gossip, he would remain where he was, but he could not be expected to stand by and suffer in silence.

Thanks to Vaudemont's valiant efforts as a go-between, Portland promised to return to the King's service, but his attitude made it clear that he was still not really satisfied. Vaudemont continued to act as a confidant for each; Portland took all his complaints to him, while William continued to tell him how distressed he was at Portland's continued coldness. William feared that the only solution to the problem was the dismissal of Albemarle, something he was loath to do as this most devoted of friends and servants had done nothing wrong, apart from inadvertently attracting an undue measure of jealousy and innuendo as well as provoking a clash of personalities between him and the man who had been the previous royal favourite. To dismiss him for no valid reason other than the dislike of an elderly rival, who made repeated insinuations yet refused to come clean about his objections, would provoke more gossip and scandal than maintaining the status quo. It was evident that a widowed king without children or close female relatives, apart from a sister-in-law in indifferent health with whom he was rarely on less than distant terms, would rely largely on male companionship. Had he not renounced his relationship with Betty Villiers, such as it was, largely out of respect to the Queen's memory?

The oft-propounded theory, accepted as fact by some, that William was homosexual is unsupported by evidence. Take away the innuendo, as likely as not motivated by Jacobite smears, put about in the hope of undermining his position on the throne, and there is nothing left to go on, apart from Burnet's oft-quoted remark that His Majesty 'had no vice, but of one sort, in which he was very cautious and secret'.[9] Though Burnet admired King William, he had always been devoted to Queen Mary and never really liked her husband. According to Nesca Robb,[10] this comment referred to the Betty Villiers scandal, which he strove to keep secret. Whereas his two uncles who preceded him on the British throne openly acknowledged their mistresses and illegitimate children, the Calvinist William preferred to conduct his extra-marital liaisons with discretion. This may lay him open to the charge of hypocrisy, if we infer that he pretended to be more virtuous than Charles and James, but Burnet's remarks – sometimes taken as indicating the King's homosexuality – are more probably referring to this, particularly as he never attempted to conceal his male friendships, knowing that they were camaraderie and nothing more.

If gossips are anxious to dissect a situation and read unpleasantness into it for its own sake, there is nothing to stop them. So it was with King William III who, by the mid-1690s, generally rose fairly late in the morning, spent much of his day hunting if the weather was suitable and, unlike most Englishmen of the time, then worked late into the night, either in his own cabinet or in the office of his chief private secretary. Until 1695 this was Portland, whose rooms and the state apartments had connecting doors. People from outside, unfamiliar with the King's regular routine and unaware of the work undertaken by him and his staff, wondered how both men spent their time. Those who disliked the King for either personal or political reasons, such as Jacobite sympathizers, strove to seek a parallel with the case of his great-grandfather King James I. His favourite, the former page boy Robert Ker, had also come to royal notice by displaying great courage in front of his sovereign after breaking a leg; having risen in royal favour he became the King's private secretary. King James's proclivities after his wife's death had been no secret. It was all too easy to draw parallels and to spread the rumour that King William, unlike the fine, upstanding, ever-philandering Catholic father-in-law whom he had dethroned, was a homosexual as well.

Further basic facts reinforce the unlikeliness of these assertions about William's character. Albemarle was notorious for his womanizing and, unless he swung both ways, was therefore unlikely to be indulging in 'the unspoken sin' with his sovereign. While it might be argued that they had every reason for denying it, none of the King's secretaries ever paid any attention to the rumours, either to confirm or deny them. Moreover, after the death of Queen Mary, a grieving, remorseful and deeply penitent king had gently dismissed his mistress. Having done so out of a feeling of religious duty, it would have been almost impossible for him to yield to a far graver sin. Had he done so, he would never have summoned a well-respected mutual friend, in this case Vaudemont, to arbitrate between him and Portland, as his tenure of the throne would not have survived the risk of exposure of any unpleasant secrets, had there been any to expose.[11] J.P. Kenyon maintained that 'there was a deep homosexual strain' in the relationship between William and Portland, while accepting it was hardly surprising that 'Jacobite muckrakers' should embellish it with additional obscene details. Both men, he argued, 'had been wedded in a David–Jonathan relationship ever since youth, never apart in council or on the battlefield', though he qualified it by suggesting that it was quite possible for this association to be 'non-physical'.[12]

At any rate a relieved Portland was content to accept that there was no basis in truth for rumours of the King's homosexuality, and personal dislike of Albemarle was no impediment to his continuing in royal service. A new opportunity was about to arise.

At the end of June William made an appeal to Portland to play an important and secret role in the peace talks with France. Portland consented, and two months later he joined the King at Dieren. But he knew that the old friendship and affection that had been a feature of their lives since their boyhood in Holland could never be rekindled, and he had to face the fact that Albemarle was now as indispensable to the King as he himself had once been. The early death of William's father and mother had left him with no one he could emotionally depend on until Portland came into his life, and even after their respective marriages William had found it hard to let his friend go. While Portland adapted himself effortlessly to life with a wife and a family of his own, William's letters to him demonstrated the resentment he felt when family business took

Portland away from his side. He may have inadvertently given the impression that he found it impossible to imagine that any woman could have a greater claim on him or Portland. However much he came to love Mary he never asked from her, or found it possible to give her, the same understanding as existed between him and Portland.

If William's feelings for Portland had homosexual overtones, they were almost certainly not reciprocated. Judging by his letters to the King during the last crisis and his reluctance to mention homosexuality by name, Portland's attitude was clearly one of horror and disgust. He hated the decadent habits of many English noblemen and once expressed a desire to remove his son, Lord Woodstock, from England, lest he should become tainted by the nobility. This same son, Portland decided, was in the event of his early death to be left to the guardianship of King William, and the boy was often allowed to stay with the King. Portland would never have allowed this if he suspected the morals of his old friend and sovereign. Though he himself might not have escaped Jacobite insinuations about his friendship with William, more reliable observers never hinted that the relationship between both men was anything but normal.

William was never very strongly attracted to women; his mother had virtually neglected him and his grandmother had been a distant and domineering figure. Throughout his life the rare women he found attractive were intelligent, witty and not always particularly feminine. The ultra-feminine Mary, some thought, seemed almost to have frightened him at first with the strength of her emotional demands. On the other hand he gave himself unreservedly in his friendship with men like Romney, Shrewsbury, Vaudemont, Portland and Keppel. His camaraderie with Ossory, whom he met when he himself was only twenty, and whose memory he cherished for years afterwards, was always important, and he made a special pilgrimage to visit Ossory's boyhood home, Kilkenny in Ireland, in 1690. To what extent these relationships were homosexual is difficult to discover. In Holland William was surrounded by servants of outstanding loyalty, and Huygens only once noted the frequent private and lengthy visits to William's rooms of Dorp, a handsome young captain of the cavalry. This was in September 1683, but when he mentioned his suspicions to one of the Prince's staff, the man at once denied that anything was going on, adding that he was not to mention it to anybody else lest the relationship be misconstrued.

Huygens was discreet in his journals less from choice than from lack of opportunity for observation. William knew of his secretary's inquisitive nature, and kept him at a distance, only sending for him when necessary. It was also apparent that, despite his involvement with Betty Villiers, William's marriage to Mary was becoming stronger, and her private papers suggested in discreet terms that his sexual relationship with her gave her grounds to continue hoping for a child. The husband–wife relationship did much to satisfy his physical needs and perhaps allowed him to suppress any homosexual inclinations he might have had. His affair with Betty may also have helped, although it is difficult to be sure how far, and for how long, sex entered into it. She never presented him with any children, yet she was in her late thirties when she married in 1695 and then she produced three children in rapid succession.

After Mary's death and Betty's departure William found comfort and compensation in the company of Albemarle, who was old enough to be talked to as an equal but still young enough to be stimulating to the tired and lonely King. While everybody noted the young man's rapid climb in favour, hardly anyone thought any more about it at first. The King's agonizing grief at Mary's death was all too evident, but even so all London was soon gossiping. In 1696 when Sir John Vanbrugh's comedy *The Relapse, or Virtue in Danger* was first presented at the Theatre Royal, Drury Lane, its homo-sexual allusions were considered daringly topical. Talk soon reached the continent, where Portland heard it at The Hague, while the Jacobites at St Germain made the most of it.

Portland at least heard enough to be alarmed about the damage the King was doing to his own reputation. Albemarle's familiar behaviour with the much older man, the King's obvious pleasure in their friendship and the hours they spent alone together seemed to a jealous man proof enough that the rumours were only too well founded. Portland's long letter of explanation looked like that of a man begging to be convinced that he was wrong. In his replies William said nothing to reassure him, preferring to dwell on the damage that Portland's resignation would inflict on the reputations of them both. He may not have been able to deny the accusation of a homosexual affair with Albemarle, or he may not have wished to. Throughout his life William always thought it beneath him to attempt to justify his actions in public. Yet the fact that he refused even his best and most long-standing friend the satisfaction of a wholehearted denial may be suggestive in itself. It is impossible to be certain. William's enemies were convinced, or perhaps wished to convince themselves, that the King *was* homosexual, and Portland's letter suggests that even his closest friends were not sure of the truth.

*   *   *

In April 1697 representatives of the other European territories assembled at Rijswijk, near The Hague, and William arrived there early in May to open formal negotiations between the representatives of France and the Allies. Talks had been in progress for nearly a year, and the concessions France had seemed ready to make, especially Louis XIV's willingness to recognize William as King of England at last, suggested a sound basis for official discussion in December 1696. Only the Emperor still retained any enthusiasm for continuing to fight, but in France, England and the United Provinces the wish for peace was almost unanimous. However, once negotiations opened at Rijswijk with Sweden as mediator, a stalemate looked likely with demand and counter-demand, concession and refusal coming from France and a pro-French Sweden on one side, and England, the Republic, Spain and the Emperor on the other. The United Provinces wanted an effective barrier against French aggression, while the English insisted on Louis's recognition of William as king. Louis promised to do so once peace was signed, but meanwhile he persisted in treating his fellow-sovereign merely as the Prince of Orange. Ever the optimist, from St Germain James had demanded to be represented at the Peace

Congress as rightful King of England. When this was refused him he sent a memorial to all the Roman Catholic powers, inviting them to join in a crusade for his restoration, but none of them took him seriously.

William watched with growing irritation, increasingly convinced that the French meant to prolong the war. Learning that the French armies were on the march again in Flanders, he hurried his forces to try to relieve the town of Ath, besieged by the French, but it surrendered on 5 June. He succeeded in forestalling a French swoop on Brussels, thus ending the active conflict, and felt it was time to be equally decisive at the conference table. Though the breach between himself and Portland at that moment was not yet completely healed, he asked his friend to put his diplomatic talents once more at his master's service. If peace negotiations were allowed to languish without any positive progress, the sooner they were broken off the better.

The delegates at Rijswijk had not even touched upon two major impediments to agreement between William and Louis. First, William insisted that Orange, his principality, should be restored to him with its civil and religious liberties intact, while Louis strongly objected to this Protestant haven, a possible centre for rebellion in the heart of French territory. Secondly, the presence of James and his court at St Germain, so near England and so accessible for discontented English Jacobites, was unacceptable to William. Though he had appeared to make light of the assassination plot of the previous year, he had never forgotten it, nor the Duke of Berwick's leading role. As long as the Jacobites had a refuge in France, and as long as their figurehead was still living there with the full sanction of the French sovereign, further plots were still possible, not to say likely. He wanted James and his family to retire to Italy, out of harm's way. However, Louis XIV, who believed strongly in the divine right of kings and who found recognition of William III a difficult concession, was reluctant to dismiss the exiled Stuart from his court and the French negotiators would not concede.

Having failed in this aspect, William took the initiative in attempting to resolve other issues. Portland had got on well with

Marshal Boufflers when the Frenchman had been his prisoner after the fall of Namur in 1695, and Boufflers himself was now high in the favour of Louis XIV. On 8 July they met near Halle, not far from Brussels, for a series of private and informal conversations which by the end of a fortnight seemed to have broken the deadlock.

At the first meeting between Portland and Boufflers, Portland gave assurances that the King was satisfied with the preliminaries. If agreement could be reached on three points which concerned him privately, he would force the Habsburgs to make peace on those terms or else abandon them. The first point was that, in the treaty, James II had to be named as an enemy of William III; the French must undertake not to aid him directly or indirectly, and they must place him under an obligation to leave for Rome or some other part of Italy. The second was that William could not consent to the return of the Jacobites from France as a group; he could not restore their estates in England, which had been confiscated by Parliament, and it must be recognized that to permit them to come back would be a threat to his personal safety, as they could not be trusted to abandon any thought of continuing to plot against him. On the other hand, once peace was signed, William would pardon individual Jacobites if they wished to live quietly in England. The third was that William should permit no Frenchman to settle in the principality of Orange, as to do so would constitute a derogation of his sovereignty as prince of the territory.

It was made clear that the Jacobite exiles would no longer be championed by Louis XIV, and that William would agree to the Orange clause orally rather than in writing. While Boufflers said on 15 July that the French could not name James, nor force him to leave France, they would insert a clause in the treaty undertaking not to give direct or indirect assistance to the enemies of the Prince of Orange. Portland accepted this, adding that William hoped, if not understood, that after peace was signed Louis would persuade James to leave France of his own free will. No firm agreement was reached and Boufflers was initially reluctant to discuss it, but at a later stage he suggested non-committally that Avignon might be a possible future residence for James. Portland took this for a commitment, and told Boufflers that the King would willingly honour the French request that an annual allowance of £50,000 should be paid to Mary Beatrice.

The King was in Brussels where he, Keppel and Portland were guests of the Prince and Princess de Vaudemont. Looking fit and happy, he was more at ease than anybody could remember in months, and he followed all news of the negotiations with great interest. When Portland returned from his last meeting with Boufflers, bringing news of Louis's concessions, William decided to spend the rest of the summer at Het Loo, waiting for the final results of the talks at Rijswijk. On 20 July the French offered favourable terms as long as a treaty was signed before 31 August; William agreed, and talked the Spaniards into signing with him. The Emperor, however, refused to sign. The date came and went, and Louis announced that the deadline for signing would be extended until 20 September, adding that he would now keep Strasbourg as the price for the Emperor's delay. On that date France, England, the United Provinces and Spain signed the peace treaty of Rijswijk; the Emperor was given another month and signed on 30 October. King Louis agreed to restore his conquests gained in the Low Countries since the Peace of Nijmegen in 1678, all her conquests in Spain beyond the Pyrenees and many of the towns conquered in the Holy Roman Empire, apart from Strasbourg. The Rhine fortresses were razed, the Duke of Lorraine's estates were returned to him and the principality of Orange was restored to William.

At last France formally acknowledged William as rightful King of England. Some of the other points discussed were not finalized. Portland was given to understand that James and his family would be required to leave French soil, and suggested that Mary Beatrice would be paid a jointure of £50,000 per annum by the English Treasury as stipulated in her marriage settlement, dependent on King Louis agreeing to all other conditions.

William was still at Het Loo when the news came. It was a disappointment to Tsar Peter of Russia, who had just arrived in Holland to pay homage and to offer William help against France. All the same his journey gave him a chance to see something of life in Europe. Fascinated by anything to do with ships, the Tsar had spent many hours with these Dutch craftsmen; though he had travelled incognito as a simple non-commissioned officer in a company of 270 people, his journey through Poland and Germany had not passed unnoticed. When he arrived in the United Provinces he sent a message to William expressing a desire to meet, and the King invited him to a private tavern at Utrecht on 11 September. The King, who had come specially from Het Loo to Soestdijk, drove to the town and received the Russian delegation, headed by three ambassadors who paid him their compliments.

Next William was led into a room where the Tsar was waiting for him and they talked together through an interpreter for two hours. The Tsar paid fulsome tribute to William's 'military genius', promising that in the event of another war with France he would be a willing ally. The latter listened gravely and with some reluctance – the man described by one onlooker as 'his Muscovitish Majesty' was not the cleanest of human beings – invited the Tsar to dine with him at Soestdijk next day. After accepting, the Tsar took fright at the inquisitive crowds, changed his mind and went back to Amsterdam. He stayed in a small boarding-house before moving to a little house on the Oostenburg wharfs where he was seen working like a common dockhand. When William sent him another invitation to dinner, this time at The Hague, he accepted. On this occasion a crowd assembled again to watch both monarchs dining. Peter's paranoia got the better of him and he offered to decapitate a few of their unwanted spectators for William. He was still in The Hague when the Dutch celebrated the peace of Rijswijk with a huge firework display. Having never seen anything like it, to the concern of William and his entourage, he borrowed a small boat and rowed fearlessly up and down the Vijver while fireworks sizzled around him.

Though the peace treaty had been ratified, there was already some concern that not all the conditions would be honoured. No more had been said by the French about sending James away to Provence, and in October Vernon noted that there was a possibility of the castles at Blois and Chambord being repaired, as if he were to retire no further away than either of those. William confessed that he too was anxious, yet he still received the French ambassadors, François de Callières and the Duc d'Harlay with courtesy on 9 November. They had been sent to compliment him on his role in the peace negotiations and he assured them that he had never intended any personal disrespect to King Louis; though circumstances had involved him in opposition, he had always sought his esteem, and he hoped they would be the best of friends from now on. William was hatless during this interview, as he was 'not King in this country', and the conversation was relaxed. When Callières expressed his surprise that William, who had appeared to him to be so fond of war, did not wish to continue fighting, the King replied that he was no longer young, he needed repose after a lifetime of toil and he knew what misery people had suffered during the last war. During the conversation the French ambassador had studied this dedicated adversary with keen curiosity and was impressed, noting that he spoke French fluently, without a foreign accent, and that his discussions kept to the point. They had heard of his illness earlier that summer and observed with sympathy that he still looked thin and weak.

Though the formalities were now over, the festivities continued. Anne, Princess de Vaudemont, had arrived in The Hague to act as hostess for William, and after his audience with the French he took her to the theatre. He was relaxed, agreeable and enjoyed the great ball she organized for his birthday on 4/14 November at Noordeinde Palace, rewarding her with a gift of diamonds.

While the Dutch and English celebrated the Peace of Rijswijk, French spirits were low. Louis XIV accepted his losses with good grace, though he probably felt embarrassed when he had to face the now negligible James II after recognizing William. Ironically, James and Mary Beatrice arrived at Fontainebleau for their annual autumn stay with the French King at the same time as the courier who had come with news of the peace from Rijswijk. Having noticed that the French court had now begun referring to her husband's son-in-law as King William, Mary Beatrice treated Louis coldly. Perhaps harbouring a sense of guilt, Louis was particularly attentive, and in order to make amends promised that they would be allowed to stay at St Germain. To King William this was a violation of one of the treaty's terms, and he refused to pay Mary Beatrice's jointure, so she and James remained financially dependent on Louis.

Liselotte still hoped that William might be persuaded to marry her daughter, and a month later her lady-in-waiting Christina de Meyercrone wrote another long letter full of elaborate compliments to Portland, stressing the admiration Liselotte had always felt for this Prince. She raised this issue only in veiled terms in a postscript. Portland obligingly passed the letter to William who answered that, though he was flattered, such a marriage would not suit him. At forty-eight he was old and in poor health. He knew that England would like him to do his dynastic duty and attempt to ensure the royal line of succession. Even the ageing ex-King James II had fathered another child at fifty-nine, a daughter Louisa Maria, born to Mary Beatrice in June 1692, so maybe they thought fatherhood not beyond him. Yet even in an age where princesses were often resigned to being married to princes or sovereigns old enough to be their father, merely for the purpose of begetting an heir, William was probably too much of a gentleman to wish himself on some poor innocent who would probably be widowed before long.

TEN

'You have so little regard for my advice'

In the brief intervals between his other business during the autumn of 1697, William returned to Het Loo to hunt. By now his health was giving ever more cause for alarm. His legs worried him particularly, and he summoned Dr Govart Bidloo, his newly appointed physician-in-ordinary, to give him a full medical examination. The doctor was appalled to see the left foot swollen up above the ankle, the right one up to the heel, and the King told him that they had been inclined to swell in this way for the past two years, adding that they had worsened of late. When Bidloo questioned him about his general health, exercise and diet, William told him almost apologetically that everyone said he did himself an injury by hunting hard. However, if he did not take sufficient exercise, his respiration would be much impaired and then his feet would swell worse than ever; after hunting the swelling would abate. The doctor asked him whether he took proper care of himself after coming in from the hunt. William's reply was that since childhood he had been used to coming in after a good day's sport soaked to the knees, and it had never bothered him. Reluctant to break the habit of a lifetime, he remained equally careless in this aspect, his only concession to advancing years being to fortify himself with a more substantial meal and then nod off in his chair.

Many of his friends were worried by his over-indulgence at table, with large meals washed down by quantities of wine and strong ale. Once respected for his moderate drinking habits, now he made no secret of his evenings over the bottle, and 'debauches' after a good day's hunting. In his youth he had disapproved of his friends' drunken revels, but with age he became more tolerant, ready to turn a blind eye within reason, and evidently prepared to agree that a

215

little over-indulgence never did much harm. His close friendship with the pleasure-loving Albemarle did nothing to discourage these habits, as they dined together two or three times a week, sitting on for hours afterwards drinking and talking. William's doctors urged him to cut down on food and drink, but in vain. As he told Bidloo during his consultation at Het Loo, anyone over the age of thirty or forty should be his own physician, and as long as he ate well he was sure it would do him no harm.

Realizing it was hopeless to try to restrain this headstrong patient, Bidloo resigned himself to letting the King drink as much as he wanted. At the same time he prescribed that the patient's swollen legs should be rubbed night and morning with a flannel covered with a powder of crabs' eyes, flour and cummin seed, and hot poultices. William accepted the first part of the advice and continued to drink as before, but refused to follow the rest on the grounds that hot poultices kept him awake. When his other surgeon Dr Radcliffe examined William some weeks later in London, his legs were no better and he also had gout in his knee. The King would not be lectured about his drinking and eating habits, and Radcliffe was dismissed.

His swollen legs and general discomfort had made him give up all ideas of making the triumphal entry into London on horseback that Portland was planning for him. London had been preparing for a glorious reception for the King ever since news of the Peace of Rijswijk had reached the city on 14 September, the day that Matthew Prior presented the treaty to the Lords Justices at Whitehall. The guns of the Tower boomed out the good news, flags were hoisted all over town and church bells were rung. Vernon noted sardonically that for once everyone was in good humour, but it would be different one year hence, when they would have to pay more taxes, would find large numbers of troops dispersed about the country, would enjoy less consumption of their goods and get only poor prices for their cattle. However, nothing could dull the festive mood and the celebrations lasted for two months. One of the most magnificent was a vast bonfire organized by the Dutch ambassador in October, in front of his house in St James's Square. Using 140 barrels of pitch, it formed a pyramid on seven scaffolds; while it blazed trumpets sounded and two hogsheads of wine were consumed.

The climax of these celebrations was intended to mark the King's return from the continent, including a reception by the Lord Mayor and aldermen of London on horseback in scarlet gowns and gold chains. Plans for large triumphal arches were made but rejected at William's request, partly as they would block the view from the upper storeys of houses on the route, partly as his dislike of such shows had been increased by what he had heard of 'the gross excesses of flattery' to which the French went in honour of their King. However, his entry was suitably regal. Landing at Margate on 14 November, he spent the night at Canterbury and moved to Greenwich the next day. Albemarle and the Prince of Denmark rode in his coach with him, while Portland waited at Whitehall and Anne watched from a window of a city merchant's house near the Exchange at Cornhill. At Southwark the King and his retinue were greeted by the Lord Mayor in full regalia, and from there the procession moved slowly through the city, with grenadiers, two city marshals, the city sword bearer, the aldermen, recorder and sheriffs all on horseback in their scarlet gowns, followed by the gentleman usher of the black rod and other dignitaries. Then came the King himself in his coach, attended by the gentlemen pensioners, footmen and equerries, followed by a procession of nobility and gentry in horse-drawn coaches.

London had not seen such crowds for many a year. They cheered themselves hoarse, and a grateful King announced two days later that 2 December would be kept as a day of public thanksgiving and a holiday for all. He had intended to celebrate it himself by attending service in the newly consecrated St Paul's Cathedral, now almost completed after Wren had doubled the number of workmen on special orders sent from Holland. Its proportions astonished visitors, and one quipped that it should be capable of stopping all the corruption of London, provided the efficacy of the sermons preached there was commensurate with the building's size. However, William had to give up the idea of attending the inaugural service of thanksgiving there, as it was pointed out to him that all London would flock to St Paul's to see him; there would not be room for them all and every other church in the city would be empty. In the end he attended the service in his own chapel at Whitehall, where Burnet gave an effusive address. That evening there was another great firework display, costing £10,000, in front of Romney's house in St James's Square, where the King dined. Several people were injured, crushed by the crowds in the small square, and at least three died.

Next day Parliament met again. If the King had imagined that the ordinary people's support would be echoed by his House of Commons, he was soon disillusioned. 'Dutch William' was no hero to many of the upper classes, who had only reluctantly accepted him as king and who resented the high taxes he obliged them to pay. A succession of bad harvests had exacerbated the general economic situation after the relatively prosperous 1680s, and the money raised by extra taxation had apparently gone straight to the army abroad, to a few Dutch favourites at home or to war profiteers. Ironically, now that peace was signed and the King's mission had been accomplished, there was a general feeling that they no longer needed William. While it seemed pointless to expect him to abdicate, particularly as he was clearly in poor health and not likely to live much longer, they felt under no obligation to make life easy for him at this stage.

Moreover, the advent of peace raised the matter of what was to be done with the large armies built up during years of conflict. The Commons looked askance at keeping so many Dutch soldiers in the country, as well as regiments of Huguenot refugees. A standing army in peacetime, they argued, was a menace to the country's liberties and a drain on public finance, and people were tired of years of war and high taxation. The debate looked set to continue for a long time, much to William's irritation.

The sudden arrival of Tsar Peter in England proved a timely diversion. When he disembarked on 10 January 1698, he ordered all the ship's crew to go below deck before he would appear. Dining later that week with William at Kensington in public he suddenly got up and left the table, complaining that he could not eat while being stared at. Respecting his wishes, William himself went to see him in private and arranged for him to watch from a small room when he came to Anne's birthday ball at Kensington on 6 February. When William called on him he was confronted with Peter's pet monkey, who jumped angrily on him as soon as he sat down. To everyone's relief the Tsar moved to Deptford, to be near the shipyards that so fascinated him, and settled into Evelyn's house, Sayes Court, which he soon turned into something resembling a pigsty. When the King came to visit him there, hurried efforts were made to put at least one room into some sort of order. Afterwards an infuriated Evelyn had to ask Wren and the King's gardener to estimate the cost of repairing the havoc, and then sent the Treasury a bill for £150.

A mock naval battle was laid on for the Tsar during a visit to Spithead, but his request for a demonstration of keel-hauling was tactfully refused. By the standards of the day he was a heavy drinker, and everyone watched in amazement one evening as he downed a pint of brandy, a bottle of sherry and eight bottles of sack before going to the theatre. He left England on 23 April, gratefully accepting the parting gift of a yacht and in exchange handing William a ruby valued at £10,000, wrapped up in a piece of brown paper.

*   *   *

On the afternoon of 4 January 1698, a maid lit a charcoal fire to dry some linen in one wing of Whitehall Palace, which had been partly restored after the fire of 1691. Within minutes the room was ablaze, and fire spread quickly through the whole complex of buildings. A hard dry frost had set in two days earlier, and much to the chagrin of the firefighters the Thames was almost completely frozen over. The King was summoned from Kensington and watched from the Park while efforts were made to save at least parts of the palace by blowing up some of the buildings. Such action was in vain and by midnight his apartments, the new wing the Queen had occupied and most of the offices had been destroyed. Next morning most of Whitehall was in ashes, apart from the one building that had survived, Inigo Jones's Banqueting House.

Though the King no longer lived there, Whitehall had still been the centre of government and many priceless art treasures were lost.

When he visited the ruins the next day, he promised that if God would spare him long enough he would rebuild it, and make it much finer than before. Labourers came to clear away the rubble, and Wren was called in to survey the ruins with a view to rebuilding. He devised a scheme for a grander new palace, with the Banqueting House as its centrepiece and a long colonnade to connect it with the Houses of Parliament. After he was shown the plans, William decided it would not be prudent to spend so much on rebuilding a palace he had never liked.

However, the scheme reawakened his interest in other palaces. For Windsor Castle, which had become his favourite country residence over the years, Wren soon devised a new Italianate addition. Large areas of surrounding land were bought up to be laid out by the master-gardener of Versailles, M. Le Notre, who came over to inspect the area. Had William lived a few years longer, and had he been assured that funds were available, the plans would surely have been executed – but fate decreed otherwise.

With his active life as a soldier and commander now a thing of the past, William became increasingly preoccupied with more aesthetic pursuits. A well-established academy of painting at The Hague had done much to encourage art in Holland, and he gave some thought to founding a similar institution in London. But not for some seventy years and four reigns would this dream come to fruition.

William rarely returned to Hampton Court after Mary's death, only going there from Kensington for three or four days at a time when he could get away. Just before the fire at Whitehall, he had taken Portland with him to Windsor to discuss an important mission, namely that of making his friend the official ambassador to Paris. As his French was faultless and his manners polished, nobody could have been better suited for such a post. Moreover, for the delicate negotiations that lay ahead, a Dutchman was preferable to an English politician who, having broken his oath to James II, would have been unacceptable to Louis XIV.

Some at court believed that there was another reason for the choice of Portland. He had found it impossible to conceal his jealousy and resentment of Albemarle, and for the King this bitter rivalry between his best friends was too painful. Portland thought the King wanted him out of the way but when he left in mid-January, his departure delayed by the fire at Whitehall, the King wrote to reassure him that he was 'more touched by your going than you could possibly believe, and if you suffered as much at leaving me as I do when I see you go, I should be very happy'.[1]

William had spared no expense for Portland's mission. The embassy in France reportedly cost £40,000, and Portland was provided with a large personal retinue, comprising a gentleman of the horse, twelve pages and fifty-six footmen. In Paris he was lent the magnificent Hotel d'Auvergne in the Rue de la Planche, but it was inadequate for official entertaining until a state dining-room had been added on. Knowing better than to compete with French cuisine and wines, Portland ordered sirloins of English beef to be sent from Dover; from Calais they were despatched by messenger to ensure they were still fresh on arrival in Paris. He also ordered large quantities of finest quality Herefordshire cider and Burton ale, which the custom-house officers on the Seine thought was vin d'Espagne and would have seized it had it belonged to a lesser citizen. When he made his ceremonial entry in March, driving in full splendour through Paris on his way to Versailles, public interest was intense, and the irony of the occasion was not lost on the Parisians when they saw the arms of England on his coach. At least one observer wryly recalled those premature celebrations after reports of William's supposed death at the battle of the Boyne in 1690. On Portland's arrival at Versailles, Louis made the unprecedented gesture of speaking first, saying how glad he was to see so many English and French together.

Once settled in his new office, the ambassador's first priorities were threefold: to try to find a solution for the Spanish succession question; to talk Louis into dismissing James II from his dominions; and to ask him to be less accommodating towards Jacobite conspirators in France. At his initial audience Portland unwisely raised the last two questions first. When Louis denied that he had ever promised to send James away, Portland replied that there could therefore be no question of the £50,000 allowance being paid to

221

Mary Beatrice, and Louis answered coldly that he could not expel the royal exiles. Portland received a similar response when he mentioned the existence (or at least likelihood) of Jacobite agents and plotters at Versailles, as the King replied that he had no knowledge of any. William was annoyed by Louis's reaction, but felt it had been tactless of Portland to raise these questions so soon. What concerned him most was that Portland's bluntness regarding the question of James would make it harder to reach agreement over the even more pressing matter of the Spanish succession. It was a while before the French monarch and the ambassador from England reached this subject, which was soon to concern every statesman in Europe.

Carlos II, King of Spain, had been a sick man since his accession in 1665. Twice married, he still had no heir, and was thought to be at death's door. The future of the Spanish empire, comprising Spain, the Spanish Netherlands, part of Italy and North Africa and large territories in the New World, hung in the balance. In the sixteenth century Emperor Charles V had divided his Habsburg empire into a Spanish and an Austrian branch, and through a series of dynastic marriages both Louis XIV and the current Emperor could now put forward strong claims to the Spanish throne. For Louis XIV the fact that his wife Marie Therese, sister of Carlos II, had renounced her rights on marriage was irrelevant, since her dowry had never been paid by Spain, and he now claimed the throne on behalf of the dauphin. The Emperor had no intention of conceding to these French pretensions, and had two candidates of his own, namely his grandson by the daughter of his first marriage, the six-year-old son of the Elector of Bavaria, and his son Charles by his third marriage. As his daughter Maria Antonia had renounced her rights and those of her little son, the Emperor's son Charles was the rightful candidate in his father's eyes, but Madrid recognized neither of these claims and had already named the Electoral Prince of Bavaria as heir to Carlos II. England and the United Provinces supported the Madrid view, since the presence of either a Habsburg or a Bourbon on the Spanish throne would destroy the balance of power in Europe.

William knew the French King would certainly not allow the entire prize to escape him, and that if war was to be prevented on the death of Carlos then at least part of the Spanish inheritance should be conceded in advance to the dauphin. He was prepared to agree to this on condition that in no case should the Spanish Netherlands, the vital barrier, fall into French hands. He was also anxious to gain England a foothold in the Mediterranean, to counterbalance a potentially dangerous new French presence there. However, his main objective was to maintain peace in Europe, and Louis appreciated that however exhausted the continent might be by war, it was unlikely that France would be allowed to lay claim by stealth to the whole Spanish empire without resistance from the Allies. Over the years he had acquired great respect for King William's abilities as a statesman and military commander, and on 14 March he sent two ministers, Pomponne and de Torcy, to Portland to ascertain his sovereign's views on the Spanish succession.

The French King and the ambassador got on well, and each time Portland came to Versailles Louis paid him every possible mark of respect. Even more gratifying to the English embassy was the admiration the French nation obviously felt for King William. Portland reported to him that he was generally more esteemed, honoured and respected at the French court than in his own countries. No such reverence was apparently shown to James, who was now hardly mentioned at court.

Madame de Maintenon, a close friend of Mary Beatrice, refused to acknowledge Portland's presence, but not all James's supporters followed her example. The Duc de Lauzun, principal counsellor to King James, was civil to Portland to a degree that surprised others, and he was equally startled to learn that James, judging by the favourable manner in which everyone said he spoke of Portland, would not have been embarrassed to find himself in his company. The ambassador himself was anxious to avoid any such encounter; his efforts to do so made his mission to Paris rather a strain, and he was relieved when it came to an end in June. On 17 June he paid a farewell visit to Louis and they had a final long meeting. The French King had already given him his portrait set in diamonds and he took a friendly interest in Portland's journey home, urging him to see some of the beauties of France on the way. Ten days later Portland was back in London, to the general acclaim of court and ministers, who agreed that he had acquitted his role as ambassador with distinction.

According to Camile d'Hostun, Comte and Duc de Tallard, sent by Louis XIV as his own envoy to William in London in the spring of 1698, King William was generally hated by the English court and nobility, though popular enough with the people. Tallard had soon gleaned a general picture of how matters stood at court, with the help of a briefing by the French courtiers, Versailles being well-informed about the political situation in England. He considered that the Secretaries of State, apart from the Duke of Shrewsbury, were basically only clerks, employed in writing dispatches without having anything to do with the contents; councils only met for form's sake and important business was not discussed in them, and everything depended on the King alone. He was warned about the importance he gave to the Dutch at court, and especially to Portland and Albemarle, the latter's star being in the ascendant, while Portland had had his day. Louis and Tallard realized that Portland's abilities and authority for negotiation were limited, and they preferred to deal directly with the King instead.

Tallard went to London at the end of March, and was soon able to confirm his brief from Versailles. It was, so he said, the friendship the King showed the Dutch, the intimacy in which he lived with them and with foreigners, the benefits which he conferred on them and his obvious preference for the Earl of Albemarle, that had made the English nobility hate their King. Commenting later on the dispute between Portland and Albemarle, he told Versailles that when Portland returned, he would be given some suitable appointment, though in England nobody believed he had any real future in public office.

Tallard had rented the Duke of Ormonde's house in St James's Square and was soon highly sought-after by society in London. When William went to the Newmarket races in April, he and his entire court took pains to put on a show for his guest, in what was to be the most glittering visit Newmarket could recall, with the Prince of Denmark, the Dukes of Somerset, Grafton, Richmond and St Albans, the Earls of Marlborough, Albemarle, Jersey, Orkney and seven other earls all present. The Dutch ambassador came with all the other foreign ministers, and Shrewsbury had risen from his sickbed to be there. William had sent his hounds to the meeting and ordered falcons to be sent over from Holland. However, the principal interest at Newmarket, then as now, was horses, and the King was proud of his. Betting was heavy and fortunes changed hands, not just on horse-racing but also on cockfights. The King himself saw six of these one afternoon before going to the races.

Throughout these proceedings Tallard was the guest of honour. His place at table was next to the King, who graciously drank his health. They made a point of not talking business here, instead waiting until their return to London before negotiations began in earnest. At first Tallard was reserved and wary in his dealings with William, but he warmed to him as he got to know him better, and was very much impressed by his direct and straightforward manner. He reported to Louis XIV that the King was quick-witted, his judgement was sound and he would not be deceived if they tried play for time and drag discussions out too long; further, that he acted with great sincerity and should he enter into a treaty with France he could be trusted to keep his word. The treaty they had in mind was one dealing with the business of the Spanish Succession, for like Portland in Paris Tallard had been asked to sound out the King's opinions and see what solutions might be agreed on between London and Versailles. Talks continued intermittently throughout the summer, and when William left for the continent in July he gave Tallard an invitation to join him later on at Het Loo, since there was still much to discuss.

William's departure in the summer of 1698 was particularly resented by the English, who could see no reason for their King to leave the country now that the war was over. Increasingly lonely, frail and disposed to postpone unpleasant business, he was determined to escape from the irritation of English politics for as long as possible. On 29 July he left from Margate, making no effort to conceal his joy at going back to his beloved Holland. Reaching Het Loo on 6 August he devoted himself to his beloved hunting, spending twelve hours a day in the saddle, until his entourage were exhausted. Courtiers who saw a tired, frail-looking man in London would have hardly recognized their sovereign as the same person, intoxicated with the thrill of being back in his old home and the freedom of doing what he really enjoyed. In September they left for Celle, with a view to arranging a possible match between the Duke of Gloucester and Sophia Dorothea, granddaughter of Electress Sophie of Hanover, to strengthen the Protestant succession and bind Hanover and England closer together. Sophie and her eldest son George Lewis, Elector of Hanover, came to Celle, and William was keen to make the acquaintance of the man who would almost certainly be King of England in due course, should the frail Duke of Gloucester fail to survive his mother.*

Before the King had left Het Loo for Celle the question of the succession to the throne of Spain had at last been agreed, and the First Partition Treaty between England, France and the United Provinces was signed in September. The Electoral Prince of Bavaria was the chosen candidate; to him was allotted Spain, the Spanish Netherlands and the colonies, while Naples and Sicily went to the dauphin, and Milan and the Milanese to the Emperor's son Charles. That neither the Emperor nor Spain would quietly sit back and accept this division of territories was regarded by both Louis and William as of little relevance. All that mattered to them was that war had almost certainly been avoided.

William had not consulted any of his English ministers before making up his mind. Chancellor Somers was only informed when the treaty was already drafted, and although he and other Whig ministers hastily wrote to William expressing their doubts as to whether the proposed division of the Spanish inheritance would help to guarantee the peace of Europe, the King went ahead. He had his misgivings, acknowledging to Tallard that they were making some arbitrary decisions in matters of which they were not the masters. At the same time he also raised the question of James's position at

* The Duke of Gloucester was dead within two years (see p. 236), and the Elector succeeded William's sister, Queen Anne, as King George I in 1714.

Versailles, but unlike his ambassador he waited until the Spanish Succession question was safely out of the way first. He chose his words with care, making it clear that he pitied King James, but reiterating that 'in truth there could not be two Kings of England'.[2] Louis was obdurate, insisting that 'Ill fortune cannot take the title or quality of King from a person who has once received it.'[3]

While at Het Loo William and Albemarle had an argument, and the young man retired from court to go and sulk in the country. The occasion of this row was Portland's triumph, his last, over his rival in the matter of William's Dutch Secretariat. Since Huygens's retirement, more of these duties had been taken over by Albemarle until now, at Portland's suggestion, the King appointed his wife's former secretary Abel Tassin d'Allonne to the post. Everyone regarded this as a snub for Albemarle. Even William's great indulgence was strained by his petulant behaviour, and although he had promised Albemarle's mother that her son would be enrolled that year in the highly distinguished Equestrian Order of Holland, he now refused to allow the ceremony to be given immediate priority, telling Heinsius that 'on account of the formalities' it could not be done before his departure for England.

Thanks to the Earl of Jersey, Portland's successor as ambassador in Paris, a compromise was found. From now on d'Allonne remained Dutch Secretary, but instructions were given to him by Albemarle and not by the King. Tallard expected this to be a source of trouble, as d'Allonne was a close ally of Portland and would not see Albemarle, but at least peace was restored in the royal household. When the King arrived back in England at the beginning of December, Albemarle was duly restored to favour and appeared at William's side once again.

In the autumn of 1698 English jealousy of the Dutch, restrained during the war by joint Anglo-Dutch interests, rose to the surface again, and in this mood William's fourth House of Commons awaited his return. A general election that summer had returned a House with a strong Tory majority which opposed the war, did not support the maintenance of a large army and was deeply suspicious of the Dutch. Though at the start of his reign William had regarded the Tories as the natural allies of the monarchy, he had come to rely increasingly on the Whigs who supported British involvement on the continent while their opponents preferred a 'Little England' naval and colonial strategy against France. By now the Tories were ready to oppose the crown at every opportunity, and when they arrived in London they were angered to learn that the King was still in Holland. When he came back and assembled Parliament on 6 December, the following week, it was the least cooperative Commons of his reign. They proposed cutting his experienced army to seven thousand, and insisted that every soldier should be a native-born Englishman.

The King was shattered at this proposal to strip England of what he saw as its necessary defences, and considered it nothing less than sheer ingratitude to the foreigners who had fought for them, like the French Huguenots and the King's own Dutch troops. In despair he seriously considered going back to Holland for good. His ministers did not believe he was serious, until in January he wrote out an abdication address in his own hand, declaring his intention to return to Holland and requesting that a regency council should be appointed to govern the country in his absence.

> I came into this kingdom, at the desire of the nation, to save it from ruin, and to preserve your religion, your laws, and liberties. And, for that end, I have been obliged to maintain a long and burthensome war for this kingdom, which, by the grace of God, and the bravery of this nation, is at present ended in a good peace, under which you may live happily and in quiet, provided you will contribute towards your own security, in the manner I had recommended to you, at the opening of the sessions.
>
> But seeing to the contrary, that you have so little regard to my advice, that you will expose yourselves to imminent ruin, I hold it neither just nor reasonable that I should be the witness of it. . . . Though I feel obliged to withdraw out of this kingdom I shall always preserve the same regard for its welfare and interests, and should I ever judge that my presence was necessary to its defence I should always be as ready to risk my life for the common good as I have been in the past.[4]

The Lord Chancellor, Baron Somers, persuaded him to reflect, and a sense of duty prevailed, as it had been his life's work to save Europe from the hegemony of France. Another peace treaty was signed at Carlowicz in February 1699 between the Austrian and Turkish governments, with English and Dutch diplomats working as mediators. A successful division of the Spanish empire had been secured, with every likelihood that there would be no further war.

Unfortunately this success was rapidly overtaken by events. Even as the treaty was being signed, the seven-year-old Electoral Prince of Bavaria, named as principal heir to the Spanish crown in the first Partition Treaty, was dying at Brussels. One afternoon he was perfectly well, then he was suddenly racked by vomiting and convulsions in the evening, sank into a coma and died early the next morning. The news caused alarm throughout Europe, as the throne would now have to go to a Habsburg or a Bourbon, and a new treaty would have to be negotiated. To the English Parliament it meant nothing, and they would not change their minds about the army. William was in despair over their apparent indifference to affairs on mainland Europe.

However, at the end of January Tallard reported to Versailles that the King of England no longer actively opposed any move to reduce his troops. The Earl of Portland, he said, had told him that a younger and more assertive King William might have stood his ground, but in his present weary frame of mind he was less concerned, and a few days later the reluctant monarch appeared in the House of Lords to sign the disbanding Bill. With admirable self-restraint, he wrote a message which was laid before the House by Lord Ranelagh, his Master of the Horse and Paymaster of the Forces, declaring that he would send the troops away immediately unless, out of consideration for their King, they might 'find a way for continuing them longer in his service'.[5] At first they wavered, but under pressure from the Commons stood firm. William was bitter, declaring that if only he had had a son himself, the troops would have stayed in England. There would be no reprieve, and in March his beloved Dutch Blue Guards, who had fought under him in every major battle of his career, marched through London on their way to embark for the journey back to Holland, as crowds – who presumably felt more gratitude to them than did their politicians – turning out to cheer them.

In a morose frame of mind and weakened by a winter of poor health, the King went to Newmarket in April for a rest. Several English noblemen accompanied him, but Portland excused himself on the grounds of ill-health, though everyone said there must have been other reasons. After his return from Paris, Portland had found that Albemarle had become almost indispensable to the sovereign, even moving into apartments adjoining the King's at Kensington which had always been Portland's. The King continued to shower favours on the young man regardless of public opinion, buying him a country estate and promoting him in the army. As Albemarle rose in the King's favour so his popularity with the English fell, and all the old gossip about their relationship was revived.

Portland had now had enough. The tension between himself and Albemarle had reached such a pitch that Tallard, who knew of Louis's admiration for Portland, was tempted to intervene on his behalf. A suggestion to Louis to this effect brought a warning to stay clear of any such private court intrigues, and to devote his attention instead to the negotiations about the Spanish Succession that Tallard had embarked on with Portland after the death of the Electoral Prince. William found it increasingly hard to keep the peace between his friends, and while he was at Newmarket Portland decided he would leave court life.

The King expected to find Portland at Kensington as usual on his return in April. When he failed to appear, William wrote to say how keen he was to see him again. Next day he received a letter from Portland's house at Windsor announcing his immediate decision to retire. The King's first reaction was measured, reminding him that the welfare and peace of Europe could depend on his negotiations with Tallard. Portland came to Kensington to justify his decision and to hand over the keys of office, which the King refused to accept. When he returned to Windsor, a letter from William followed him, begging him to reconsider. He also sent d'Allonne to Windsor after him to try to bring him back, but in vain, and on 5 May d'Allonne returned with Portland's keys.

Nevertheless the sovereign and his lifelong companion never made a total break. Though their old friendship was now a thing of the past, they still dined together occasionally and kept in touch about progress with the Second Partition Treaty. William continued to take an affectionate interest in his old friend's children and grandchildren, especially after the lonely widower remarried. Maria, the new Countess of Portland, whose first marriage had also ended in widowhood, began to raise a second family while her husband spent most of his remaining years in contented retirement at Byfield House, Windsor. As Ranger of Windsor Great Park and Supervisor of the Royal Gardens, he still earned an annual salary of £2,600 and annual expenses of £10,000.

With Albemarle at his side, William left England on 3 June, his main concern being to seek agreement for a second Partition Treaty. It had been drafted in negotiations between Tallard and Portland, and provisional agreement was reached a few days later, with Spain and the Indies being ceded to Archduke Charles, while the dauphin would take all the Spanish territories in Italy. William hoped Austria might accept the Treaty this time, but the Emperor at once refused on the grounds that there would be too much French influence in Italy. Amsterdam initially supported him, to the embarrassment of William, who was being pressed for Dutch agreement by the French, but conceded in January 1700 and the Treaty was signed by England, the Republic and France in March. Minor exchanges of territory took place involving Lorraine, Milan, Naples and the two Sicilies, designed largely to prevent the French from acquiring complete control of Italy.

While these negotiations continued throughout the summer of 1699, the King spent much time hunting at Het Loo with Albemarle in constant attendance. In England he was exhausted, but in Holland his spirits always revived. By now he was slowing down, but traces of the young William and his zest for life showed through when he set foot on Dutch soil once again. Nevertheless his health was deteriorating; his legs were bothering him again, and the slightest change in temperature could bring on a feverish chill. He was finding some of the hunters in his Dutch stables too much for him, and orders were sent to England to find 'more temperate' mounts. An aide, Henry Ireton, reported that the King could only ride animals 'with a very easy motion in their gallop'.⁶ Although he had many fine steeds in his stable, by now he was 'almost quite in foot', a considerable restriction for someone who was already so lame. Tallard had noticed in England that after a day's hunting the King had to be carried upstairs. When London's most celebrated physician, Dr Radcliffe, was summoned to Holland to attend Albemarle's mother, it was rumoured that he had really gone to attend the ailing King. However, William, still believing he was his own best doctor, refused to be fussed over.

He returned to England on 27 October, arriving at Margate. Suddenly he took a renewed interest in his domestic building projects, on the assumption that if the English would not spend their national wealth on armies, it might as well produce some splendour instead. At Hampton Court work on the new buildings was speeded up, while in the park a hare and pheasant covert was planted. William's forty-ninth birthday was celebrated at court in fine style. In the morning he was complimented by the nobility and gentry; in the afternoon he dined with Anne and George at Kensington and then watched a concert, and in the evening there were bonfires, illuminations and a ball at St James's in his honour. Five days later he held a military review for the Duke of Gloucester, and while the little boy watched the King and Prince George inspected the three troops of Horse Guards in Hyde Park in the presence of their commanders, Ormonde, Rivers and Albemarle. In November the King asked Parliament to pay Prince George's mortgage debts in their entirety. While most of the Tories attacked this request, after a series of debates the measure was approved in January 1700.

Before Christmas William began to entertain regularly at Kensington, for the first time since Mary's death. On 27 November the first of a series of 'apartments', or gambling parties, was held. Members of Parliament, their wives, daughters and others were among the guests at his drawing-rooms, which he would enter from his own apartments, generally leading in Princess Anne who acted as his hostess. His doctors were anxious that the smoke from so many candles would be bad for him, but he remained comparatively unaffected. After an exchange of bows and curtsies, people sat down to cards, basset and other gambling games. William, who still detested ceremony, succeeded in keeping the atmosphere relaxed and informal, walking about and chatting to his guests, who were asked to remain seated when he approached, and playing a few hands at each table. For the safety of the winners, several small guardhouses were erected throughout the park, lest any opportunist footpads might be lurking in the shadows at the end of the evening.

Nevertheless there were those who felt that William had now effectively lost contact with the English. Even among the common people his popularity had fallen, mainly because of his constant journeys overseas, even though the war was over. Politically he was almost isolated, now that the Whig ministers who had presided over the government in the last years of the war had gone. A new, much weaker ministry of mediocre politicians could not handle the aggressively Tory House of Commons, and that autumn they mis-handled the matter of the King's grants in Ireland to his favourites. The House of Commons had already tried to settle the matter in February 1699, when a Bill was introduced to annul all grants of crown property made since the revolution. Some of William's ministers artfully stopped the Bill from going any further by suggesting that it did not go far enough, and should be widened to include *all* grants of crown lands made since the Restoration. As many Tory leaders in the House owed their fortunes to the lavishness of Charles II or James II, they dropped the Bill. But William's ministers were now unable to save him from the humiliation of an inquest on his generosity to his friends.

After the pacification of Ireland in 1691, more than a million Irish acres had been forfeited. Some had been returned to their former owners, but the rest had been presented by William as personal gifts to those who had served him in Ireland, and to his favourites, Albemarle, Portland and Romney. A commission of seven MPs was now appointed by the House of Commons to inquire into the grants, and from the outset the majority was openly hostile to the King, especially after discovering that he had given 90,000 acres of the Irish estates, formerly belonging to King James II, to Betty Villiers. Three of the commissioners objected, saying it was an insult to William. The parliamentary debates lasted all winter, coming to an end in February 1700 when the House voted that the grants should be taken back and put into the hands of trustees, so that the national debts could be paid out of the revenue. The King made a last futile effort to justify the grants, and in April 1700 Parliament sent fourteen commissioners to Ireland to dispose of the forfeited estates there, the money raised being put towards payment of the debts incurred by the state during the war.

Adding insult to injury, the House then voted that an address should be presented to the King asking him to demand the resignations of all foreigners except Prince George from his councils. It was too much for the long-suffering William, who hurried down from Kensington to the Treasury, put on his robes and crown, and prorogued Parliament before they knew what was happening. He was too angry to make even the shortest of speeches from the throne. Defiantly he announced that the Order of the Garter would be given to Albemarle, ordering that the installation should be performed with greater splendour than had ever been known before and that all foreign ambassadors should be invited. The ceremony duly took place on 5 June.

Everyone saw that the King looked pale and feverish, and he was longing to get away as soon as possible to Holland. In Scotland too, animosity against the King was stronger than ever, after the collapse of the Scottish colonial adventure at Darien. His northern kingdom was on the verge of revolution; his own evident impatience and lack of sympathy had done nothing to improve the situation. Despite an address the previous October from the desperate leaders of Scotland, he had refused to call his Scottish Parliament earlier than March, and then put it off again. The Scots sent a delegation to Kensington at the end of March, but William, about to leave to hunt at Hampton Court, received them coldly and dismissed them after a few minutes. One delegate was determined not to have his country's grievances brushed aside in this careless manner, and told the King that the address they brought him was not just a petition for

Parliament but also evidence of the deep discontent in Scotland. The King replied that that would be seen when the Parliament met in May. But when the Scottish Parliament met on 24 May, it was for just a week, and the King, who had ordered Holyrood House in Edinburgh to be fitted up for his reception earlier that year, was conspicuous by his absence.

Such an offhand attitude from their sovereign only added to Scottish discontent and fury. The King's patience with his northern kingdom was now exhausted, and he was concerned that the whole business was unnecessarily delaying his departure from England. It was the selfishness of a sick man, tortured by persistent colds and fevers, swollen legs and constipation. After seeing him in June, Dr Radcliffe told the court that he thought the King could barely live three months. James Vernon, under-secretary to Shrewsbury, who went to see William every day, told him to go as soon as possible to Het Loo. William was sure he would get better if only the doctors would stop giving him remedies. His English doctors, unable to agree on the most effective treatment, carried their arguments into the sickroom. Radcliffe thought William had dropsy, and prescribed purges and asses' milk; another doctor, Sir Thomas Millington, said such treatment was completely wrong and suggested garlic. Millington wanted to call in Dr Hutton, the King's first physician, for consultation, but at the mere mention of his name Radcliffe went out of the room in a passion, and they broke up resolving nothing.

In the end William made his own decision and after a final inconclusive consultation with his doctors in the first week of July he left Hampton Court for Holland. The next day he sailed from Margate, arriving on 27 July at The Hague after a stormy crossing, during which he was very sick. Once he arrived in The Hague he began to feel better, and when the Earl of Jersey saw him at Het Loo in August he noted with satisfaction that the King seemed very well, except for his legs, which were still swollen.

Yet another family tragedy was about to overshadow his visit. Soon after a party for his eleventh birthday on 25 July the Duke of Gloucester became seriously ill. It was believed that he had smallpox, although his doctors could not agree in their diagnosis, and he died on the morning of 30 July. The King had always been very fond of his namesake and nephew, and only two months earlier he had given him Mary's apartments at Kensington. London went into mourning, and the crush to see the lying-in-state of Anne's only child and heir was so great that the Lord Chamberlain ordered that only persons dressed in mourning should be admitted. He was interred at Westminster Abbey on 9 August at 9 p.m., a guard of honour lining the route with lighted torches in their hands.

William was in Holland when the news was brought to him. Though he had not expected the frail lad to reach maturity, he was so stricken with grief that he remained in seclusion for two days, shutting himself up in his room to be alone in his abject misery. He wrote to Anne:

> I do not believe it necessary to use many words to tell you of the surprise and sorrow with which I learned of the death of the Duke of Gloucester. It is so great a loss for me and all England that my heart is pierced with affliction. I assure you that on this occasion and on any other I shall be glad to give you any marks of my friendship.[7]

Throughout Europe speculation began immediately about the future of the English throne. In January Anne's seventeenth pregnancy had terminated with yet another miscarriage, and while she still hoped for children she never conceived again. For five years she had been so lame that she could not climb stairs or stand straight, and at thirty-five she was an invalid unable to walk unaided for any distance. It was said that, like her husband, she sought solace from the bottle, and Liselotte wrote to the Electress of Hanover that Princess Anne was 'said to drink so heavily that her body is quite burnt up. She will never have any living children, and King William's health is so delicate that he can't live long. So you will soon sit on your grandfather's throne.'[8]

In England some had not given up hope that William might consider remarrying again and providing England with an heir. There were several potential candidates: the Princess of Denmark;

the daughter of the Landgrave of Hesse-Cassel; and the widow of Hendrik Casimir (who died in 1696), who was the mother of Friesland's Stadholder Jan Willem Friso. Though France's opinion counted for nothing in England (apart from the Jacobite faction), the French state was eager to champion the rights of the Prince of Wales at St Germain as heir, and should he die without leaving an heir himself, to plead for the Savoy family whose duke had married the daughter of Charles I's sister Henrietta. Trusting that his people would prefer a prince from Germany than one from France, William hoped that the Hanoverians, as the immediate Protestant successors after Anne, would be recognized by Parliament as soon as possible.

As he was not prepared to trust France, William needed no persuasion to endorse the Hanoverian claim. Dowager Electress Sophie of Hanover, a granddaughter of King James I, was the senior Protestant claimant. She and her daughter Sophie Charlotte, wife of the Elector of Brandenburg, visited William at Het Loo in October. It was no easy task for William to convince Sophie that she should accept the succession to the English throne for the sake of Protestant Europe. At sixty-eight, she was reluctant to leave her country and family, and though she readily admitted that he had made many foolish mistakes she still felt a sense of loyalty to her hapless cousin ex-King James. But William persuaded her, promising Sophie Charlotte that he would also support her husband in his elevation from Elector of Brandenburg to enthronement as the first King of Prussia.

Duty accomplished, and with the knowledge that the English succession would be safely in Protestant hands after he and his sister-in-law were dead, William left Het Loo to return to England. He had relented in his attitude to Scotland, and plans were made for him to go to Edinburgh for the opening of Parliament there in October. His presence north of the border, he was assured, would do nothing but good. However, events in Europe would not only frustrate his plans to pay even the briefest of visits, but were also about to precipitate one final crisis in foreign affairs during his reign.

ELEVEN

'You can bear me up no longer'

By the beginning of the eighteenth century King William was ageing fast, and there were times when he longed for eternal rest. From 1699 onwards he wrote very few letters in person; those in his own hand and not dictated to secretaries were executed in a shaky, weary sprawl. As he was increasingly lame, his attendants usually had to help him up and down stairs in the sedan chair. Like many elderly people he clung tenaciously to the old days. There was an air of comfortable familiarity to be found in meeting and dealing with those whom he already knew, unless they had displeased him in the past, but newer faces were less assured of a welcome.

His meagre appetite for food had not changed, and he ate even less in his last years. Breakfast was usually a dish of chocolate, and he rarely touched 'confections or sweetmeats'. He enjoyed fish, stews, vegetables and fresh fruit, taken with soft drinks, white wine, bottled beer (well iced except in winter) or cider. Bidloo suggested it would do his constitution good if he had more sherry, claret and madeira. Though he was no drunkard, the King now tended to indulge more, especially on feast days. Whenever he was at Het Loo on his last visits to Holland visiting friends could always be sure of hospitality and a good carousing atmosphere till the early hours, and William's health always improved rapidly at such times – a sure sign that a little merriment did more good than harm.

He was always fastidious about personal matters and hygiene. Table equipment and cutlery had to be spotlessly clean and carefully set out, with food properly prepared so that hot things were hot and cold things cold. He washed his feet once a week in Spanish wine, and insisted on a clean shirt at least once a day.

Outdoor leisure activities still occupied his spare time. He continued to hunt, shoot, fish and walk as much as his failing strength would permit, and sometimes played bowls on the green in his private gardens. Gentle exercise helped to reduce the swelling in his legs, and each spring when the weather became milder he went outside whenever possible. Where indoor activities were concerned he was interested in adding to his art collection, and his collection of microscopes testified to an interest in science. His own private library was a continual source of personal satisfaction, and account books show regular bills of £40 to his bookseller, with books on religion, travel and history, among them Paffenrode's *Wars of the Greeks and Romans* and Plot's *Natural History of Oxfordshire*, on his shelves. During a spell of ill-health when he was confined to bed, Dr Radcliffe was impressed to find him absorbed in an English translation of Aesop's *Fables*.

Once a week, as he had done since youth, he checked his household accounts. While casual acquaintances and most of his ministers found him prudent if not downright tight with his money, he was unfailingly generous to those in his immediate circle, not just Portland and Albemarle but also his devoted valets, clerks and pages.

*   *   *

For the war leader who had become a man of peace in his declining years, there was to be another prescience of coming conflict. On 1 November he learnt of the long-expected death eleven days earlier of King Carlos II of Spain, who had left his entire inheritance to Philippe, Duc d'Anjou. The immediate question was whether Louis XIV, Philippe's grandfather, would stand by the Second Partition Treaty that had named Archduke Charles of Austria heir to King Carlos and handed the Spanish possessions in Italy to the dauphin. After discussions with Madame de Maintenon and his son the dauphin, Louis XIV decided to accept the terms of the will, and presented his grandson Philippe to the Spanish ambassador and the whole court as the new King of Spain. It was clear that the Emperor would probably not accept this settlement, and Louis was said to be ready to defend his grandson's claim by war if necessary.

Louis hoped that England and the United Provinces might be persuaded to accept his grandson as King Philip V of Spain, and wrote to the States-General in December that he had acted in the spirit of the Partition Treaty to preserve peace. He was confident that they would be grateful to him for sacrificing to the common good the considerable states which he could have added to his crown, and he made it known that the crowns of France and Spain would never be united. A sceptical William, who feared the only logical outcome would be a Franco-Spanish world empire, was not prepared to accept this assurance, and warned the more trusting English and Dutch as much. The Grand Alliance was now no more than a name, and England and Holland had to resist the French King's aggrandizement. Early in 1701 the Spanish Regency Council rashly invited Louis XIV to govern Spain for the time being on behalf of his inexperienced sixteen-year-old grandson. Proclaiming that he no longer recognized the Pyrenees as a national border, he sent a contingent of troops to occupy the fortresses in Flanders. By the terms of an agreement between the Dutch and the Governor of the Spanish Netherlands, Maximilian of Bavaria, these had been previously garrisoned by troops from the States of Holland. Now they were under orders to leave at a day's notice, and every European power except one was shocked by this brazen occupation at a time of peace.

At Westminster the Whigs, then in opposition, viewed France's attitude with particular alarm. French power would now be firmly entrenched throughout much of Europe, with a stranglehold on trade throughout the continent. The Whigs had several merchants among their number, and to them war seemed the only way to bring King Louis to account. As France also held most of the Channel ports, a new era of Jacobite plots and threats of invasion seemed likely, and as the country had recently been stripped of much of its army it seemed woefully unprepared.

A general election had just returned a Parliament with a small Tory majority. To William's dismay, the Tories seemed determined to turn a blind eye to this threat to European stability. Instead they chose to dwell on the immediate past, in particular by supporting the House of Lords' indirect attack on the King whereby they tried to impeach Portland for his role in negotiating the Second Partition Treaty without consulting Parliament. Portland did not improve the situation by his defence in the House in which he named four ministers as having been equally involved. It was clear to everyone that the Englishmen had been brought in too late to do more than rubber-stamp a treaty that they considered, in the light of subsequent events, to have been disastrous for European peace. The House of Commons gave their support to the Lords' attack on one of the detested Dutchmen, and only one voice was raised in his defence.

The impeachment of the three Whig ministers held most responsible – Somers, Orford and Montagu, Lord Halifax – was still being discussed in Parliament when the English people lost patience. Apart from following the Dutch example in recognizing the Duc d'Anjou as King of Spain, Parliament had done nothing about the approaching European crisis. The Kentish people, more worried than most by rumours of French invasion as they would be the first to be threatened, were quick to voice their anger and composed a petition begging the House to stop quarrelling, to provide for the safety of the country and to vote supplies allowing the King to come to the defence of England's allies. When the petition was handed in on 8 May, the furious MPs had the five gentlemen who presented it handed over at once to the Sergeant-at-Arms and detained in the gatehouse.

Such high-handed reaction could have had no better effect from William's point of view, and the Kentish petition was followed by a far more impressive memorial, drafted by the satirist and journalist Daniel Defoe. As 'the voice of the people', he condemned the Kentish petitioners' arrest, attacking Parliament for its inertia and shortsightedness, for illegally detaining the Kentish petitioners, for failing to vote supplies, for demanding that the King should remove his ministers on as yet unproven accusations, and for deserting the Dutch when the French were at their gates. He demanded that if the French King would not listen to reason King William should declare war on him. Englishmen, he concluded, were no more slaves to parliaments than to a king. Having signed his memorial 'Legion –

for we are many', he presented it in person at the head of a delegation of sixteen gentlemen. The House was too astonished to arrest him, but continued to quarrel all the same.

In mid-May the States-General sent a petition to William to ask for English assistance in the face of growing French aggression in Flanders. The hated Avaux had arrived at The Hague in March to try to negotiate a separate treaty between France and the Republic. The States reported to William that they had refused to enter into separate negotiations, as England and the Republic had a common interest in keeping the general peace, but they desperately needed support. France was daily strengthening its position in Flanders, working hard to secure allegiance from the former allies of England and Holland and trying to foment discord in Germany.

William sent a copy of this document to both Houses. The Commons were still too preoccupied with their impeachment proceedings to take much notice, and spent the next six weeks arguing over petty questions of procedure with the Lords. Having a better grasp of priorities, the latter rose to the occasion, sending an address to the King asking him to implement the treaties between England and Holland and to open negotiations for a triple alliance between the Dutch, the English and the Emperor. The King reported to Heinsius that he had a partial mandate from Parliament for a war he had tried to avert.

Before he could sail for Holland and begin consulting with the Allies, there was some unfinished business to be settled by Parliament, namely the impeachment of the three ministers and the question of the English succession. The first was dealt with at the beginning of June by the Lords, who acquitted each in turn. The second was resolved on 12 June, when the King gave his royal assent to the Act of Settlement, naming the House of Hanover as heirs after Anne to the English crown, and including eight articles providing for new limitations on the royal power, several clearly dictated by Parliament's resentment of William's Dutch ways. A future monarch could not be allowed to leave the country without Parliament's permission, and his or her chief advisers had to be English. Too ill and weary to argue, William thanked the House gracefully.

Anne's heiress, and therefore second in succession to the throne, was Dowager Electress Sophie. At seventy she was almost twice Anne's age, but she was in considerably better health and it was quite likely that the elder woman would outlive the younger.* Her eldest son and heir George Lewis was Elector, and though he had divorced his wife in scandalous circumstances they had a son† and daughter, the son being expected to continue the family line. King William proposed to bring the Elector to England for a visit in the autumn of 1701, but his plans were largely defeated by Anne's spurious claim that she was pregnant again and the excitement would be bad for her. The Tories had tried to convince her that William planned to establish the Prince as his heir and to supplant her as well as the Prince's mother.

The King was not only tired and unwell but also increasingly lonely. Most of his old friends and relatives were either dead or living in Holland; like him, most were in such indifferent health that they were unlikely to see him again. Apart from Albemarle, he had nobody in whom to confide regularly. Portland was generally there in a supportive role, though the old bonds had lapsed. He had always felt ill at ease with the etiquette and obsequiousness of court life in London, finding the simplicity and informality that prevailed at The Hague far more to his taste. This resentment of state and ceremony, the management of a large household of fawning officers, functionaries and servants, increased with age. Without family and with so few friends, life in England was drab indeed. In July Albemarle married Gertruida Quirina van der Duyn, the daughter of one of the King's Dutch officers. Though he may have felt a twinge of sadness at seeing his closest friend and helpmeet marry, William generously gave the couple his blessing and provided the penniless bride with jewels and a dowry.

---

* Both women died in the summer of 1714, Sophie in June and Anne in August, seven weeks later.
† Later King George II.

On 14 July William arrived at The Hague, accompanied by Marlborough as ambassador extraordinary. While relations between both had often been difficult in the past, William knew that Marlborough, the husband of Anne's closest friend, would become the most important man in England outside the royal family, and for all his faults he was surely one of the most capable. It made sense to involve him more deeply in European affairs, and to train him as the future leader of the Allied coalition against France. He left it to the earl, therefore, after presenting him at The Hague to the foreign ambassadors, to begin talks with Heinsius and others, while he went to inspect the Dutch armies that he knew he would never lead in person again.

William's Dutch and English friends were reluctant to let him go. The alarming decline in his health was apparent to all, and they noticed that he was sparing himself public appearances as much as possible. People in the Dutch capital who had not seen him for months were horrified by the sight of him. His legs were now so swollen that he could only walk with difficulty, and the painful gout that had attacked his left hand since March made it equally hard for him to ride, as he had trouble holding the reins. After the physical ordeal of the inspection tour he was exhausted, retiring to Het Loo to rest and following negotiations at The Hague from a distance.

Despite their recent differences Portland had softened again towards his old friend, whom he sensed was not much longer for this world. While William was at The Hague, Portland's son Lord Woodstock came to see him, to pay his respects and bring news of the family, including a new baby half-sister, the child of Portland's second marriage.

Meanwhile Avaux had made a last effort to reach agreement on the partition of the Spanish empire, but the French terms were unacceptable to the Allies and the ambassador was recalled to Paris on 11 August. This move lent added urgency to the Allied discussions, and a few weeks later, on 7 September 1701, a new Grand Alliance was signed at The Hague. With the aim of securing the Spanish possessions in Italy and the Spanish Netherlands – the Dutch Barrier – for the Emperor, the Republic undertook to raise an army of 120,000 men, England 40,000 men and the Emperor 90,000. The Allies also pledged themselves to ensure by concerted action that the crowns of France and Spain should never be united, and it was decided that other European princes should be invited to join them. They left the door open for peace by negotiation, but it was firmly closed by an obdurate Louis XIV.

*   *   *

At St Germain Europe's most famous exile, now aged sixty-seven, had been unwell for several months. In the spring of 1701 the former King James had a minor stroke but made a fair recovery. That summer Liselotte observed sardonically that he would 'do himself a mischief one day with his boundless piety'; a couple of days earlier 'he spent so long kneeling and praying that he fainted clean away, and he was unconscious for so long that everyone thought his last hour had come'.[1] Less than a fortnight after the Grand Alliance was signed in September, James took to his bed and knew he would not recover. On his deathbed Louis told him that the Prince of Wales, aged thirteen, would now, in his eyes, be the rightful King of England. After hearing this royal promise to recognize his son, and declaring that he pardoned all who had injured him, especially the Prince of Orange and Princess Anne, James died.

Louis's recognition of the Prince of Wales as King James III was the most calculated insult he could have offered William. The news, sent to him at Het Loo by Lord Manchester, the English ambassador to Paris, arrived as he was dining with friends and he was furious. Instructions were at once sent off to Lord Manchester to leave France as ambassador, and to London to expel his opposite number Poussin. Whigs and Tories were united in their condemnation of France, and Jacobites who took it upon themselves to act as heralds and proclaim the accession of the young Catholic king were pelted with rotten eggs in the streets.

In spite of this angry reaction, William was human enough to spare a thought for the dead man, the father-in-law who had perhaps been his own worst enemy. After Mary's death James had forbidden his court in exile to go into mourning. William refused to be so ungracious himself, and ordered partial, or violet, mourning as if for a relative. Princess Anne had received a letter from Mary Beatrice, telling her that her father had expected the court to go into full mourning, as she herself had already done. However, when William's instructions arrived she had to take down the signs of observance from her apartments at St James's. She did so, grumbling at 'the ill-natured, cruel proceeding of Mr Caliban', complaining at being made to 'do so monstrous a thing as not to put my lodgings in mourning for my father'.[2]

Anne's indignation at William's decision only to put on violet mourning was not shared by most of the English. Their fury was directed at Louis's interference in the succession to their crown. He had gone back on his word given at Rijswijk, and at a stroke had united the English in their determination to make war on France. Impatiently they waited for their King to return to London so they might demonstrate their loyalty to him in person.

William made preparations as usual to leave Holland in October, but his health delayed his departure. A recurrence of asthma, headaches and digestive disorders made him feel wretched most of the time, and these were exacerbated by a painful eruption on one side which may have been shingles. A few days before he was due to leave Het Loo for The Hague, he went for a last long day of hunting at Dieren. It was pouring with rain and when he arrived at his host's house at Voorst, he was soaked through and shivering with cold. After a hot drink he went early to bed and was up the next morning for another dawn to dusk session in the saddle. It rained hard all day but the King was not deterred, boasting the next day after a sound night's sleep that he was much better, and knew the activity would do him good. But he caught a heavy cold, with a sharp touch of fever, lost his appetite and eventually had to leave Het Loo for The Hague to see his doctors.

Like everybody else they were amazed that a man in his broken state of health could even contemplate going hunting. His legs had now almost completely failed him. Since November 1700 the doctors in England had tried all kinds of remedies to reduce the swelling, including frictions with elder-flower water, 'spaw-water', pills made of extract of gentian and lesser centaury, powder of crabs' claws compound, and Epsom salts in chicken broth; they had purged him with rosin of jalap and extract of rhubarb, and dosed him with tincture of steel. But his legs remained as swollen as ever, while his cough worsened. The French ambassador, who had seen him in May coming out of St James's Church, had noticed how decrepit he looked and the great difficulty he had getting into his coach.

Immediately before his departure from England, his English doctors had held a lengthy consultation, writing down their findings and the treatments they had prescribed for him as guidance for any doctor he might see in Holland, and asking some of their Dutch colleagues to send their opinions by letter. They reached no conclusions as to the cause of his ill-health, though they suggested it might be scurvy or incipient dropsy. Within the last few years, they reported, his 'asthmatic paroxysms' had become less severe, though expectoration had increased. They had been impressed by the patient's resilience. He had no headaches or upset stomach, was a good sleeper and was 'never troubled with a looseness and but seldom with a costiveness'.[3] He suffered occasionally, they noted, from feverish colds in winter, but his appetite was still good, although more moderate than it used to be, and they were more disturbed by his drinking habits than they liked to admit.

For the swollen legs they had once recommended tight bandaging, which just drove the abscess higher. According to one doctor, it was a soft pale swelling that retained pits in the skin after being pressed with a finger, and they now suggested massage and resting for an hour or so with his feet up when he came in from hunting. This did not help and by July, when he was at Het Loo, his legs were worse than ever, while the dosings, purgings and spa-water cures had exhausted him and ruined his appetite. Appalled by these symptoms of his own decline, he anxiously asked Bidloo whether he thought the disease was dropsy. After Bidloo had consulted with his colleagues, the Dutch doctors took him off the purgatives, prescribed a fortifying medicinal wine made with herbs and citron peel, infused with Rhenish wine, and begged him to eat less fruit and moderate his iced drinks. For his legs they suggested massage twice daily with a warm flannel, or Hungary water and bandaging with more flannel, and in winter wearing breeches lined with English lamb-skins. Their treatment had some success; within a few weeks, to William's relief, his legs were much improved.

Some in Holland suspected his illness might be diplomatic. They knew he was anxious for the States to appoint the young Prince Jan Willem Friso of Nassau-Dietz, Stadholder of Friesland since the death of his father Hendrik Casimir, as his sucessor for the Stadholdership of all the United Provinces. He had already made the boy sole heir to most of the huge Orange estates. But when William started to talk at The Hague about him, he met with little response, and some suspected that his illness was feigned in order to enlist a sympathetic response from the States of Holland.

In October, when William returned to The Hague on his way back to England, it was clear that he was seriously ill. On his arrival he was for some days in so bad a condition that they feared he was in terminal decline. His amazing constitution pulled him through once more, but he looked dreadful. One eye-witness remarked to one of his doctors that he was leaving them 'at a very great pace', to which the doctor answered, 'Even quicker than you would think.'[4] Another, watching him riding down the Voorhout in his coach, felt instinctively that he had seen his Stadholder for the last time.

After the crossing to Margate William was carried off the boat in a state of virtual collapse and was put straight to bed once they reached Greenwich. London had been preparing a rapturous welcome for their King for weeks now, but the reception was cancelled as it would have exhausted him. Instead of riding through the City he went directly to Hampton Court, arriving on 5 November. It was a pathetic contrast with the landing of a younger, more energetic 'William the Conqueror' at Torbay, just thirteen years earlier to the day. Even so, people insisted on celebrating his return home with bonfires and pealing bells, while deputations from all parts of the kingdom travelled to Hampton Court to deliver their speeches and addresses. He could not decently refuse to see them, but afterwards complained bitterly to Heinsius how tiresome it had been.

As ever, fresh air and exercise proved the best medicine, and within a week he was telling everyone proudly that he was riding and eating well, and feeling much the better for it. This was an exaggeration, for everyone around him realized that he was in failing health. Yet he continued to discharge his duties as king, holding councils and giving audiences. He could still ride and now walked fairly easily, and on his better days he could exert himself more than his doctors thought good for him. When he entertained Princess Anne and Prince George at Hampton Court one evening, everyone noticed a new gentleness in his manner to them. Whereas he had been to some the personification of outward coldness and surliness, he now seemed more accommodating, even softer.

He lived quietly now at Hampton Court, surrounded by friends like Albemarle and his wife, who were looking forward to the birth of their first child. He still took a lively interest in the world around him. Bidloo was impressed when they had a long conversation one evening about recent discoveries and advances in medicine, surgery and anatomy. He took a considerable scientific interest in his own illness, and always wanted to know the whys and wherefores of everything. Though he knew he would not live to see the completion of Wren's work on Hampton Court, he always wanted to inspect the most recent progress on the stately rooms and gardens. The latter remained a source of endless pleasure, and that autumn he ordered some new Italian statuary for them.

Portland came down regularly from his Ranger's lodge in Windsor Great Park, where he was living with his second wife and their first child. Though he had not resumed his old offices, he and William had regained something of their old intimacy. Even more encouragingly, the quarrels between Albemarle and Portland seemed to be a thing of the past, even if it was no more than a truce observed merely so as not to upset their sovereign. During a stroll in the gardens at Hampton Court one day that winter, William confided to Portland that he did not expect to live another summer, begging him at the same time not to repeat what he had said.

This remark was made after his legs had suddenly swollen up again. Sending for Bidloo, the only doctor he really trusted, he asked once more if it was dropsy and if there was really nothing to be done. Bidloo had a little stove specially made, a box made of oak, lined with flannel, on either side of which burned little lamps filled with spirits of lavender. It was large enough for the King to sit with his legs and thighs inside. William was delighted with it at first, and when Romney, Ormonde and other friends came to see him, he proudly demonstrated it to them. Soon the novelty wore off and he could not be bothered to go on using it regularly, and his legs swelled again.

Ill-health could not prevent him following political developments in England with the closest attention. At his return he had been impressed by the degree to which public opinion was now with him in his opposition to French imperialism. It encouraged him to dissolve the quarrelsome, factious Parliament of the previous year and to issue writs for a general election at the end of the year. After spending Christmas at Hampton Court he moved to Kensington. On 31 December 1701 a new House of Commons assembled with a Whig majority of about thirty, and the King's new ministry was once more largely Whig in composition, headed by Somers. He went down in person to open Parliament, and made what many MPs thought the most effective and moving speech they had ever heard from him. 'He laid it upon them to "consider the dangers they were in, and not to increase these by new divisions among themselves", wrote Burnet afterwards, and "he expressed a readiness to forgive all offences against himself, and wished they would as readily forgive one another, so that no other divisions might remain but that of English and French, Protestant and Papist".'5 He reminded them of their responsibilities, warning them that 'the eyes of all Europe' were upon Parliament, and all matters were at a standstill until their resolutions were known. 'If you do in good earnest desire to see England hold the balance of Europe, and to be indeed at the head of the Protestant interest, it will appear by your right improving the present opportunity.'6 Parliament and people alike were moved by the appeal from this shadow of a man, and the Commons took to heart his words about the dangers of party divisions at this time, unanimously voting for all necessary supplies for the preservation of Europe.

William's speech was printed and translated into French and Dutch. Belatedly, in this moment of crisis, even the English forgot their national prejudices and realized for the first time that their once-detested Dutch King was the man to whom Protestant Europe looked for leadership. Daniel Defoe, always an admirer of William yet no sycophant, was one of the instigators of this new wave of appreciation that swept the country with the publication of his 'True-Born Englishman'. In biting terms he castigated the xenophobia of his fellow citizens, pouring scorn on their resentment of the King's foreign advisers and their fickleness. The pamphlet became an instant best-seller and William, unused to hearing himself referred to by his English subjects in such effusive terms, read it and summoned Defoe to Kensington to thank him in person.

Now with the full backing of Parliament and people, he began to make preparations for the campaign that would be inevitable that summer. The French were fortifying themselves in Flanders, at the same time penetrating deep into the Rhineland around Cologne, while the Austrians were already fighting the Spanish in Italy. At this time the Allies presented a formidable coalition against France, especially as the original core of Austria, England and the Republic had been strengthened by Denmark, Hesse and Munster. Sweden and Poland were on the verge of joining them, and Portugal seemed likely to, yet no general strategy had been decided upon. Negotiations about military preparations were going slowly at The Hague; in February the King sent Albemarle over to try to expedite the discussions and to help coordinate the Allied plans. It was as if this new round of activity had somehow briefly rejuvenated him and put new energy into his tired frame.

On 20 February he left Kensington for Hampton Court. After lunch he went riding on a new horse called Sorrel. As he urged her into a gallop she stumbled on a molehill and fell to her knees. He tried to pull her up by the reins, but she lurched forwards and then sideways, and William fell on to his right shoulder. His collarbone was broken and his surgeon Dr Ronjat set it at Hampton Court.

William insisted on returning to Kensington that evening as planned, with his arm in a sling, and during the long coach-ride the bone was jolted out of place again. Bidloo had to reset it, and afterwards William went to bed and slept well, apparently unaffected. Next day he felt well enough to work as usual, and continued to deal with business, writing a little with his left hand. On 22 February the archbishop held a service in his room as he did not feel strong enough to attend chapel. Bidloo adjusted his bandages regularly, especially when they made breathing difficult, and Portland called every day to keep him company. Nevertheless he thought no more of his fall until 27 February when they took the bandages off. It was discovered that the fracture had not mended and was slightly swollen, while his right hand and arm looked odd and puffy as well.

Refusing to take much notice of this, or of his growing weakness, William dictated letters as usual, including one to the Duke of Mecklenburg to thank him for joining the Allies. Next day he sent a message to the House of Commons apologizing for not being there in person but urging them to bring about a union between his kingdoms of England and Scotland to avert the war which he felt to be otherwise inevitable. With the help of Bidloo he limped about Kensington House, and sometimes he even felt strong enough to leave his rooms and walk slowly through the galleries to look at his favourite paintings.

On 2 March he appointed a commission of five lords to deal with some urgent outstanding parliamentary matters, among them the Abjuration Bill to exclude the Pretender Prince of Wales from the succession. Afterwards he took a gentle stroll around his gallery, but this time the effort was too much for him. Exhausted, he sat down on a chair to get his breath. Asking his attendants to leave him, he fell asleep in the gentle spring sunshine beside an open window. When he woke up the sun had long since gone in and he was chilled and shivering, coughing and feverish. The next day he developed a fever and in the evening the doctors had to be called to his bedside again. That night he slept badly, coughing a great deal, and he was clearly very ill. His doctors prescribed every remedy they thought might be effective, but he refused them all.

On 6 March he was too weak to keep his food or medicine down. New remedies were tried but to no effect, and when the doctors begged him to eat a little to keep his strength up, he replied impatiently that forced feeding did him no good. That night he became so ill and vomited so much that everyone felt the end must be near. In the morning he was given quinine for his fever; he drank some milky tea and a cup of chocolate. The Commons had just assembled to discuss the Union of England and Scotland, and when told of his worsening condition wondered if he would be able to sign his assent to the Abjuration Bill. Somehow he found the strength that evening to put a specially prepared stamp on the parchment giving a commission the power to act for him, and the Bill became law.

Albemarle had hurried back from Holland, arriving at the King's bedside in the morning of 7 March. When he reported how well the Allied discussions were going at The Hague, he was alarmed that the King showed little interest, only remarking wearily, *'Je tire vers ma fin'* ('I draw near my end').[7] Only a few days earlier he had told a friend that he had never been afraid of death. There had been times when he wished to die, but now there was a future and he would prefer to be spared a little longer. By this stage, though, he knew his time was running out. Members of the Privy Council were assembled in his bedroom, and they questioned the doctors anxiously about his condition. All eight doctors present shook their heads, declaring that their hopes depended on his taking some food and their remedies. Some of the noblemen urged Bidloo to try to persuade the King to eat a little. This time William gave in, asking them to lift him up, and saying he would take as much as he could.

Later he slept a little, only to wake at 3 a.m. on 8 March and send for Bidloo again, complaining he could not sleep as he was struggling to breathe. The doctor propped him up in bed and, leaning against him, the King remarked he could sleep in this position. For over an hour the devoted doctor sat without moving, until William woke, realized how uncomfortable Bidloo must have been, and protested 'You can bear me up no longer.'[8] After that two servants, one of them his page Sewel, took it in turns to support him with pillows. The doctors consulted together soon afterwards and agreed to summon Archbishop Tenison, who arrived at 5 a.m. with Burnet to give him the Sacrament.

As word spread through London, the dying King's sickroom filled with friends and courtiers. He remained calm. He said farewell to his closest friends, to Overkirke and Albemarle, to whom he handed his personal keys, and some of his servants were summoned to be specially thanked. At 7 a.m., struggling for breath, he took Bidloo by the hand, thanked him for all his faithful services, and asked him how long it could last. The doctor reassured him he might last another hour or more, 'though you may be snatch'd away in the Twinkling of an Eye'. When Bidloo felt his pulse, he held on to him, saying: 'I do not die yet, hold me fast.'[9]

About an hour later Portland arrived at the King's bedside. Some said afterwards that Albemarle had refused to send for him earlier, but according to another account the servant dispatched to fetch him lost his way to Windsor in the dark. By the time William saw him he had more or less lost the power of speech, but with a look asked him to approach. Portland bent down, putting his ear to the King's mouth, but could distinguish only a few incoherent words. With a last gesture, William took Portland's hand and pressed it weakly against his heart. Then his head fell back, he closed his eyes and gave two or three soft gasps. The struggle was over.

When his emaciated body was undressed, the attendants found Mary's small gold ring on a black ribbon round his neck. He had had it made into a locket in 1684 and it contained a lock of brown hair. After an autopsy, his body was enbalmed and taken to the Prince's Chamber, Westminster, to lie in state. The doctors were surprised to find more blood in the lungs than in the rest of the body. His legs and right arm were still swollen, and the upper half of one lung was infected, the immediate cause of death, though the stomach, liver, gall-bladder, spleen and kidneys were all in good condition.

Portland retired to Windsor to nurse his grief in private for a few days, while Albemarle mourned bitterly for several weeks. Liselotte, always intrigued by the close relationship between the King and the young man, wrote to the Dowager Electress of Hanover, now heir to the English throne, of rumours that he was 'on the point of following his master, he was ill to death with grief'.[10]

Anne and Prince George had visited William three times since his accident, but they were not present at his deathbed. She was with Sarah Churchill at St James's, waiting for the half-hourly bulletins sent to her by Lord Romney of the approaching end. Burnet was the first to hurry there with the news and throw himself upon his knees before the woman who was England's new sovereign. Several delegations followed, while Vernon formally notified both Houses of Parliament that the King was dead, and one member rose to pay tribute to 'a great King'. That afternoon Anne was proclaimed in the presence of both Houses and was received with loud cheers. She emphasized that the black mourning she wore was for her father James, with only violet trimmings in her brother-in-law's memory. It was a sweet revenge.

The sadness felt throughout the country was far less intense than the grief which had followed Mary's death. 'Dutch William' had never loved England as he had Holland. The year of 1689 was the only one in which he had never left his kingdom, and to the end of his days he was regarded as a foreigner. For years English Jacobites would drink a toast to the 'little gentleman in black velvet', the mole on whose hill his horse had stumbled. Without any evidence they said that the King had left nothing but debts, that Mary's funeral bills were still unpaid, that the crown jewels had been pawned or spirited away and that William had schemed to have Anne arrested so that the Hanoverian dynasty could succeed him immediately.

Yet William had a posthumous and highly articulate champion in Daniel Defoe. In his satire *The Consolidator* (1705), he berated the English for their shabby treatment of the man who had 'left a quiet, retired, completely happy condition, full of honour, beloved of his country,' to come and deliver them from the encroachments and tyranny of their then sovereign. He became their 'mere journeyman', their servant, their soldier of fortune; 'he has fought for you, fatigued and harassed his person, and robbed himself of all his peace for you; he has been in a constant hurry, and run through a million of hazards for you'. His reward was to be treated with jealousy, suspicion, reproaches and abuses of every kind, until such treatment 'ate into his very soul, tired it with serving an unthankful nation, and absolutely broke his heart; for which reason I think him as much murdered as his predecessor was, whose head was cut off by his subjects'.[11]

While his wife had been buried with pomp and glory, William's own funeral on 12 April was a modest occasion taking place in private at midnight. Beginning at Kensington, the procession went at a solemn, dignified pace to Westminster, with a wax effigy on the funeral chariot, and his coffin was added at Westminster Palace. The pall was carried by six dukes, with Prince George as chief mourner. Moving silently through the dark streets, the procession reached the doors of Westminster Abbey where it was met by the Dean and conducted to the Henry VII Chapel, where the service was read by the Dean and the Bishop of Rochester. Then the vault was opened, the coffin was lowered into it and the officers of the dead King's household broke their staves and threw them in, shouting 'God Save Queen Anne'.

* * *

King William III's place in English and European history rests on two factors. He provided the political climate for modern government in England, and he was a staunch defender of the United Provinces in Holland. Respected and admired at home and abroad, despite all his achievements and qualities he was never really loved by the English during his lifetime. No colourful despot, eccentric, madman, fool, spendthrift, drunkard or debauchee, he appeared dull, cold and reserved, and unlike the unreliable, philandering yet lovable rogue King Charles II he made little effort to win English hearts. His frequent long absences in Holland, his offhand treatment of the English nobility and his contempt for ceremonial display alienated too many people. Only on his infrequent personal appearances did his popularity rise.

Nor was his death felt as a personal loss in Holland. In his last years he had become increasingly remote to the Dutch, away on campaigns or in England, or a recluse at Het Loo. They remembered him less as the Saviour of the Fatherland of 1672 than as a war leader who had led them into exhausting conflicts that ruined trade and forced them to play second fiddle to England. Yet without the House of Orange there would have been no United Provinces, and without William III the Republic would probably have become little more than an insignificant outpost of the French empire. Within the Republic itself, his rule resulted in no major constitutional or administrative improvements. Though he was accused of hastening the decline of Holland by his warlike policy and heavy taxation, any other leader facing the threat of King Louis XIV would probably have done the same. He left the Dutch with an army respected throughout Europe, with a more powerful and better-equipped navy and, most of all, with a sense that it was their national duty to defend their frontiers and to maintain the barrier of the Spanish Netherlands. With relief they learned that even after his death England's new sovereign intended to continue the struggle against their common enemy, France, as confirmed by Anne's dispatch of Marlborough to The Hague to reassure her Dutch allies that there would be no change in policy.

Later in the eighteenth century William received due recognition in Britain, where towns and cities commemorated him with statues financed by public subscription in St James's Square in London, Bristol, Glasgow, Petersfield and later still, on the bicentenary of the invasion of 1688, at Brixham. The Whig histories of the time celebrated him 'almost as an honorary Englishman, for many Englishmen felt that only through him had their liberties been secured'.[12] In time there was a reaction to this mood of adulation, and 'King Billy's' position as champion of the Ulster Unionists made him a dubious hero, if not an embarrassment to many.

Nevertheless, the achievements of the years 1689 to 1702, and the part he played in them, should be observed. It was in the reign of William and Mary together, and then of William alone, that Parliament began assuming the role in British government over the monarch that it was never again to lose. After the capricious Charles and the tyrannical James, Westminster ensured that no English sovereign should enjoy such absolute powers again, and Parliament acquired new responsibilities. At first parliamentary government was far from stable, owing mainly to party strife, personal antagonism between ministers and senior parliamentarians, and subsequent rapid ministerial changes. Yet a more steady administration developed, as did the constitutional devices which provided and ensured greater efficiency and stability in parliamentary authority, not least the growth of cabinet government.[13] Ministers also gradually began to play an active part in formulating English foreign policy, previously the sovereign's role, as well as managing home affairs. By voting William supplies for only one year at a time, they forced him to summon Parliament on a regular basis, and no matter how much he privately resented it he was wise enough to accept this curb on the royal prerogative.

To William, England was primarily a weapon to be used against the imperialist designs of France, and he needed her naval and military strength. In 1688 England was largely preoccupied with her own internal and political conflicts; thirteen years later she was a force to be reckoned with in Europe, was a leading member of the Grand Alliance, had established herself in the Mediterranean and boasted a disciplined army capable of fighting its corner in any foreign war. According to David Ogg, King William had reigned over a country which had been 'a community of divided and quarrelsome adolescents' but under his guidance had acquired 'the unity and maturity of a nation'.[14]

The nine years' war, often known as 'King William's war', permanently transformed England. As a result the country was equipped with the military, political and diplomatic machinery, to say nothing of national self-confidence, that laid the basis of her development and expansion in the eighteenth century. At least one modern historian, A.H. Jones, has argued that the war, far more than the events of 1688–9, 'constitutes the really significant revolution of the late seventeenth century'.[15]

Others have said that William III took England into Europe, and that he was the first European. He was probably the first European statesman, crowned or otherwise, to have a firm grasp of the principle of the balance of power throughout the continent, a principle which dominated European thinking from the treaty of Utrecht in 1713 to the outbreak of the First World War in 1914. While he was often called the Protestant Champion, this was the tribute of a Europe that still thought in medieval terms. He was no religious zealot, and the wars against France into which time and again he plunged Europe were no crusades, their sole aim being to check the French King's imperial ambitions. Yet he appreciated French culture, got on well with individual Frenchmen, had a respect for the nation which was often reciprocated, and envisaged her as a potential friend and ally – but not on France's own expansionist terms. At her worst France was a menace to be resisted, but at the same time she was an integral part of Europe which could not be destroyed or eliminated lest a vacuum be created which brought in its train something far less palatable. It would take a descendant of the Duke of Marlborough to acknowledge that it almost seemed 'that a being had been created for the sole purpose of resisting the domination of France and the Great King'.[16] This justified the invasion of 1688 and the Glorious Revolution, in William's eyes, both being essential if England were to be retained in the Protestant camp on the side of the Allies; and the fact that they necessitated the deposing of his own father-in-law was a necessary evil at worst.

Often thought of as a soldier king, he was one of the last European monarchs to lead his armies in person, but on the battlefield he was constantly outmatched by the larger armies of Louis's generals and their superior strategy. Yet he was noted for outstanding personal courage; as his French adversaries recognized, it was a rare royal commander who readily risked his own life at the head of his troops on the battlefield, though this could not compensate for an initial lack of experience, mediocre military skill and troops who were often demoralized and ill-equipped. Where he excelled was in diplomatic warfare, and he built up from nothing a strong and determined coalition against France. He was born to lead; in childhood he was already aware of his destiny, which he pursued to the end of his days. Physically weak, he mastered disability with the strength of will to carry out what he saw as his life's purpose, and let nothing stand in his way.

Ironically he died before he could see the power of Catholic France curtailed, a cause to which he had devoted much of his life, though he had helped to deal the first blow to her predominance of Europe. By the standards of his time he was humane, though he was certainly no saint. He cared little if anything for public opinion: criticisms of his generosity or rumours of homosexuality never disturbed him, and his few close friends respected and appreciated his loyalty.

William and Mary were no intellectuals, but they were sensitive and intelligent and shared a genuine taste, even a passion, for fine paintings, craftsmanship, architecture and gardening. If he had had more time to cultivate these interests, and she had lived longer, they would certainly have left England and the Dutch with more than Kensington House, Het Loo and some unfinished schemes to remember them by. The interest they took in their dwellings was not merely inspired by the pleasure of creation, nor for William by a desire to compete with the Sun King, but were the simple enthusiasms of a man and a woman who valued the quality of home life and a degree of privacy, at variance with the constant sense of public spectacle in which previous kings and queens of England had generally lived.

This went hand in hand with their efforts to lend a higher moral tone to English public life by rejecting decadence and immorality at court. Mary, according to Clive Bigham, was 'a conscientious woman of blameless rectitude', and 'the most honest and discreet of the Stuarts', who shone out 'as a rare type of domestic virtue and piety' in a notoriously corrupt and immoral age,[17] while William's Calvinism was offended by profanity and ostentatious loose living. Though sometimes ridiculed for their efforts, their influence left its mark, as did their tolerance in religious matters. Had Parliament allowed it, William would certainly have led the way in creating a climate of greater tolerance for Catholics and dissenters in public life. Though his achievement was limited, his example of tolerance helped to reduce English religious conflicts, and he left a country in which minority groups like Jews and Quakers could practise their religion according to conscience.

Perhaps the final word should go to G.M. Trevelyan, who observed that unlike his wife the King 'never sought the love of contemporaries or of posterity, and he has not obtained it; but he sought their welfare and freedom, and these he achieved'.[18] While he reigned during the decade in which Parliament came into its own, ironically he succeeded in being his own prime minister, admittedly long before the age when such a post was officially recognized, as well as his own Secretary of State for Foreign Affairs. Industrious, wise and courageous, he was much more capable than his predecessors, was by far the most able monarch of the house of Stuart and was considerably underestimated as a sovereign. The achievements of his self-effacing yet intelligent and cultured Queen should likewise be duly recognized, and all credit accorded her for the influence she brought to bear on his character and the way in which he discharged his duties as King of England.

THE HOUSE OF STUART

JAMES VI and I   m.   Anne of Denmark
1566–1625   1574–1619

Henry
1594–1612

CHARLES I   m.   Henrietta Maria of France
1600–49   1609–69

Elizabeth
1596–1662

FREDERICK V
Elector Palatine
1596–1632   m.   Sophie
1630–1714

Charles Louis
1617–80

Ernest Augustus
Elector of
Hanover
1630–98

Elisabeth
Charlotte
('Liselotte')
1652–1722

GEORGE I
1660–1727

House of Hanover

Mary
1631–60   m.   WILLIAM II
of Orange
1626–50

CHARLES II
1630–85   m.   Catherine of
Braganza
1638–1705

Anne Hyde   m.   (1) JAMES II   m.   (2) Mary Beatrice
1637–71   1633–1701   of Modena
1658–1718

Henry, Duke
of Gloucester
1639–60

Henrietta
1644–70

WILLIAM III
1650–1702   m.   MARY
1662–94

ANNE
1665–1714   m.   George
of Denmark
1653–1708

James
('The Old
Pretender')
1688–1766

Louisa
1692–1712

William, Duke of Gloucester
1689–1700

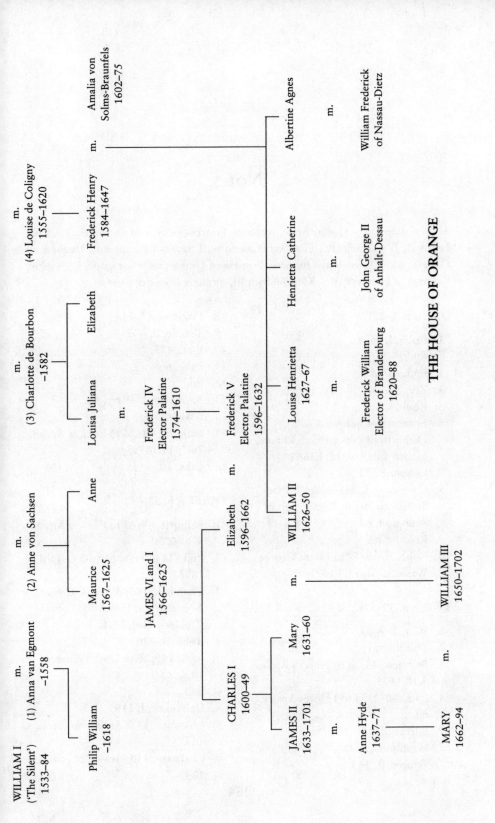

THE HOUSE OF ORANGE

WILLIAM I ('The Silent') 1533–84

m. (1) Anna van Egmont –1558

m. (2) Anne von Sachsen

m. (3) Charlotte de Bourbon –1582

m. (4) Louise de Coligny 1555–1620

Philip William –1618

Maurice 1567–1625

Anne

Louisa Juliana m.

Elizabeth

Frederick Henry 1584–1647

m. Amalia von Solms-Braunfels 1602–75

Frederick IV Elector Palatine 1574–1610

JAMES VI and I 1566–1625 m. Elizabeth 1596–1662

Frederick V Elector Palatine 1596–1632

WILLIAM II 1626–50 m.

Louise Henrietta 1627–67 m. Frederick William Elector of Brandenburg 1620–88

Henrietta Catherine m. John George II of Anhalt-Dessau

Albertine Agnes m. William Frederick of Nassau-Dietz

CHARLES I 1600–49

JAMES II 1633–1701 m. Anne Hyde 1637–71

Mary 1631–60

WILLIAM III 1650–1702 m.

MARY 1662–94

Notes

Abbreviations: A – Queen Anne, formerly Princess George of Denmark; J – King James II; L – 'Liselotte', Elisabeth Charlotte, Princess Palatine and Duchess of Orléans; M – Queen Mary, formerly Princess of Orange; nd – not dated; S – Sophie, Electress of Hanover; W – King William III, formerly Prince of Orange

ONE (pp. 1–29)

1. Robb, I, 65.
2. Ibid., 99.
3. Ibid., 100.
4. Zee, 27.
5. Robb, I, 102.
6. Elizabeth of Bohemia, 342: Elizabeth to Prince Charles Louis, Elector Palatine, 11.4.1661.
7. Chapman, 53.
8. Courtenay, I, 285–6: Sir William Temple to Henry Bennet, Earl of Arlington, nd.
9. Reresby, 82.
10. Robb, II, 39: W to Count George Waldeck, May (?) 1675.

TWO (pp. 30–51)

1. Weir, 259–63.
2. Hamilton, 10.
3. Bathurst, 43: M to Frances Apsley, 3.10.1675.
4. Ibid., 60–1: M to Frances Apsley, nd.
5. Burnet, II, 16.
6. Hamilton, 27.
7. Temple, II, 343.

8. Courtenay, I, 114.
9. Temple, II, 432.
10. Ibid., 433.
11. Lake, 6.
12. Ibid.
13. Anon, *Royal Diary*, 33.
14. Lake, 8.
15. Bathurst, 81: M to Frances Apsley, 26(?).11.1677.
16. Lake, 10.

THREE (pp. 52–75)

1. Bathurst, 89: M to Frances Apsley, 3.3.1678.
2. Ibid.: M to Frances Apsley, April 1678.
3. Chapman, 106; d'Avaux, Comte, *Négociations*, Irish MSS. Comm. (Dublin 1934), I, 31.
4. Robb, II, 220.
5. Ibid., 149: W to Lord Arlington, 18.8.1680.
6. Ibid., 204.
7. Dalrymple, I, 119.
8. Chapman, 115; Avaux, op. cit. II, 124.
9. Chapman, 115; Avaux, op. cit. II, 124.

264

Notes

FOUR (pp. 76–99)

1. Public Record Office, SP 8/3, 119/228: J to W, 6.2.1685; Callow, 298.
2. Weir, 260.
3. Watson, 189–90.
4. Evelyn, II, 473, 18.7.1685.
5. Anon, *Royal Diary*, 10.
6. Bodleian Library, Rawlinson MSS, C983/106: Dr Stanley to Bishop Compton, 22.12.1685; Hamilton, 165.
7. Waller, 114–15.
8. Burnet, III, 133–4.
9. Bowen, *Mary*, 295: M to J, 26.12.1687.
10. *Letters of Queen Anne*, 29–30: A to M, April 1687.
11. Robb, II, 254.
12. Echard, 119.
13. Bowen, *Mary*, 117.
14. Dalrymple, II, 216.
15. Ibid., 293.
16. Ibid., 107–10.
17. Waller, 158.
18. Bowen, *Mary*, 125.
19. Hamilton, 188–9.
20. Haile, 192.
21. Strickland, X, 378.
22. Haile, 197.

FIVE (pp. 100–18)

1. Hamilton, 194; *Proceedings of the States of Holland and West Friesland*, October 1688.
2. Pearce, 14.
3. Clark, 138.
4. Ogg, *England*, 223.
5. Bromley, 207; *Journals of the House of Commons*, 28.1.1689.
6. Doebner, 4–5.

7. Burnet, III, 390.
8. Doebner, 7–9.
9. Ibid., 9–10.
10. Ibid., 10.
11. Marlborough, 18–19.
12. Doebner, 11.
13. Ibid., 10.
14. Robb, II, 283; Japikse, *Correspondentie van Willem III en Hans Willem Bentinck*, 5 vols (The Hague, 1927–37), II, iii, 102: W to Princess Albertina of Nassau-Dietz, 11.3.1689.
15. Dalrymple, II, 15.
16. Chapman, 170.
17. Oldmixon, III, 780.
18. Zee, 279; *London Gazette*, 14.4.1689.
19. Whiston, 653.

SIX (pp. 119–44)

1. Burnet, IV, 152–3.
2. Doebner, 17.
3. Bowen, *Mary*, 222.
4. Zee, 293; Bentinck, 109, 116.
5. Burnet, IV, 60–1.
6. Marlborough, 21.
7. Doebner, 18.
8. Zee, 297.
9. Doebner, 21.
10. Foxcroft, II, 244.
11. Robb, II, 300; Japikse, op. cit., II, iii, 113: W to Portland, 11.2.90.
12. Robb, II, 303; Muller, *Wilhelm III von Oranien und Georg Friedrich von Waldeck*, 2 vols (1873, 1880), II, 215: W to Waldeck 14.2.90.
13. Gregg, 79.
14. Doebner, 25–8.
15. Burnet, IV, 82.
16. Doebner, 29.
17. Chapman, 183–4.

SEVEN (pp. 145–65)

1. Bentinck, 123–4.
2. Ibid., 97.
3. Doebner, 88–9.
4. Kroll, 57: L to S, 20.8.1690.
5. Doebner, 48.
6. Grew and Sharpe, 197.
7. Churchill, I, 355–6.
8. Marlborough, 32.
9. Burnet, IV, 163.
10. Doebner, 354.

EIGHT (pp. 166–88)

1. Doebner, 61.
2. Bentinck, 149–50.
3. Bowen, *Mary*, 237.
4. British Museum Add. MSS 35618: M to Duchess of Hamilton, nd; Zee, 382.
5. Robb, II, 360; Heinsius, *Archives ou Correspondance inedited de la Maison d'Orange Nassau*, I, 1689–97, 374.
6. Burnet, IV, 277.
7. Zee, 348; Japikse, op. cit., II, 346: W to Charles, Prince de Vaudemont, 25.12.1694.
8. Anon, *Royal Diary*, 11.
9. Tenison, *A sermon preached* . . .
10. Ailesbury, I, 298–9.
11. Hill, 348.
12. Burnet, IV, 249–50.
13. Robb, II, 361–2.
14. Zee, 389; *Journal of the House of Lords*, 15.
15. Gregg, 101; Ranke, VI, 264; Bonet report, 28.12.1694.
16. Historical Manuscripts Commission, Bath Papers: A to W, 29.12.1694; Gregg, 102.
17. Sandars, 368; Macpherson Papers.

18. Robb, II, 365: W to Prince de Vaudemont, 5.2.1695, 15.2.1695; Japikse, II, iii, 347, 349.

NINE (pp. 189–214)

1. Kroll, 70: L to S, 12.10.1695.
2. Anon, *Royal Progress*, 12.
3. Miller, *James II*, 239.
4. Ogg, *England*, 427.
5. Wickham Legg, 67.
6. Robb, II, 396: W to Earl of Portland, March 1697; Japikse, I, i, 197.
7. Ibid., II, 398: Earl of Portland to W, 30.5.1697; Japikse, I, i, 198.
8. Ibid., II, 399: W to Earl of Portland, 1.6.1697; Japikse, I, i, 200.
9. Burnet, IV, 439.
10. Robb, II, 402–3.
11. Baxter, 352.
12. Kenyon, 7, 179.

TEN (pp. 215–37)

1. Grimblot, I, 145.
2. Ibid., II, 183.
3. Ibid., 187.
4. Coxe, 574.
5. Ralph, II, 809–10.
6. Vernon, II, 357.
7. Pierpont Morgan Library, Rulers of England, Box XI, William and Mary #22, W to A, 4.8.1700; Gregg, 121.
8. Kroll, 96: L to S, 17.4.1701.

ELEVEN (pp. 238–61)

1. Kroll, 101: L to S, 4.9.1701.
2. Green, 86–7.
3. Zee, 468.

Notes

4. Ibid., 469.
5. Burnet, IV, 296.
6. Ogg, *England*, 483.
7. Strickland, XII, 32.
8. Zee, 475.
9. Kroll, 107: L to S, 9.4.1702.
10. Cannon & Griffiths, 443.

11. Barclay, 'Puffing Billy'.
12. Plumb, 102–3.
13. Ogg, *England*, 485.
14. Jones, 258.
15. Churchill, I, 341.
16. Bigham, 400.
17. Trevelyan, 449.

Bibliography

I MANUSCRIPT SOURCES

Bodleian Library, Oxford, Rawlinson MSS
British Museum, Additional MSS
Historical Manuscripts Commission, Bath Papers
Pierpont Morgan Library, New York. Rulers of England, Box XI
Public Record Office, The King's Chest

II BOOKS AND OTHER PRINTED SOURCES

The place of publication is London unless stated otherwise

Ailesbury, Thomas, Earl of. *Memoirs*, ed. W. Buckley, 2 vols, Roxburgh Club, 1890
Anne, Queen. *Letters of Queen Anne*, ed. Beatrice Curtis Brown, Cassell, 1935
Anon. *The life of William III, late King of England, and Prince of Orange*, London, 1703
—— *The Royal Diary: or King William's Interior Portraiture*, London, 1705
—— *The Royal Progress; or a Diary of the King's journey*, London, 1695
Appleyard, Revd J. *William of Orange and the English Revolution*, Dent, 1908
Ashley, Maurice. *James II*, Dent, 1977
Barclay, Andrew. 'Puffing Billy', in *History Today*, December 2002
Bathurst, Benjamin (ed.) *Letters of Two Queens*, Robert Holden, 1924
Baxter, Stephen B. *William III*, Longmans, 1966
Bentinck, Mechtild, Comtesse (ed.) *Marie, Reine d'Angleterre, Lettres et Mémoires*, The Hague, 1880
Bigham, Clive. *The Kings of England 1066–1901*, John Murray, 1929
Bluche, François. *Louis XIV*, tr. Mark Greengrass, Basil Blackwell, 1990
Bowen, Marjorie. *The third Mary Stuart: Mary of York, Orange & England, being a character study with memoirs and letters of Queen Mary II of England, 1662–1694*, John Lane, 1929
—— *William, Prince of Orange (afterwards King of England), being an account of his early life up to his twenty-fourth year*, John Lane, 1928
Bromley, J.S. (ed.) *The New Cambridge Modern History, Vol. VI: The rise of Great Britain and Russia, 1688–1715/25*, Cambridge, University Press, 1970

Bibliography

Burnet, Gilbert. *History Of His Own Times*, 6 vols, London, 1833

Callow, John. *The Making of King James II*, Stroud, Sutton, 2000

Cannon, John & Griffiths, Ralph. *The Oxford illustrated history of the British monarchy*, Oxford, University Press, 1988

Chapman, Hester W. *Mary II, Queen of England*, Jonathan Cape, 1953

Churchill, Winston S. *Marlborough, his life and times*, 2 vols, London, 1933

Clark, Sir George, *The later Stuarts, 1660–1714*, 2nd edn, Oxford, Clarendon, 1956

Courtenay, T.P. *Memoirs of the Life, Works and Correspondence of Sir William Temple, Bart.*, 2 vols, London, 1836

Coxe, William (ed.) *Private and Original Correspondence of Charles Talbot, Duke of Shrewsbury, with King William, &c.*, London, 1821

Dalrymple, Sir John. *Memoirs of Great Britain and Ireland*, 3 vols, Edinburgh and London, 1771–88

Doebner, Dr R. (ed.) *Memoirs of Mary, Queen of England*, Leipzig, 1886

Echard, Laurence. *History of England*, London, 1707

Elizabeth, Queen of Bohemia. *Letters*, comp. L.M. Baker, Bodley Head, 1953

Evelyn, John. *Diary*, 4 vols, ed. W. Bray, London, 1906

Foxcroft, H.C. (ed.) *The Life and Letters of George Savile, 1st Marquess of Halifax*, 2 vols, Longmans, Green, 1898

Fraser, Lady Antonia. *King Charles II*, Weidenfeld & Nicolson, 1979

Green, David. *Queen Anne*, Collins, 1970

Gregg, Edward. *Queen Anne*, Yale University Press, 2001

Grew, Edwin & Sharpe, Marion. *The court of William III*, Mills & Boon, 1910

Grimblot, Paul. *Letters of William III and Louis XIV*, 2 vols, Longman, 1848

Haile, Martin. *Queen Mary of Modena: her life and letters*, Dent, 1905

Hamilton, Elizabeth. *William's Mary: a biography of Mary II*, Hamish Hamilton, 1972

Haswell, Jock. *James II, soldier and sailor*, Hamish Hamilton, 1972

Haynes, John. *Kensington Palace*, Historic Royal Palaces Agency, 1995

Hibbert, Christopher. *The Marlboroughs: John and Sarah Churchill, 1650–1714*, Viking, 2001

Higham, F.M.G. *King James the Second*, Hamish Hamilton, 1934

Hill, C.P. *Who's who in history, Vol. III, England, 1603 to 1714*, Oxford, Basil Blackwell, 1965

Hudson, Derek. *Kensington Palace*, Peter Davies, 1968

Jones, J.R. *Country and court: England 1658–1714*, Edward Arnold, 1978

Kenyon, J.P. *The Stuarts: a study in English kingship*, Fontana, 1970

Kroll, Maria (ed.) *Letters from Liselotte: Elisabeth Charlotte, Princess Palatine and Duchess of Orléans, 'Madame', 1652–1722*, Victor Gollancz, 1970

Lake, Dr Edward. *Diary*, Vol. I, Camden Society, 1847

Marlborough, Sarah, Duchess of. *Memoirs*, ed. W. King, Routledge, 1930

Bibliography

Miller, John. *James II: a Study in Kingship*, Methuen, 1989

—— *The Life and Times of William and Mary*, Weidenfeld & Nicolson, 1974

Ogg, David. *England in the reigns of James II and William III*, Oxford, University Press, 1955

—— *William III*, Collins, 1956

Oldmixon, John. *History of the Stuarts*, 3 vols, London, 1730

Pearce, Frank. *The book of Brixham: portrait of a harbour town*, Tiverton, Halsgrove, 2000

Plowden, Alison. *The Stuart princesses*, Stroud, Sutton, 1996

Plumb, J.H. *The growth of political stability in England 1675–1725*, Macmillan, 1967

Ralph, James. *The History of England during the reign of King William III*, 2 vols, London, 1744–6

Ranke, Leopold. *History of England*, 6 vols, Oxford, University Press, 1875

Renier, G.J. *William of Orange*, Peter Davies, 1932

Reresby, Sir John. *Memoirs*, ed. Andrew Browning, Glasgow, Jackson, 1936

Robb, Nesca A. *William of Orange: a personal portrait, Vol. I, 1650–1673*, Heinemann, 1962

—— *William of Orange: a personal portrait, Vol. II, 1674–1702*, Heinemann, 1966

Sandars, Mary F. *Princess and Queen of England: Life of Mary II*, Stanley Paul, 1913

Sidney, Henry. *Diary and Correspondence of the Times of Charles The Second, etc*, ed. R.W. Blencowe, 2 vols, Bickers, 1843

Strickland, Agnes. *Lives of the Queens of England, Vols VIII–XI*, Colburn, 1845–7

Temple, Sir William. *Works*, 4 vols, London, 1814

Tenison, Archbishop Thomas. *A sermon preached at the funeral of Her Late Majesty Queen Mary*, London, 1695

Traill, H.D. *William the Third*, Macmillan, 1915

Trevelyan, G.M. *England under the Stuarts*, Methuen, 1904

Turner, F.C. *James II*, Eyre & Spottiswoode, 1948

Vernon, James. *Letters illustrative of the reign of William III, from 1696 to 1708, addressed to the Duke of Shrewsbury*, ed. G.P.R. James, 3 vols, London, 1841

Waller, Maureen. *Ungrateful daughters: the Stuart princesses who stole their father's crown*, Hodder & Stoughton, 2002

Waterson, Nellie M. *Mary II, Queen of England, 1689–1694*, Durham, NC, Duke University Press, 1928

Watson, J.N.P. *Captain-General and Rebel Chief: The Life of James, Duke of Monmouth*, Allen & Unwin, 1979

Weir, Alison. *Britain's royal families: the complete genealogy*, Bodley Head, 1989

Whiston, William. *Memoirs*, London, 1749

Wickham Legg, Leopold G. *Matthew Prior*, Cambridge, University Press, 1921

Zee, Henri & Barbara van der. *William and Mary*, Macmillan, 1973

Index

Abbreviations: M – Mary II; W – William III

Ailesbury, Thomas Bruce, Earl of 180
Albemarle, Arnout Joost van Keppel, Earl of
148, 170, 181–2, 184, 187, 199, 216, 217,
220, 224, 227, 232, 233, 234, 239, 243,
249, 251; relationship with W 200–5,
207–8; at W's deathbed 254
Albemarle, Countess of, formerly Gertruida
Quirina van der Duyn 243
Albert, Prince Consort 177
Albertina von Nassau-Dietz, Princess of
Orange 115
d'Albeville, Ignatius White, Marquis 86
d'Allonne, Abel Tassin 201, 227, 230
Almonde, Lt-Admiral Philip van 157
Amalia von Solms-Braunfels, Princess 3, 11,
14, 16, 64, 173
Anne of Denmark, Princess [daughter of Queen
Anne] 88
Anne of Denmark, Princess, later Queen 47,
49, 51, 58, 60, 61, 63, 77, 83, 11, 132, 151,
183, 195–6, 197–8, 219, 232, 249; birth 30;
childhood and education 32–4; marriage 72;
James II's preference for 79; and death of
daughters 87–8; and birth of Prince of Wales
90–2; declared W and M's heir 111; at
coronation 116; relations with W and M,
and allowance problems 129–31, 135–6;
and final break in relations with M 158–62;
and M's death 179; ill-health 236; and Act
of Settlement 242; and mourning for James
II, 246, 255
Anne, Duchess of York, formerly Anne Hyde 9,
18; marriage 30–1; death 32
Apsley, Frances, later Lady Bathurst 34, 50, 55,
64, 71
Apsley, Sir Allen and Lady 34
Argyll, Archibald Campbell, Earl of 78
Arlington, Henry Bennett, Earl of 40, 43
d'Avaux, Jean Antoine, Comte 61, 68, 74–5,
91, 97, 242, 244

Barbesieux, Marquis de 150, 155, 162
Barclay, Sir George 193–4
Barillon d'Amoncourt, Paul, Marquis de 42
Bath, Marquis of 103
Bathurst, Sir Benjamin 71
Bellasyse, Lady 35
Berwick, James, Duke of 193–4, 209
Beverweerd, Lodewijk van Nassau, Heer van
54
Bidloo, Dr Govart 215, 238, 247, 250, 252–4
Bigham, Clive 260
Blair, James 168
Blancard, Sieur 146
Blaythwayt, William 195
Bonet, Friedrich 183
Bornius, Dr Hendrik 12, 14
Boufflers, Louis-François, Duc de, Marshal
148, 189, 210, 211
Bourdon, Daniel de 81, 84
Brandon, Charles Gerard, Lord 73
Bristol, Bishop of 116
Brooke, Lord 190
Buckhurst, Lord 169
Buckingham, George Villiers, Duke of 19
Burnet, Gilbert 84, 90, 91, 103, 114, 128, 133,
136, 161, 176, 177, 181, 203, 218; at W
and M's coronation 117; at W's deathbed
254, 255

Callières, François de 213
Campbell, John, Earl of Breadalbane 154
Carlos II, King of Spain 17, 27, 222, 239
Carmarthen, Sir Thomas Osborne, Marquis of
128, 136, 149, 187
Carstares, William 102
Casimir, Hendrik 248
Castanaga, Marquis de 147
Catherine, Queen, formerly Catherine of
Braganza 31, 37, 48, 50, 59, 107, 139
Catherine Laura of York, Princess 37

271

Index

Mary, Princess of Orange (W's mother) 17, 30, 52, 174; and birth of W 1, 3; visit to France 5; introduces W to people of Amsterdam 7–8; visit to England and death 8–9

Mary, Queen 18, 77, 103, 168, 189, 204, 257; birth 31; childhood and education 35, 37; first spoken of as wife for W 38–9; character, interests and routine 41–2, 53–5, 63–5, 83–4, 175, 260; introduced to W 43–5; betrothal and wedding 46–9; leaves for Holland 50–1; state entry into The Hague 52; pregnancies 55–9; letters to Frances Apsley 55; and Duchess of York's visit 58; ill-health 62–3, 173–4; and Monmouth in Holland 60–1, 72–5; and Exclusion Bill 68; told of James II's accession 76; and Monmouth's rebellion 78–9; concerns over English succession 79–80, 85–6; and Betty Villiers scandal 81–2; and Huguenot persecution 82–3; and Burnet 84–5; and James II's attempts to convert her to Catholicism 86–7; and birth of Prince of Wales 89–2, 94–5; and prospect of W's invasion 96, 98–9; reproached by James II for disloyalty 99; and W's departure from Holland 100–1; formally offered crown as joint sovereign 110–11; receives news of his arrival in England 111–12; returns to England 113; and Declaration of Rights 114; coronation 115–18; at Hampton Court and Kensington 119–20; and royal household 123, 125; and Wren's building programme, artistic and literary interests 125; and W's threat to leave England 127–8; relations with Anne 128–30, 133, 139, 148, 158–62; and Anne's allowance 130, 135–6; in charge of England during W's absence 134, 138–9; and Earl of Shrewsbury 145; and Whitehall Palace fire 149; world-weariness 151–2; and Kensington House fire 152–3; and massacre of Glencoe 155; and threat of French invasion 156–8; and plot on W's life 162–3; tries to set moral example 163–4; and merchant ships controversy 167; and Duke of Gloucester 169; jewellery 173–4; last illness and death 176–80; rumours of letter left for W 181; mourning for, lying in state and funeral 182–8

Mary, Queen, formerly Princess Mary Beatrice d'Este of Modena 47, 48, 50, 57–8, 67, 77–8, 88, 156, 211, 213–14, 223; marriage 35–6; exiled from England 60; pregnancy and birth of Prince of Wales 89–92; and English court mourning for James II 246

Maurice of Orange, Prince 54
Maximilian, Elector of Bavaria 147, 240
Mecklenburg, Duke of 252
Meyercrone, Christina de 197, 214
Middleton, Charles, Earl of 184
Millington, Sir Thomas 235
Modena, Laura, Duchess of 88
Monmouth, Anna Scott, Duchess of 35, 48, 50, 58
Monmouth, James Scott, Duke of 35, 43, 59, 70, 76–7, 93, 96, 104; in Holland 60–2, 72–5; and Exclusion Bill 68–9; rebellion and execution 78–9
Montagu, Charles, Earl of Halifax 172, 190, 241
Mordaunt, Lord 86
Morgan, Father 86
Mytens, Jan 11

Needham, Eleanor 35
Neufville, François de, Marshal Villeroi 189
Newcastle, Duke of 190
Nottingham, Daniel Finch, Earl of 115, 120, 128, 136, 139, 140, 150, 156, 157, 190

Oates, Titus 58, 59
d'Obdam, Mademoiselle 146
Odijk, Adriaen Willem van Nassau, Heer van 54
Ogg, David 258
Orkney, Lord George Hamilton, Earl of 224
Ormonde, James Butler, Duke of 149, 170, 224, 232, 250
Ortwinius 84
Ossory, Thomas Butler, Earl of 54, 66, 170, 206
Overkirke, Hendrik van Nassau, Neer van 18, 25, 54, 80, 254

Pembroke, Earl of 136, 187, 189
Pendergrass, Captain 193
Penn, William 86, 149
Pepys, Samuel 31
Peter the Great, Tsar of Russia 211–12, 218–19
Peterborough and Monmouth, Earl of 35, 136
Petre, Father 88
Philippe, Duc d'Anjou, later King Philip V of Spain 239
Pomponne, Simon Arnould, Marquis de 223
Portland, Maria, Countess of 231
Portland, Willem Bentinck, Earl of 18, 28, 47, 54, 78, 85, 134, 148, 151, 152, 159, 169–70, 178, 184, 191, 193, 198, 227, 233, 239, 241, 243, 249; created Earl of Portland